EXTRAVERSION
AND
INTROVERSION

THE SERIES IN CLINICAL AND COMMUNITY PSYCHOLOGY

CONSULTING EDITORS:

CHARLES D. SPIELBERGER and IRWIN G. SARASON

Averill	Patterns of Psychological Thought: Readings in Historical and Contemporary Texts
Becker	Depression: Theory and Research
Bermant, Kelman, and Warwick	The Ethics of Social Intervention
Brehm	The Application of Social Psychology to Clinical Practice
Cattell and Dreger	Handbook of Modern Personality Theory
Endler and Magnusson	Interactional Psychology and Personality
Friedman and Katz	The Psychology of Depression: Contemporary Theory and Research
Iscoe, Bloom, and Spielberger	Community Psychology in Transition
Janisse	Pupillometry: The Psychology of the Pupillary Response
Kissen	From Group Dynamics to Group Psychoanalysis: Therapeutic Applications of Group Dynamic Understanding
Klopfer and Reed	Problems in Psychotherapy: An Eclectic Approach
London	Personality: A New Look at Metatheories
Manschreck and Kleinman	Renewal in Psychiatry: A Critical Rational Perspective
Morris	Extraversion and Introversion: An Interactional Perspective
Olweus	Aggression in the Schools: Bullies and Whipping Boys
Reitan and Davison	Clinical Neuropsychology: Current Status and Applications
Smoll and Smith	Psychological Perspectives in Youth Sports
Spielberger and Diaz-Guerrero	Cross-Cultural Anxiety
Spielberger and Sarason	Stress and Anxiety, volume 1
Sarason and Spielberger	Stress and Anxiety, volume 2
Sarason and Spielberger	Stress and Anxiety, volume 3
Spielberger and Sarason	Stress and Anxiety, volume 4
Spielberger and Sarason	Stress and Anxiety, volume 5
Sarason and Spielberger	Stress and Anxiety, volume 6
Ulmer	On the Development of a Token Economy Mental Hospital Treatment Program

IN PREPARATION

Cohen and Ross	Biology and Psychopathology
Krohne and Laux	Achievement, Stress, and Anxiety
Sarason and Spielberger	Stress and Anxiety, volume 7
Spielberger, Sarason, and Milgram	Stress and Anxiety, volume 8

EXTRAVERSION AND INTROVERSION

An Interactional Perspective

Larry Wayne Morris

Department of Psychology
Middle Tennessee State University

With a Foreword by

H. J. EYSENCK

Institute of Psychiatry
University of London

● HEMISPHERE PUBLISHING CORPORATION

Washington   New York   London

A HALSTED PRESS BOOK

JOHN WILEY & SONS

New York   Chichester   Brisbane   Toronto

Hemisphere Publishing Corporation
1025 Vermont Ave., N.W., Washington, D.C. 20005

Distributed solely by Halsted Press, a Division of John Wiley & Sons, Inc., New York.

1 2 3 4 5 6 7 8 9 0   L I L I   7 8 3 2 1 0 9

Library of Congress Cataloging in Publication Data

Morris, Larry Wayne.
    Extraversion and introversion.

    (The Series in clinical and community psychology)
    1. Extraversion. 2. Introversion. 3. Personality.
I. Title.
BF698.M67   154.2'3   79-16168
ISBN 0-470-26805-0

Printed in the United States of America

To Nancy

CONTENTS

Foreword   *H. J. Eysenck*   xi

Acknowledgments   xv

1   Extraversion–Introversion and Person–Environment
Interaction   1

Personality Theory and Research   1
Extraversion–Introversion   5
Interactional Perspective   8
Personality Traits and Interactionism   15
Interactional Personality Research   17
Plan of the Book   20

2   Meanings and Measurements of Extraversion
and Introversion   23

Eysenck Scales   24
16 Personality Factor Questionnaire   28

Guilford–Zimmerman Temperament Survey   30
California Psychological Inventory   31
Comrey Personality Scales   32
Minnesota Multiphasic Personality Inventory   33
Psychological Screening Inventory   35
Myers–Briggs Type Indicator   36
Bendig's Pittsburgh Scales   37
Classroom Behavior Inventory   38
Interpersonal Style   38
Conclusions   40

3   Extraverted and Introverted Interpersonal Attitudes
    and Behaviors   43

Social Expectations and Priorities   44
Interpersonal Agreement and Disagreement   47
Person Perception and Interpersonal Attraction   50
Observable Differences in Social Behavior   53
Sexual Behavior   54
Interpersonal Communication   56
Miscellaneous Research Topics   61
Observations from an Interactional Perspective   63

4   Extraversion–Introversion and Other Important
    Personality Traits   65

Internal and External Control of Reinforcement   67
Miscellaneous Interpersonal Variables   72
Sensation Seeking   74
Field Dependence   75
Repression–Sensitization   77
Social Self-esteem, Social Anxiety, and Shyness   81
Social Attitudes: Conservatism and Dogmatism   85
Summary: Meaning of Extraversion–Introversion   88

5   Educational and Vocational Achievements of Extraverts
    and Introverts   91

Academic Performance   92
Teaching Strategies and Personality   99
Vocational Preferences   102

Miscellaneous Vocational Studies   106
Work Behavior   108
Plan of the Book: A Reminder   111

6   Psychological Disorders of Extraverts and Introverts   113

General Maladjustment   114
Anxiety-related Disorders   115
Depression and Suicide   117
Psychotic Disorders   119
Criminal Behavior   121
Antisocial Behavior of Children and Youth   128
Aggression and Hostility   132
Looking Ahead   135

7   Role of Extraversion–Introversion in Other
Problematic Social Behaviors   137

Cigarette Smoking   137
Alcohol   142
Narcotics   146
Marijuana and Other Soft Drugs   150
Summary: Strengths and Weaknesses of Extraverts
and Introverts   152

8   Genetic Influence and Extraversion–Introversion   157

Stability of Personality   158
Global Personality Batteries   161
Specific Extraversion Scales   165
Temperaments and Personality Traits: Concluding
Thoughts   168

Bibliography   173

Author Index   203

Subject Index   213

FOREWORD

There is fairly widespread discontent in psychology with the present status of the concept of personality. This discontent is mirrored in the usual textbook treatment of this area; the student is often offered nothing but a list of totally different and irreconcilable theories, each offered uncritically and with no attempt at evaluation, comparison, or detailed analysis of empirical findings. There seems to be a complete absence of what T. S. Kuhn, the famous philosopher of science, describes as the essential feature of "normal" science: a *paradigm*, an agreed set of concepts and working models, accompanied by a set of methods for obtaining empirical verification or falsification of relevant theories. Is the position really as desperate as all that? Are we this far removed from becoming a proper science?

I would say that there is far more agreement than might appear at first sight; the reason why this agreement is not always apparent is that psychologists value originality above all else, so that they scorn the use of agreed terms and would rather coin new names for old concepts than employ an agreed nomenclature. Whether this kind of originality is worthwhile is, of course, doubtful; it irritates and mystifies the student and makes it more difficult than need be to find the required paradigms in the welter of disorganized neologisms. There are very many concepts in the field of personality research that are closely related to extraversion–introversion but that are called by many different names. The author of this book has performed a most useful service in clearing up this confusion by surveying in detail and with rigor the large literature that has accumulated, in clarifying the exact empirical meaning of the terms by reference to observational and experimental studies, and in showing the social relevance and significance of the personality dimensions so labeled.

Extraversion–introversion is particularly important in demonstrating that paradigms in the personality field are capable of being developed; it covers an unusually wide and socially important area and has perhaps produced more literature than any other concept with the possible exception of neuroticism. Term and concept were already in popular use in the nineteenth century, and descriptive and causal theories were introduced into psychology by O. Gross in Vienna and G. Heymans in the Netherlands long before C. G. Jung published his *Psychologische Typen*, which for many people made these terms household words. There is now much evidence to connect the types of behavior associated with extraversion and introversion with psychophysiological mechanisms that can be studied in great detail in the laboratory; only in this way can we surmount the circular arguments presented by correlational and factor-analytical approaches and arrive at causal theories that predict the outcome both of laboratory experiments and of social observations and studies. The concept is certainly relevant to many aspects of social functioning, such as neurosis and criminality, and also extends to education and many other areas. Its central status in this respect is well emphasized and represented in this book.

The author has been particularly successful in demonstrating the close relation that exists between extraversion–introversion and many other concepts that have played a part in recent discussions and experiments. Equally important is the demonstration that other concepts that superficially might seem to be linked with extraversion–introversion, such as internal and external locus of control, are in fact quite independent. Empirical data alone can decide such questions, and fortunately there is now a large body of such data available, never before brought together in such a careful and up-to-date fashion.

If psychology remains the hope of a science rather than a science, as William James said, it would nevertheless seem that we are getting closer to the point where the one merges into the other. Both from the descriptive and the causal points of view, concepts like extraversion–introversion are now sufficiently well understood to serve as building stones for a science of personality. This is not the only dimension of personality, and many others will have to be studied in equal detail before we can say that we properly understand personality and can predict individual differences in behavior. But the study of extraversion–introversion has shown how to proceed in these studies and that the possibility exists of looking at personality through the use of the scientific method. This is an important advance.

H. J. Eysenck
Institute of Psychiatry
University of London

ACKNOWLEDGMENTS

The completion of this book was dependent on many factors, and I am indebted to many for their various contributions. First of all, my wife Nancy to whom the book is dedicated has provided the love, patience, and encouragement that form the necessary foundation for any accomplishment of mine. But her contributions also included valuable insights about the content and organization of the material, as well as a multitude of specific helpful suggestions. My children Kae, Jeni, and Scott have each in his or her own way enriched my life during this time. Jane Rust's typing skills were more than sufficient to produce final copy after numerous rough drafts, and I am appreciative of her pleasant attitude, dependability, and friendship. Many colleagues have supplied the personal day-by-day reinforcement that is so important in maintaining consistent work habits, but I am particularly grateful to Glen Littlepage, Jim Rust, Terry Whiteside, and Beryl West for their personal and professional encouragement. I wish to thank the Department of Psychology for a reduced teaching load during one semester. Last but not least, a crucial contribution came in the form of a generous faculty research grant to cover the cost of preparing the manuscript.

Larry Wayne Morris

EXTRAVERSION
AND
INTROVERSION

1

EXTRAVERSION-INTROVERSION AND PERSON-ENVIRONMENT INTERACTION

One of the best ways to learn about personality is to start with one central concept and explore its relationships with many other concepts and processes that are applicable to the study of personality. This book does precisely that, using the vehicle of extraversion–introversion to explore the psychology of personality. The result is exposure to such diverse topics as clinical disorders, reasons for smoking cigarettes, vocational interests, and currently popular personality traits. The primary aim is to gain an understanding of the meaning and usefulness of extraversion–introversion in the light of the most current research, but the potential secondary gains are numerous.

PERSONALITY THEORY AND RESEARCH

Traditionally personality researchers and theorists have been those specialists within psychology who devote their time and energies to the study of life-styles and to the study of variables that affect the development and maintenance of life-styles. All psychologists are ultimately interested in the understanding, prediction, and control of behavior, but each specialty within psychology places qualifications on the types of behaviors that are of primary interest. To the personality psychologist, the behaviors of greatest importance are those that are (1) relatively pervasive in the person's life-style in that they show some consistency across situations, (2) relatively stable in the person's life-style across time, and (3) indicative of the uniqueness of the person. The underlying principle is that the study of personality is the study of the totality and organization of persons' behaviors, the study of the characteristic behavior patterns that differentiate individuals from one another. In a word, the study of personality is the study of life-styles.

Pervasiveness and stability are important defining qualities of behaviors of primary importance to the personality psychologist because behaviors that do not meet these qualifications are not very helpful in understanding a person's general life-style. A behavior pattern that is expressed at only one time and place in a person's life, to take an extreme example, is rarely informative about his or her personality. Such behavior is, in fact, often misleading to observers because it is uncharacteristic of the person. The behavior tells us more about the special situational forces and special pressures of the external environment operating on the person than it does about the person. Thus it is of primary interest to the social psychologist, for example, but not the student of personality. Furthermore, behavioral patterns that show some stability over time but are limited to highly specific situations and behavior patterns that show some cross-situational pervasiveness but are confined to a relatively short time span are of somewhat limited importance in the study of personality.

For example, the style of life evidenced by a person during one year in graduate school seems all important at the time of its occurrence, but in the perspective of one's entire lifetime spent in many different situational contexts these behaviors fade in importance. They continue to be important in the study of the individual's life-style to the extent that they express the continuity of the personality that may be seen with some degree of consistency across a longer span of time and a variety of situational contexts. Other examples of the same phenomena include periods of upheaval in one's life such as divorce and the ensuing adjustment period, major illness or injury and the time spent in recuperation, and relatively temporary exposure to atypical social groups and influences. In this context it is interesting to note that some personality theorists would see such stressful situations as cutting to the core of the personality and revealing realities that are usually not in evidence in the life-style.

Uniqueness or individuality is an important defining quality of the behaviors that are of primary importance to the personality psychologist because understanding of one person's life-style is heightened by the contrast with others' life-styles. That is not to say that there is no interest in the commonalities inherent in human nature and imparted by common sociocultural influences but that there is more intense interest in the individual differences emerging in the expression or inhibition of these common tendencies. Considering the graduate student again, the student of personality is less interested in the behaviors that are more or less common to all graduate students and more interested in those behaviors that set a given student apart from some, most, or all of the other students. That this particular student wears clothes or studies or dates is of some interest if one is comparing different species, vocational groups, or age groups, respectively, but the study of personality thrives on the particular ways of dressing, studying, and dating that identify this person as an individual. And it is no coincidence that those behaviors in one's life-style that evidence the most pervasiveness and stability are also the ones that best reflect the individuality and uniqueness of the life-style. Together they reflect the global picture of the individual in which the personality theorist is interested.

The meaning of personality as an area of study for the psychologist is paralleled by a definition of personality as applied to individuals. One's personality may be taken to be the combination of his or her more or less pervasive and stable behavior patterns that are reflective of his or her individuality as a person. A major implication of the foregoing discussion is that such a global approach to the study of human behavior, which emphasizes patterning and organization in behavior, leads one directly into the study of private purposes and intentions. This is because of the inevitable connection between behavioral continuities and consistencies on the one hand and goals, priorities, and purposes in life on the other.

Therefore in addition to the study of observable behavior the study of personality also involves the study of internal, private experience, which may be conceptualized in terms of three levels of internality. At the very least there is a consideration of the conscious thoughts and emotions that are directly related to ongoing behavior (Level 1), such as the thoughts and feelings that occur in connection with a verbal conversation one has with a friend. These consist of expectancies, perceptions, and interpretations one has of the other as well as intentions, related thoughts, and associated emotions. These private events influence the content of the conversation but are not entirely reflected in it.

The work of most personality theorists has been concerned with a slightly more internal dimension of personal experience, involving more general cognitive, emotional, or attitudinal processes (Level 2). Included here are such variables as general self-esteem, specific beliefs about oneself and others, characteristic ways of thinking about problems, and general attitudinal or emotional tendencies. Using our example of two people engaged in a conversation, these processes would not be obvious but would tend to add a characteristic flavor to a person's conversations in general. Thus there would be favorite (and avoided) topics of conversation and tendencies toward optimism, pleasantness, distrust, or antagonism, and so forth. Most of the adjectives that we use to describe others and most of the traits used by personality theorists to describe others suggest this level of assumed internal processes. Many theorists would carry this line of thinking a step further to include internal processes that operate totally at an unconscious level (Level 3), affecting ongoing conversational content in subtle ways but never coming to the awareness of the parties involved. Some of the processes that could operate at this level are unrecognized biological or psychological needs, unverbalized frustrations and conflicts, and internalized values that are so well ingrained that the person no longer thinks about them but nevertheless acts upon them.

Almost by definition, the level of the internality of the processes considered above is related to the pervasiveness and stability of the tendency in the life-style. The first level, conscious thoughts and emotions directly related to ongoing behavior, involves processes that are highly situation specific and readily changeable. The second and third levels are progressively less so; that is, they apply to a wider range of situations and are more difficult to alter markedly. Thus the definition of personality is inevitably broadened to include various internal processes that reflect or influence the development and maintenance of lifestyles.

To be sure, much experimental personality research is conducted in artificial laboratory situations in which highly specific situational influences on minute segments of behavior are explored. Often, no attention is given to the relationship of current behavior to past and future behavior or to the general life-style of the subject. In many instances this approach is desirable in that precise experimental control of variables is necessary to clarify effects and relationships. But the perplexing problem to the personality researcher is how to get life-style considerations into the laboratory in order to see their influence on and interaction with situational variables. The answer has been to include demographic variables, such as sex and age, and personality variables, such as traits and needs, in the experimental design. To the extent that such variables, alone or in combination, capture the pervasive, stable, and unique characteristics of the subject's life-style, personality becomes a part of the laboratory study.

EXTRAVERSION–INTROVERSION

Among the most widely used personality variables is that of extraversion–introversion, and a major purpose of this book is to evaluate its usefulness in research conducted in the recent past. Although there are not yet sufficient data from which firm conclusions may be drawn, it seems likely first of all from information presented throughout the book that the presence of extraverted and introverted tendencies in one's behavior is pervasive in nature, that is, it applies to his or her behavior in a variety of situations and may be seen expressed in various areas of life. Second, extraverted and introverted tendencies appear earlier in childhood and evidence more stability through the developmental years than most personality characteristics (see chapter 8). Third, individual differences ranging along a continuum from one extreme to the other are clearly identifiable, allowing the possibility that one's uniqueness can be partially identified by his or her placement on the continuum. It would be foolish to suggest that this variable alone could capture the essence of one's life-style, but it may well be one of a few that can best be utilized to this end. The following chapters indicate that there is a correlation between persons' introversion-extraversion scores and numerous tendencies that are operative in their life-styles.

The importance of extraversion–introversion in personality theory and research has long been recognized and is widely accepted. Most of the current thinking about this concept is traceable historically to the work of either Carl Jung or Hans Eysenck. In the early part of this century, after breaking with Freud, Jung developed a complex theory of intrapsychic processes called analytical psychology (see Jung, 1923). In developing the idea of many polarities (such as conscious versus unconscious, thinking versus feeling, and progression versus regression) existing within each personality, emphasis was placed on the opposing tendencies of extraversion and introversion. The basic difference between the two lies in persons' preferences for attending to the inner world of subjectivity with an emphasis on reflective, introspective cognitive activity (introversion) versus preferences for attending to the outer world of objective events with an emphasis on active involvement in the environment (extraversion). Both of the opposing tendencies were seen by Jung as necessary and healthy, and one would do well to develop both attitudes simultaneously so that a proper balance is achieved. However, there is typically a preponderance of one of the two tendencies in any given individual, which is important in understanding his or her life-style. Jung's theories have had considerable impact on clinically oriented psychologists in particular, and derivatives of Jung's thoughts are encountered frequently in the research literature. A recent detailed treatment of this subject is available in a book by Shapiro and Alexander (1975).

Hans Eysenck's work (e.g., H. Eysenck & Eysenck, 1969) on extraversion–introversion, spanning the last three decades, has had a similar impact on experimentally oriented psychologists and thus has stimulated much research on the topic.

(Incidentally, Eysenck's atypical spelling of the word extraversion became the accepted spelling in the subject index of *Psychological Abstracts* beginning in 1974.) Although Eysenck's orientation is more biological and behavioral in contrast to Jung's intrapsychic approach, the influence of the two has been largely complementary. Eysenck contends that there are three major personality dimensions, extraversion–introversion, neuroticism–stability, and psychoticism, which are largely independent of each other and which together convey a wealth of information about individuals' life-styles. Eysenck defines the basic difference between extraverts and introverts as biological, rooted in the reticular activating system of the brain. This is the system that monitors incoming neural impulses resulting from environmental stimulation and that either stimulates (excites) or inhibits responses of higher brain centers to the stimulation; the system thus controls the arousal level of the cortex of the brain. Extraverts and introverts are held to differ in the relative strength of the opposing processes of excitation and inhibition such that introverts typically have higher levels of cortical arousal compared with extraverts.

The differing levels of arousal result in behavioral and attitudinal preferences and tendencies. Assuming that each person desires and functions best at a moderate level of arousal most of the time, it follows that introverts should most often be found seeking a reduction of external stimulation, inasmuch as external stimulation increases arousal, whereas extraverts should be found most often seeking an increase in stimulation from the environment. Furthermore a high arousal level facilitates learning in the presence of noxious stimuli, which are particularly arousing and thus particularly aversive to introverts. A massive array of research has been done in the areas of perception, learning, and performance of simple tasks, effects of sensory deprivation and overstimulation, and so on, which is largely supportive of the biological theory advanced (see H. Eysenck, 1976e). For the reader who would like to pursue these biological differences further, Gray (1972) has advanced a slightly different biological theory. The implications are the same as those of Eysenck, but the emphasis is on arousability rather than arousal per se. Examples of research addressing these issues include Wigglesworth and Smith (1976) and Fowles, Roberts, and Nagel (1977).

The resulting behavioral differences are perhaps most apparent in social situations. Both the presence of other persons and social activities per se are typically arousing and thus more likely to be sought out and enjoyed by extraverts than by introverts. Furthermore introverts learn more social inhibitions than do extraverts (H. Eysenck, 1976c), which affects their activities in social settings. Eysenck's extravert then is described as sociable, lively, impulsive, seeking novelty and change, carefree, and emotionally expressive. In contrast, the introvert is quiet, introspective, intellectual, well ordered, emotionally unexpressive, and value oriented; prefers small groups of intimate friends; and plans well ahead.

INTERACTIONAL PERSPECTIVE

It is becoming abundantly clear that any complete understanding of human behavior must incorporate the insights of environmental, social, ecological, and behavioristic psychology along with insights from the study of personality. Perhaps the major contribution of the past decade of research and theory concerning personality has been the conceptual advance variously termed interactionism, person–environment or person–situation interaction, trait–state interaction, or the cognitive-learning perspective. Carlson (1975), Sechrest (1976), and Phares and Lamiell (1977) have all noted this development in their recent *Annual Review of Psychology* articles on personality. Although the conceptualization is not new, earlier attempts to deal with the issues involved were nevertheless unable to avoid resultant theories that were either heavily person oriented, as in the case of Henry Murray's personology and Kurt Lewin's field theory, or heavily environment oriented, as in the case of Roger Barker's ecological psychology.

The recent trend is one that gives more nearly equal weight to person and environment in determining both overt behavior and private experience. The question of which is most important is, one hopes, being supplanted by much better questions: Which environmental factors interact with which person factors to produce which behaviors? How may we best conceptualize the interaction? Stated thus, the person–environment interaction becomes a common meeting ground for psychologists of many different theoretical persuasions.

Social-learning theory, as developed in the writings of Bandura (1969), Krasner and Ullmann (1973), Mahoney (1974), Rotter, Chance, and Phares (1972), and Staats (1975), represents perhaps the most complete current statement of the nature of the person–environment interaction, but the movement is not limited to any one theoretical school of thought. In fact, it seems possible to incorporate and move toward interactionism within all extant theoretical systems. The common denominators are emphases on (1) cognitive processes and (2) social processes and inter-personal relationships. Focusing on the latter seems inevitably to lead to an emphasis on the former, and the combination of the two offers the best tool for understanding person–environment interactions. Within behaviorism the historical development begins with the early radical behaviorists, followed by neobe-haviorists who begin to admit the importance of social and covert processes, and culminates in the current social-learning theory of Bandura (1977), the cognitive social-learning theory of Mischel (1973; 1977), and the cognitive-learning perspective of behavior therapists in general (see Lazarus, 1977).

A similar though less dramatic development may be seen in other schools of thought. For example, most neo-Freudian theorists differed from Freud in their increased emphasis on social and cultural factors in personality development and on cognitive (ego) processes. Robert Carson (1969), tracing his lineage back to one of the neo-Freudians, Harry Stack Sullivan, completed the transition to an interactional position that is consistent with many of the tenets of social-learning theory. Within humanistic or phenomenological theory, the current move toward interaction may be seen in the popularity of George Kelly's (1955) cognitive (personal construct) theory as well as in recent attempts to understand the self or self-concept as a cognitive system (Epstein, 1973) and as a social construct (Horrocks & Jackson, 1972; Ziller, 1973).

There is much to be said for an interactional psychology that is broader than any of these developments, for each school of thought has unique contributions to make. Behavioral social-learning theory contributes an understanding and analysis of situational determinants and environmental variables; neo-Freudian interactional theory contributes explorations of developmental processes; and phenomenological theory contributes insights concerning the involvement of emotions in the process. Although all of these theoretical developments cannot be traced here, the interested reader will find ample detail in Walsh's (1973) review of four such theories and related research and in edited works by Endler and Magnusson (1976) and Magnusson and Endler (1977) containing numerous recent contributions to both theory and research methodology. Discussion of two positions will be satisfactory for our purposes.

Walter Mischel's (1973; 1977) cognitive social-learning theory focuses attention on the individual's cognitive activities and behavior patterns, studied in relation to the specific conditions that evoke, maintain, and modify them, which in turn are changed by the cognitive activities and behavior patterns. Five person variables are identified by Mischel; all of these relate to the cognitive activities of the person. They are operative in his or her perception, interpretation, and reaction to situations and in attempts to change those situations. Mischel maintains that such individual differences in cognitive activities are the person variables most likely to show some consistency across situations. They are (1) cognitive and behavioral construction competencies, capacity or potential for generating a variety of ways of interpreting and responding to social situations; (2) encoding strategies and personal constructs, the specific ways one processes available information and uses it to form interpretations of environmental events; (3) behavior–outcome and stimulus–outcome expectancies, the expectancies one holds concerning the consequences of particular behaviors and the reinforcements available in particular social settings; (4) subjective stimulus values, the value one places on various situations, potential consequences of behavior, and incentives; and (5) self-regulatory systems and plans, including self-imposed goals, standards, and reinforcements operative in a situation as well as organized plans for the initiation, sequencing, and termination of complex behavior.

Thus Mischel conceptualized person variables as ongoing cognitive and behavioral processes rather than static qualities of the individual. These have been acquired through direct and vicarious social-learning experiences and are modifiable by current environmental forces. The way the person–environment interaction works is that the person is an information processor with characteristic ways of gathering, processing, interpreting, and drawing behavioral implications from the available information. These characteristics of the person are the cognitive social-learning person variables. The role of the environment is to provide information to the person for processing. Thus any behavior that occurs is produced jointly by the person's information processing system and the environmental information provided. Behavioral patterns produced consistently by this interaction constitute the person's life-style or personality.

At times the person variables exert powerful effects on the individual's behavior, and at other times the situation is the dominant influence. These differential situational effects may be understood within Mischel's framework by differentiating between strong and weak situations. The former dominates behavior by minimizing the influence of person variables, that is, by utilizing commonly held competencies; inducing uniform interpretations, expectancies, and values; and minimizing self-involvement in the situation. An example would be a driver approaching a red traffic light: individual differences in response are negligible. In contrast, weak situations are characterized by ambiguity, unclear expectations, and numerous alternative responses and create an environment in which individual differences (that is, effects of person variables on behavior) are maximal. The operation of these processes is seen most clearly in social situations, in which the most profound influence on life-style is to be found. In these situations the most important determinant of the strength or weakness of the situation is the degree of role structure present. Where roles are clearly defined, individual differences are minimal; where they are loosely defined, individuality becomes apparent.

Robert Carson's (1969) interactional approach to personality focuses directly on interpersonal behavior. He presents convincing evidence that the two independent dimensions within which the varieties of interpersonal behavior may best be described are (1) dominance–submission and (2) love–hate. This system may be elaborated into a circumplex having eight distinctive, behaviorally defined segments. Incidentally Lorr and Youniss (1973) have developed an inventory to assess interpersonal style that is based largely on this rationale and that is discussed in detail in the next chapter. The system is highly useful in discussing person–environment interactions because it represents simultaneously (1) a description of one's typical mode of interpersonal behavior across situations, (2) a description of one's current mode of behavior in a single interpersonal situation, and (3) one's reactions to interpersonal responses initiated by other persons. The first two represent influences of a person on his or her environment, whereas the third represents environmental effects on the person. Thus a person may engage in dominant-loving interpersonal behavior in a particular relationship because it reflects a strategy, plan, or intention to influence the other toward submissive-loving behavior (either as a general life-style strategy or as a specific-situation strategy) or because this behavior is a reaction to submissive-loving behavior initiated by the other. Most interpersonal behaviors result from both forces operating concurrently. Loving and hating behaviors tend to be reciprocated in kind whereas dominating and submissive behaviors tend to evoke their opposites. Knowledge of such relationships existing within a common culture thus forms the framework for both effecting changes or maintaining desired behavior patterns in others and simultaneously for interpreting others' expectations of us and reacting appropriately. The reciprocal person–environment interaction is thus rendered more understandable.

Carson proceeds to discuss in considerable detail the processes of dyadic relationships, interpersonal transactions and contracts, and implications for understanding abnormality and therapeutic processes. He emphasizes the learning that occurs in social contexts and the cognitive processes operative in interpersonal encounters as crucial in understanding human behavior and personality. His discussion of learning includes both action learning (i.e., alterations of observable behavior) via classical and operant conditioning and observational learning, and cognitive learning (alteration of cognitive processes), with the latter occupying a relatively more important position in the theory. An important variable that appears when considering learning in a social context is that of complementarity. It is highly reinforcing for one's behavior to cause another person to respond in kind or according to one's intentions; and it is highly aversive for a behavior to fail to have its desired effect on the other person.

In discussing cognitive processes, Carson follows the theoretical model proposed by Miller, Galanter, and Pribram (1960). At the most general and internal level of personality one has an image, defined as the totality of one's knowledge and the content of one's cognitive processes acquired through past experience. At the intermediate level of generality there are strategic plans, which are abstract and general life-style considerations of priorities and purposes. Tactical plans represent the day-to-day adaptation of strategic plans to specific situations and thus constitute the most identifiable and situation-specific level of cognitive functioning. Images and plans are constantly modified by experience with various specific situations as a result of being applied and evaluated. Thus tactical plans in particular develop situational specificity and are highly modifiable, whereas strategic plans and images are progressively more stable and pervasive.

The interactional approaches of Mischel and Carson appear highly complementary and evidence considerable agreement. Together they cover the major points of emphasis of most current interactional theorists and thus serve as good examples for our purposes. Interactionists generally agree that cognition is the primary mediator between whatever person and environment variables are operative. Thus physiological, motivational, and emotional states of the person, along with past experiences, feed information into the ongoing cognitive processes, as do cues, reinforcements, instructions, examples, and other environmental influences. The cognitive system processes the information, interprets it, weighs priorities, formulates strategies, and through a problem-solving process dictates behavioral reactions.

There is one additional point that bears some clarification and that involves the meaning of the term *interaction*. On the one hand, it is used to describe a theoretical position regarding the causes of behavior. Statements of this position range from the mere assertion that there are both person variables and environment variables that can affect behavior to the much stronger assumption that all behavior is codetermined by interacting person and environment variables. This is not a difficult form of interactionism to accept because it simply means that environmental forces are powerful determinants of behavior but are nevertheless modified in their effect (strengthened or weakened) by the person's perception and interpretation of those forces and by his or her own intentions.

On the other hand, there is a more challenging and comprehensive meaning of interaction, which is concerned with the effects of persons and environments on each other rather than on behavior per se. In the place of simpler notions that either persons shape their environments or environments shape persons, interactionism may be taken to mean that both person variables and environment variables continually change to some degree because of the interaction between the two. Each operates, either successively or simultaneously, on the other. The assumption is that neither person nor environment variables remain static but that both are affected in reciprocal fashion by the behaviors that they produce. Persons choose and change their environmental surroundings selectively, and social-learning experiences change personalities. It appears that both Carson and Mischel agree with this more comprehensive meaning of the term, although not all interactionists would. Clearly agreement with the first meaning concerning effects on behavior does not imply agreement with the second meaning concerning effects of person and environment on each other, nor does evidence for the first meaning in the research literature constitute evidence for the second. In fact, some hold the two meanings to be basically contradictory (Buss, 1977; Overton & Reese, 1973). It does seem unlikely, however, that a theorist would hold the more comprehensive second position without also agreeing with the first.

Our interactional perspective includes both meanings, recognizing them as separate but complementary positions. We hold that (1) behavior is jointly determined by person variables and environment variables operating concurrently, (2) the effects of each on behavior are simultaneously affected (facilitated or inhibited) by the other, (3) the content of each is simultaneously shaped by the other, and (4) the resulting behavior has a reciprocal effect in modifying both the person and environment that produced it. Consider again our two friends involved in a conversation: (1) the next statement out of one's mouth is determined jointly by aspects of the situation (including but not limited to the last statement of the other) and by the cognitive, emotional, and behavioral characteristics of the one about to speak; (2) these situational and personal aspects have simultaneous moderating effects on both the strength and content of each other as the person seeks to interpret and respond in the conversation; and (3) the statement, once verbalized, has an effect on both the speaker (person) and the listener (environment). Both are changed and the complex interaction of causes and effects continues to develop interdependently.

PERSONALITY TRAITS AND INTERACTIONISM

Where does all this leave trait theory in general and the study of extraversion–introversion in particular? Traits are person variables, and yet trait theory has come under heavy attack in recent years, often from the theorists cited above. The problem is that traits have traditionally been defined in ways that imply static and unchanging personality characteristics. It is clear that trait psychology must adapt to the incontrovertible evidence of the relative situational specificity of behavior if it is to remain a viable force in personality theory. It must move in the direction of defining traits in less general terms, that is, as persons' predispositions or tendencies to think and behave in specific types of ways when they are exposed to specific types of situations. The concept of situational specificity is almost always implied in current trait theories (e.g., Cattell, 1965, pp. 246–250), but the implication is seldom specified sufficiently to enhance the usefulness of particular traits. Another direction in which trait psychology must move is toward a specification of the conditions under which a given trait may be acquired, modified, or extinguished.

Mischel, one of the most outspoken critics of trait theory (e.g., 1968), nevertheless speaks of person variables and argues that the variables most likely to show consistency within a person's life-style are cognitive social-learning variables, that is, cognitive variables operative in social contexts. If he is correct, trait psychology needs to move in the direction of specifying and assessing these person variables and to move away from less fruitful variables. Traits that can be demonstrated to be related to ongoing cognitive processes in social situations should have preeminence. A move in this direction has been taken by Nideffer (1976), whose Test of Attentional and Interpersonal Style (see chapter 2 for further details) assesses both cognitive processes and interpersonal behaviors and attitudes.

Stagner (1976, 1977), a staunch defender of trait theory, agrees that a trait should be "conceived as a schema, or a cognitive rule, that guides behavior in a variety of situations perceived as belonging to this schema or subject to this rule" (1976, p. 116). Similarly Cantor and Mischel (1977) view traits as "prototypes (or normative conceptual schemata)" that are used in processing and organizing information available to us from our social environment. They are concepts about the similarities and differences that we have observed about the behavior of ourselves and others, which are developed and operate according to the cognitive principles of concept abstraction and concept utilization. Acquired trait labels therefore function as cognitive elements in our perception of other people. At the same time they function as traits directing our behavior in the sense that they constitute and embody expectations concerning future behavior. Applying a trait label to another implies expected behavior patterns, which monitor our interactions with the person so labeled. Likewise attributing a trait to oneself implies self-expectations consistent with the prototype and thus exerts an influence on future behavior.

The data collected by Cantor and Mischel make two important points. First, the constructs of introversion and extraversion do operate cognitively as prototypes. Second, these particular concepts or schemata are pervasive in our culture and are naturally occurring in the sense that their presence in the thinking of the subjects could be assumed from prior learning rather than being taught in the experimental setting. The experimental procedure consisted of a memory task in which 76 college students were presented 10-sentence descriptions of each of four characters, then given an interfering numerical task, and finally tested for recognition memory of the characteristics of the four characters. One of the characters was described as predominantly extraverted, another had predominantly introverted qualities, and the other two were random-mixture controls. When the extraverted and introverted prototypes were suggested either implicitly or explicitly in connection with the memory task, consistent memory biases occurred, which evidenced the cognitive operation of the trait prototypes.

INTERACTIONAL PERSONALITY RESEARCH

The overriding conviction involved in the preparation of this book is that extraversion–introversion has great potential in future personality research. But the move must be made from traditional trait psychology to the perspective of the person–environment interaction in order to explore the limits of that potential. The remainder of this chapter is devoted to a discussion of studies that deal simultaneously with the topic of extraversion–introversion and with issues facing the personality researcher seeking to work within the interactional perspective.

Simple yes and no answers to the question of cross-situational consistency are, it is hoped, a thing of the past, but attempts at adequate conceptualization of this issue remain of paramount importance. One approach is to view transsituational consistency as a personality dimension in its own right. Campus (1974) found that there were individual differences in the degree of consistency revealed in subjects' self-ratings of their needs across 16 hypothetical situations and that consistency of self-ratings across situations was related to the predictability of behavior from personality variables (needs). Long, Calhoun, and Selby (1977) also found individual differences in the degree of consistency of social behavior in various anxious and nonanxious situations. These studies make the point that the behavior of some individuals is more consistent and predictable across situations than that of others, as though the behavior of some is controlled more by person variables and the behavior of others is more situationally determined. If so, it will be interesting to see which personality traits are related to this consistency dimension. Neither study showed a noteworthy relationship between extraversion and consistency.

Another approach was taken by Bem and Allen (1974), who reasoned that each person probably has some traits that are expressed consistently in behavior but that the consistent traits would vary from person to person. Thus any given personality trait would have the quality of cross-situational consistency for some people but not for others. The important question then is how to determine which individuals are consistent on which traits. Bem and Allen assumed (correctly) that scores on the personality trait itself would not provide the answer because there would be both consistent and inconsistent persons scoring at all points along the continuum from low to high scores on the trait. In their study of extraverted behavior, Bem and Allen asked, "How much do you vary from one situation to another in how friendly and outgoing you are?" They conducted multiple assessments of how friendly and outgoing subjects were, including global self-ratings, a self-report questionnaire, parents' and peers' ratings, verbal behavior during a group discussion, and conversation while waiting with a confederate. Responses to the consistency question were related to other indices of consistency (intercorrelations among measures, standard deviations), and, as expected, consistency of both types was unrelated to scores on the self-report friendliness scales. Correlations of the dependent variables with a measure of extraversion were significantly higher and quite impressive in the self-rated consistency group. The implication is that extraversion-introversion is a good predictor of the friendliness exhibited in various situations for some people but not for others, and the difference is not reflected in extraversion scores per se. When both groups of subjects are utilized without differentiation, the presence of the latter group waters down the results. Similar results were found for the trait of conscientiousness. Turner (1978) conducted a similar study using another variable relevant to the study of extraversion–introversion: interpersonal dominance. He divided college students into consistent and inconsistent groups depending on whether they rated themselves as either "dominant" or "deferential" (both consistent) or marked "depends on the situation" (inconsistent). Subjects were asked to write a story describing their typical degree of dominance exhibited in group discussion situations. The story was used to predict actual dominance displayed in group discussions conducted at least one week later. Again, prediction was superior for the consistent group compared with the inconsistent group. The implication is clear. However, it remains to be demonstrated that the subjects who were consistent on the trait under investigation were inconsistent on other traits, and vice versa. Another needed study involves identifying the personality traits most likely to be expressed consistently in the life-styles of the largest number of people. It would not be surprising to find extraversion-introversion near the top of such a list.

Many investigators have reacted to the recent attacks on trait psychology by affirming their confidence in the value of personality traits and by seeking to improve the methods used to assess them. For whatever reason much of this attention has been directed toward the measurement of interpersonal dominance or assertiveness. Turner's (1978) study went a step beyond the above discussion to show that a change in assessment technique, that is, asking subjects to write a story about the maximal (rather than typical) degree of dominance that they could possibly display in the group discussion, improved the predictability of the inconsistent group up to the level of the consistent group. In fact, although the major finding was of the interaction between groups and assessment techniques, the maximal story procedure was generally more useful in predicting actual behavior than was the typical story procedure, a finding consistent with that of Willerman, Turner, and Peterson (1976) in a study of emotional expression. In essence, the maximal approach asks subjects about their capabilities or competencies, much as in the assessment of ability, rather than asking about their characteristic or typical behavior.

Another study addressing the assessment problem is that of Dworkin and Kihlstrom (1978), who developed a measure of dominance following the situation–response format, which has received considerable attention among interactionists. This measurement approach was initiated and popularized by Endler and his colleagues in the study of anxiety (e.g., Endler, Hunt, & Rosenstein, 1962). Dworkin and Kihlstrom cited 12 specific situations and 11 responses (or response modes) that could be employed or experienced in each situation, and subjects rated the probability of each response occurring in each situation on a 7-point scale. Thus each situation, each response mode, and specific combinations of the two may be scored for a group of subjects and for each individual; in addition, a total dominance score may be derived for each person. In a sample of college students, total scores correlated positively with a traditional dominance questionnaire. The percentage of the variance in inventory scores accounted for by the person–situation inter-action was extremely high compared with the variance that could be attributed to either persons or situations separately. In other words, predicting a person's assertiveness is enhanced considerably by assessing his or her characteristic level of domi-nance in a particular type of situation rather than analyzing behavior only as a function of the situation or only as a func-tion of a personality trait. The types of situations that were differentiated on the basis of factor analysis were (1) situations involving friends, (2) situations involving others in the com-munity such as a grocer, and (3) group situations involving impositions from others in which dominance was displayed. While situation–response inventories clearly reflect the spirit of interactionism, the assessment approach, in comparison with traditional assessment techniques, is not without its critics (e.g., Knudson & Golding, 1974).

Another noteworthy point concerning the prediction of dominant behavior in specific settings from self-report measures of dominance involves what Jaccard (1974) calls the *multiple-act criteria*. He examined female dominant behaviors in a sample of college students related to scores on two questionnaire mea-sures of dominance. When predicting single behaviors, the ques-tionnaire meaures failed; however, strong predictive relationships emerged when specific behaviors were summed to constitute a multiple-act criterion. The point is well taken, considering that personality researchers are often interested more in predicting average, typical, or characteristic behavior rather than a specific behavior at a specific time and place.

PLAN OF THE BOOK

The major aim of this first chapter has been to introduce the conceptual framework of interactionism. The studies dis-cussed in the last several pages are mainly of methodological and metatheoretical importance in that they explore the most advantageous ways of conceptualizing and conducting inter-actional personality research. The fact that extraversion and related variables (friendliness and dominance) have been used in some of these studies may be taken as an indication of the

assumed potential of extraversion–introversion in future interactional research. Unfortunately, most of the research to be
reported in this volume is not explicitly interactional in design,
although noteworthy exceptions are sprinkled throughout. The
reader who is eager to see the design and results of good interactional research involving extraversion–introversion is referred
to chapter 3 in particular and also to parts of chapters 5 and 7.
Most such studies find the personality trait to interact with
situational variables in affecting behavior.

The content of the remaining chapters has been determined
almost entirely by the content of studies on extraversion–
introversion published in the years 1972–1977 (and 1978, as
much as possible). A concerted effort has been made to include
every such study, regardless of design or finding, concerned
with personal or interpersonal attitudes or behavior. (Studies
concerned solely with physiology, perception, and learning in
laboratory settings were systematically excluded; inclusion
of these would probably have doubled the size of the volume.)
Studies conducted before 1972 were selectively included in
order to clarify particular points, and no comprehensive coverage
of earlier research is intended. The intention in preparing this
volume is to present as unbiased an account as possible of the
current status of extraversion–introversion in the various research areas represented and to provide a resource to which
researchers, theorists, educators, and students may go for both
a comprehensive overview and specific details of one another's
work.

Chapters 2, 3, and 4 discuss current studies involving the
content areas of global personality assessment, social behavior,
and currently popular personality traits, respectively. Emerging
profiles are drawn that help to clarify the basic attitudinal and
behavioral characteristics of more extraverted and more introverted individuals. Simultaneously conceptions of other important
personality variables and processes are sharpened as their relationships to extraversion–introversion are explored. In chapters 5,
6, and 7, these insights are applied and elaborated upon in the
context of discussions of the achievements, clinical problems,
and social problems, respectively, of more extraverted and more
introverted persons. Some of the strengths and weaknesses of
each life-style come to light, and, simultaneously, there is insight

to be gained concerning the achievements and problems themselves as the relationships are explored. Finally, chapter 8 considers the evidence concerning the degree to which these differences are genetic in origin.

It is hoped that both professional and student researchers will be able to identify numerous research topics embedded in the following pages, including examples of how to (or how not to) address particular topics. There are crucial questions left unanswered in virtually every area discussed. There are hypotheses suggested by the findings of poorly done studies; such hypotheses should be examined with more refined research methods. And there are topics not represented in the following pages at all because there is no current research addressing them.

The assumptions and emphases of the interactional perspective discussed earlier suggest that more research is needed on the following topics:

1. Interactive effects of person and environment variables on behavior: For persons scoring high or low on extraversion-introversion, what environmental conditions facilitate or impede the expression of extraverted and introverted behavior? Or, conversely, what situational inducements to engage in extraverted or introverted behaviors are facilitated or impeded by the person's extraversion or introversion? What behaviors are most affected by interactions involving extraversion-introversion?

2. Interactive effects of person and environment variables on each other: What are the antecedent and continuing conditions under which tendencies toward extraversion or introversion are acquired, modified, and extinguished? What differential selections of and modifications of their environments do more extraverted and more introverted persons make? What types of behaviors, once engaged in, have the greatest reciprocal effects in changing the degree of the actor's extraversion or introversion?

2

MEANINGS AND MEASUREMENTS OF EXTRAVERSION AND INTROVERSION

It is generally agreed that extraversion–introversion or some similarly labeled trait is one of the major descriptive dimensions in the study of personality. Invariably analyses of personality test batteries reveal that extraversion emerges as one of a few factors that account for much of the common variance shared by specific items or specific personality dimensions. Although this is not a new finding (Carrigan, 1960; Peterson, 1965), current research with improved test batteries continues to provide an accumulation of data that support the centrality of extraversion-introversion in the study of the structure of personality as assessed by global self-report measures (see Wilde, 1977).

There continues to be lively discussion centered around such issues as how many major personality variables such as extraversion there are, how they relate to each other, whether extraversion is too general a dimension that should be discarded in favor of its subcomponents, and how best to measure extraversion-introversion. As we explore the research relating to these questions, our major purpose is to gain insight into the meaning(s) of the construct as it is currently used in personality research and theory and to identify available measuring instruments.

EYSENCK SCALES

Hans Eysenck has long contended that there are two major personality dimensions, extraversion–introversion and neuroticism-stability, which are independent of each other (H. Eysenck, 1944). He later added a third, psychoticism (H. Eysenck, 1953; H. Eysenck & Eysenck, 1976b). His initial conclusions were reached on the basis of factor analysis of rating scale data from several hundred neurotics in England and supported by numerous subsequent studies. Eysenck's position is that the extraversion and neuroticism factors appear under various labels (sociability and impulsiveness, anxiety and emotional stability) in all personality assessment schemes that adequately sample the entire range of personality variables. The implications for personality research are twofold: first, that measures of extraversion-introversion and neuroticism convey the most information about a given personality of any trait scores that could be utilized; and second, that these dimensions must be considered central to any full description and analysis of the individual differences that we call personality.

The research technique most often used in addressing the issues raised above is factor analysis, a statistical method for reducing a complex mass of data to the simplest set of common elements (factors) within it. A large number of subjects complete a personality battery, and scores on all items are correlated with each other. Factor analysis identifies clusters of items the scores of which covary, and emerging dimensions that fit the correlated clusters are called primary factors. Similarly clusters of primary factors may be identified by further intercorrelation and factor analysis, leading to the emergence of second-order factors. Through this process it is likely that 500 items may be reduced to 10–15 primary factors and further to 2–6 second-order factors. Eysenck's extraversion and neuroticism factors are usually best matched by second-order factors on most personality batteries. Factor analysis may be used further to select the best items representing a personality factor in order to improve the scale designed to measure it.

Applying this technique, Eysenck has continued to refine scales to measure extraversion, neuroticism, and psychoticism. Successive versions of Eysenck's scales are the Maudsley Personality Inventory (H. Eysenck, 1959), the Eysenck Personality Inventory (H. Eysenck & Eysenck, 1968), the Psychoticism-Extraversion–Neuroticism Scale (S. Eysenck & Eysenck, 1972), and the Eysenck Personality Questionnaire (H. Eysenck & Eysenck, 1976a). Versions are available for children and adolescents (S. Eysenck, 1965) and have been translated into the languages of Afrikaans (Orpen, 1972), Ghanaian (Kline, 1967), Hebrew (Handel, 1976), Hindi (Gupta, 1971; Singh, 1966), Persian (Mehryar, 1970), and Turkish (Irfani, 1977). These scales and the attendant definition of the concept of extraversion-introversion are the most popular in current use, and their usefulness is supported by data such as those presented by Handel (1976) that the scales have considerable equivalence across age groups and across cultures.

Several elements are involved in Eysenck's differentiation between extraverts and introverts. The two major dimensions are sociability and impulsivity, but components such as jocularity and quick-wittedness may also be identified (H. Eysenck & Eysenck, 1969). S. Eysenck and Eysenck (1963) factor analyzed responses of 300 subjects to 66 of their extraversion and neuroticism items and found that the extraversion items split evenly into two categories representing sociability and impulsivity. The two subcomponents correlated .50 with each other, a relationship that could be regarded equally as evidence for combining them into one variable (extraversion) or for maintaining their separate identities. In any case, they were clearly not independent dimensions.

If desired, the extraversion scale can be scored separately for these two major components. Gibson (1974) used the impulsivity and sociability items so identified in the above study and total extraversion scores to predict sociometric ratings and test impulsiveness (guessing at test items when placed under time pressure) among 24 members of a freshman psychology class. As expected, sociability scores predicted sociometric ratings (being ranked among the best known or least known in the class) better than impulsiveness scores did; however, total extraversion scores predicted them equally well. Unexpectedly the same

pattern held for test impulsiveness. This study replicated the
earlier correlation reported between the two subcomponents
of extraversion ($r = .47$).

Another view of the various aspects of extraversion–introversion
is provided in a series of studies by Howarth and his colleagues,
who have been quite critical of Eysenck's extraversion scale.
Howarth (1973) reanalyzed H. Eysenck's (1944) original rating
scale data of 700 neurotic soldiers, from which the neuroticism–
extraversion conceptualization emerged, using a more sophisti-
cated form of factor analysis, the hierarchical oblique method.
He concluded that although there was an adjustment–emotionality
factor similar to but not limited to Eysenck's neuroticism, no
clear-cut extraversion factor could be identified. In two factor
analytic studies of the Eysenck Personality Inventory, the conclusion was reached that the extraversion dimension is not sufficiently unitary to be useful and should be approached from a
multivariate point of view. Howarth (1976a) concluded that
the extraversion scale, unlike the neuroticism scale, does not
have satisfactorily high item–scale correlations, satisfactorily
low cross-correlations with the neuroticism scale, or satisfactory
commonality in the higher order factor analytic solutions. More
specifically Howarth and Browne (1972) identified 15 inter-
pretable factors, 5 in the domain of extraversion and 7 in the
domain of neuroticism. Two sociability factors, impulsivity,
jocularity, and social conversation were identified and judged
to be sufficiently independent to defy combination into the
broader concept of extraversion. The neuroticism factors were
interpreted similarly. Nevertheless, the two major factors that
accounted for the most variance were sociability and adjustment–
emotionality.

There is general agreement among researchers that the sociability aspect of the extraversion–introversion dimension, either
alone or in combination with other subcomponents of extraversion, emerges as one of the two or three personality factors
that account for a major proportion of the variance in the particular
data being analyzed. Where more than one extraversion factor
emerges, the sociability dimension is consistently the most salient,
as in the study described above. Thus there is little argument
about the centrality of the trait of extraversion as defined specifically as sociability, that is, the participation in and enjoyment

of social activities. Arguments arise at the point of deciding whether to include other elements such as impulsiveness, and if so which ones, into a broader personality dimension. For example, Vagg and Hammond (1976) administered a combination of items from three personality batteries (Eysenck's, Cattell's, and Guilford's) to large samples, factor analyzed the responses, and concluded that the extraversion confactor that emerged consisted entirely of social extraversion with no element of impulsivity included. In all, four confactors were identified: neuroticism, extraversion, sensitivity, and morality.

There are two authors (Barratt, 1972; Schalling, 1977) who disagree with the placement of sociability as the most central component of extraversion and place impulsiveness in that position instead. Both insist that the two major orthogonal dimensions in personality assessment are impulsiveness and anxiety and that impulsiveness but not sociability has a physiological basis similar to that claimed by Eysenck for the trait of extraversion. In particular Schalling contends that Eysenck's theories of delinquency and criminality and of cigarette smoking (see chapters 6 and 7) hold for impulsiveness only.

Actually the word impulsiveness as used in the current literature has many different meanings, some of which are and some of which are not related to extraversion and introversion. For example, Bentler and McClain (1976) investigated the relationship between the currently popular reflection–impulsivity dimension, as measured in children by the Matching Familiar Figures Test, and other measures of impulsivity and extraversion. Utilizing self-reports, peer ratings, and teacher ratings of each variable in a sample of fifth graders, they found that extraversion was positively related to impulsiveness when the latter was defined as a tendency to be restless, to horse around, to lose control and to enter into activities with great vigor. However, neither of these variables was related to the reflection–impulsivity dimension. Cairns (1973) likewise failed to find a relationship between Junior Maudsley Personality Inventory and Matching Familiar Figures Test scores (cf. Messer, 1976).

In the most thorough study to date of the relationship between extraversion and impulsiveness, S. Eysenck and Eysenck (1977) conducted three factor analytic studies of impulsiveness items gathered from various sources and identified four replicable factors. In addition to a narrow definition of impulsivity (acting on impulse), there were factors defined as risk taking, non-planning, and liveliness. The total of the four was labeled broad impulsivity. Of the four factors, only risk taking and liveliness were related to sociability and extraversion. Narrow impulsivity and nonplanning seem to be indications of maladjustment (psychoticism), and broad impulsivity was also more highly related to psychoticism than to extraversion. It is clear then that the trait of impulsiveness in its fullest meaning is too broad to be subsumed under extraversion but that the two traits overlap partially. Further support for this position is found in a study by Plomin (1976b), who correlated Maudsley Personality Inventory scores with three factors of impulsivity; impulse control, sensation seeking, and decision time. He concluded that Eysenck's impulsiveness items on the Maudsley Personality Inventory were not impressively related to any of the three and could best be labeled liveliness, which correlates positively with sociability. The Eysencks suggest that researchers investigating this area use a separate impulsivity scale, available from them upon request, in addition to the Eysenck Personality Questionnaire.

Thus the descriptions given earlier need to be modified on the basis of this latest study. Extraverts apparently do not plan less or act more on impulse in the strict sense than do introverts but appear more lively and spontaneous and are more likely to take risks than introverts. The issue of the sociability-impulsivity relationship is raised in many of the following studies and in later chapters as well. It will be necessary for us to recall and apply the insights of the present discussion at those points in order to understand better the meaning of extraversion scales developed by investigators other than Eysenck.

16 PERSONALITY FACTOR QUESTIONNAIRE

Cattell's 16 Personality Factor Questionnaire (16PF) (described in great detail by Cattell, 1973) is probably the most widely used and accepted instrument for the global assessment of normal personality. The 16 primary scales or factors were derived from factor analyses of item intercorrelations and are assumed to represent the basic source traits of personality. The primary factor accounting for the greatest proportion of variance is a sociability factor, labeled affectia. The primary scales of sociability (affectia), dominance, surgency (happy-go-lucky, gay, enthusiastic), venturesomeness (parmia), and group adherence (as opposed to self-sufficiency) are interrelated and combine to form a second-order factor of extraversion (exvia versus invia). Thus the 16PF may be scored for the primary scales related to extraversion–introversion as well as for the global extraversion–introversion factor (Cattell, Eber, & Tatsuoka, 1970).

There is agreement between Eysenck and Cattell that the data show extraversion (exvia) and neuroticism (anxiety) to be the two dimensions in global personality assessment that account for the most variance (Cattell, 1973; Nerviano, 1974). There is also agreement on the basic content of the two dimensions. However, Cattell emphasizes the multidimensionality of extraversion–introversion as represented in the five primary scales, as well as the existence of at least eight second-order factors. The differences in conclusions and in research methods are basic, technical, and complex (Cattell, 1972, 1973; H. Eysenck, 1972b; H. Eysenck & Eysenck, 1969). Nevertheless, the practical point of agreement is underscored by findings such as that of Hundleby and Connor (1968) that Eysenck's Maudsley Personality Inventory extraversion scores correlated highly ($r = .73$) with Cattell's second-order extraversion scores.

In research on the 16PF, Howarth and his colleagues are critical of Cattell's basic factor structure. While agreeing that sociability is a major dimension of the 16PF, they deny that a second-order extraversion factor exists. Howarth (1976b) presents a reanalysis of Cattell's (1947) original data, beginning with his unrotated factor matrix, from which he concludes that there are only six identifiable primary factors: cooperativeness, emotional maturity, conscientiousness, emotional stability, sociability, and surgency (energetic, talkative, nonintrospective, cheerful, emotional, adventurous, and self-willed).

Howarth and Browne (1971) used another approach to determine the factor structure of the 16PF, factor analyzing the intercorrelations among the specific items of the battery rather than beginning with the 16 primary scales. Using a sample of 567, they extracted 10 primary factors that are at variance both in number and content from Cattell's assumed 16 personality factor structure; however, see Cattell's (1973) reply. The first factor, adjustment versus emotionality, resembles Eysenck's neuroticism. Additional factors germane to the current discussion are sociability (the third factor), impulsiveness, social shyness, and rhathymia (carefreeness and light-heartedness), all of which were relatively independent of each other.

A number of questionnaires with the same basic structure as the 16PF have been developed in Cattell's laboratory for use with special populations (High School Personality Questionnaire, Children's Personality Questionnaire, Early School Personality Questionnaire). The Clinical Analysis Questionnaire (Delhees & Cattell, 1971) adds 12 primary scales useful in clinical populations to the original 16. Krug and Laughlin (1977) factor analyzed the responses of almost 2,000 normals and abnormals, including inpatients and outpatients with a variety of diagnoses, to this instrument and found results similar to those reported above. For both sexes, the first of 10 second-order factors was extraversion–introversion, consisting of a combination of sociability, surgency, adventurousness, and group adherence. In addition, introversion was consistently associated with the seven depression scales included.

GUILFORD–ZIMMERMAN TEMPERAMENT SURVEY

During the years between 1934 and 1949, J. P. Guilford and his colleagues conducted a systematic research program that resulted in the identification of 13 primary personality factors and the eventual construction of the Guilford–Zimmerman Temperament Survey (GZTS) designed to assess them. In an excellent review and discussion of factor analysis and extant personality batteries, Guilford (1975) dissects the evidence for higher order factors in the GZTS. He presents a positive evaluation of Eysenck's neuroticism dimension, a second-order factor that he labels emotional stability. Combined with paranoid disposition, these form a third-order general adjustment factor. However, Guilford is very critical of Eysenck's extraversion dimension. There are five primary scales of the GZTS that are related. General activity, ascendance or social boldness, and sociability or social interest combine to form the higher order factor of social activity. The higher order factor that Guilford calls introversion–extraversion consists of the primary scales of restraint or seriousness versus impulsiveness (rhathymia), and thoughtfulness or reflectiveness. Thus again, the two dimensions of social activity and impulsiveness have been identified, and the question is raised of whether they combine into a third-order factor of extraversion in the broadest sense, as Eysenck suggests. Guilford disagrees; furthermore, he says that Eysenck's extraversion scale does not represent any of the specific extraversion dimensions well. According to Guilford, Eysenck's scale combines one element of social activity (sociability) with one element of introversion–extraversion (impulsiveness) in a way that prompts Guilford to call it a shotgun wedding. It is interesting that when Eysenck first began to construct a measure of extraversion he began with Guilford's rhathymia (carefreeness) scale as the best index available to him at the time.

As with the 16PF the GZTS can be administered in its entirety and then scored for each of the five primary extraversion factors as well as the higher order factors of social activity and introversion-extraversion. There is one element in Guilford's measurement of extraversion that has not been given much weight in the foregoing discussion and that may be deserving of closer scrutiny. It is the thoughtfulness or reflectiveness scale, a measure of thinking introversion. This dimension relates to the intellectual, meditative, self-stimulating, and introspective aspect of introversion, which is related to but not synonymous with a lack of impulsiveness and certainly is not synonymous with a lack of sociability.

CALIFORNIA PSYCHOLOGICAL INVENTORY

The California Psychological Inventory (CPI) consists of 18 scales aimed at assessing the normal personality (Gough, 1975; Megargee, 1972). Two recent factor analyses (Burger, Pickett, & Goldman, 1977; Johnson, Flammer, & Nelson, 1975) agree that there are five primary factors represented: adjustment by social conformity, social poise or extraversion, capacity for independent thought, conventionality, and nurturance or emotional sensitivity or femininity. In both studies extraversion is the second factor that emerges and includes the dominance, capacity for status, sociability, social presence, and self-acceptance scales. The CPI extraversion score thus seems to be composed entirely of the sociability dimension. Romine and Crowell (1978) refer to the two most important of the five primary factors, labeled above as adjustment by social conformity and social poise or extraversion, as value orientation and person orientation, respectively. In either case, the first involves elements such as adjustment, socialization, responsibility, and conformity to societal values, and the second involves extraversion in the sense of sociability. Romine and Crowell (1978) scored the California Psychological Inventories of 211 college students for these two factors and correlated them with Eysenck Personality Inventory scores, finding moderate relationships between person orientation and extraversion and between value orientation and stability (the opposite of neuroticism).

Two recent investigations have compared the content of the CPI and the 16PF scales. While Nerviano and Weitzel (1977), using a small sample (205) of army recruits, were unimpressed with the similarities between similarly named scales on the two tests (for example 16PF sociability and CPI sociability), Stroup and Manderscheid (1977) found considerable agreement in the factor structure of the two. Each was administered to a separate group of approximately 2,000 freshmen college students. Anxiety or adjustment, extraversion, and three other common factors were identified, again indicating the pervasiveness of these dimensions in global personality assessment, despite differences in items and in the content of specific scales.

COMREY PERSONALITY SCALES

One of the most recent developments in the global assessment of personality is the development of the Comrey Personality Scales (CPS) (Comrey, 1970), designed for the same purpose as the 16PF, GZTS, and CPI. Eight primary factors are assumed to cover the scope of normal personality: trust, orderliness, conformity, activity, emotional stability, extraversion, masculinity, and empathy. Vandenberg and Price (1978) verified this factor structure in the responses of 377 subjects, and found in addition that the stability and extraversion scales correlated highly with the appropriate Eysenck Personality Questionnaire scales. The Comrey extraversion dimension is defined by clusters of items reflecting the opposite of reservation, seclusiveness, and shyness, together with talkativeness. The extraversion factor correlates positively with the activity, stability, and empathy factors but is not related to orderliness.

MINNESOTA MULTIPHASIC PERSONALITY INVENTORY

The Minnesota Multiphasic Personality Inventory (MMPI), unlike the batteries discussed heretofore, was designed for use with clinical populations (Dahlstrom, Welsh, & Dahlstrom, 1972). It is used to identify one's similarity to various clinical diagnostic groups and was validated according to that criterion. Therefore it is particularly noteworthy that factor analyses of the MMPI have also revealed neuroticism and extraversion-introversion dimensions similar to those identified in the other batteries. Block (1965) developed two scales to represent these dimensions: ego control (introversion) and go resiliency (the opposite of neuroticism). And Welsh (1956) devised a scoring system for the MMPI that yielded anxiety and repression (introversion) scores. The use of the label repression is an interesting choice to describe the introversion end of the dimension, but the implication is that the introvert is inhibited and overcontrolled, the opposite of impulsive. Another dimension assessed by the MMPI that has been found to relate consistently to this personality dimension is represented at the extraversion end by hypomania. Apparently the outgoing, active, impulsive manner of the moderately manic individual is closely related to the concept of extraversion.

Two measures of the sociability aspect of extraversion-introversion have been derived from different combinations of MMPI items. One is the extraversion scale developed by Giedt and Downing (1961), and the other is the social introversion scale developed by Drake (1946), indicating primarily the extent of social participation and secondarily the degree of general psychological adjustment. A factor analysis of the 70-item social introversion scale conducted by Graham, Schroeder, and Lilly (1971), using a heterogeneous sample of over 400 patients and normals, revealed the following factors: social inferiority and discomfort, affiliation, social excitement, social sensitivity, interpersonal trust, and concern about physical and somatic inferiorities. Graham and Schroeder (1972) later used this analysis plus additional data to construct a briefer (18-item) social introversion scale with comparable content. In comparison with Eysenck's scale, the social introversion scales appear to include a stronger element of neuroticism or maladjustment and little or no impulsiveness.

Blackburn (1968) administered the MMPI to groups of neurotics and psychopaths and concluded from correlations that the repression and hypomania scales form one extraversion cluster (overcontrol versus impulsivity), whereas the social introversion and the extraversion scales form another that is related but nevertheless distinct. Thus the question of combining impulsivity and sociability appears again. In one factor analysis of the MMPI, Kassebaum, Couch, and Slater (1959) distinguished between the two (social withdrawal versus social participation, impulsivity versus intellectual control). The former contrasts maladjusted introversion with normal extraversion and includes both the social introversion and depression scales, whereas the latter contrasts maladjusted extraversion with normal introversion and includes impulsivity and hypomania. Repression had sizable loadings on both factors. However, both Hundleby and Connor (1968) and Goorney (1970), using normal subjects, found both hypomania–depression and social introversion to be significantly related to extraversion scores as measured by the Maudsley Personality Inventory (Eysenck's). Likewise, both Corah (1964) and Blackburn (1972a) reported high correlations between repression and extraversion, and placed them both on a single extraversion factor. A surprising finding of Blackburn was that neither repression nor extraversion was related to a separate impulsivity scale, a finding which may be a function of the population tested, that is, male psychiatric offenders.

Two studies (Wakefield, Bradley, Doughtie, & Kraft, 1975; Wakefield, Yom, Bradley, Doughtie, Cox, & Kraft, 1974) draw an interesting comparison between the Eysencks' psychoticism-extraversion-neuroticism model and the scales of the MMPI. Using large adult samples of normal males and females, factor analysis revealed (among others) a female introversion factor consisting primarily of social introversion and depression and a male introversion factor consisting of social introversion, depression, and hypomania. Assuming that social introversion represents Eysenck's extraversion, that hypomania is neuroticism and extraversion combined, and that the psychopathic deviate scale represents a combination of extraversion and psychoticism, they constructed a conceptual three-dimensional framework and compared the empirical placement of the MMPI scales in factor space. The statistical association of the conceptual and empirical placements was significant for both females and males. There is one consistent unexpected finding throughout these studies, that is, that there is no relationship between extraversion per se and the psychopathic deviate scale.

Johansson (1970) used the MMPI social introversion scale as a criterion to construct an additional scale of extraversion. He separated subjects into high, medium, and low social introversion groups, administered the Strong Vocational Interest Blank (which is widely used in the process of vocational counseling), and identified items on the latter that differentiated between introverts and extraverts. The result was a 69-item Occupational Introversion–Extraversion (SVIB–OIE) scale that may be scored for an individual following administration of the SVIB. Johnson, Nelson, Nolting, Roth, and Taylor (1975) have identified a common factor emerging from both the SVIB and the Minnesota Counseling Inventory as a social introversion-extraversion factor that is reflected in the SVIB–OIE scale and relates to the social relations and leadership scales of the Minnesota Counseling Inventory.

PSYCHOLOGICAL SCREENING INVENTORY

The Psychological Screening Inventory (PSI) is a brief inventory developed recently (Lanyon, 1970, 1973) for use in mental health-related settings. Lanyon accepted the extraversion–neuroticism factorial structure of such inventories and determined to construct brief scales of each, labeled expression and discomfort, respectively, as well as scales of alienation, social nonconformity and defensiveness. Whereas the alienation and social nonconformity scales were designed to assess the similarity of an incoming client to psychotic and psychopathic groups, respectively, the expression (extraversion) and discomfort (neuroticism) scales are composed of items selected primarily on the basis of internal consistency. The resulting emphasis of the expression scale was on verbal and social dominance and fluency, although the original definition also included the element of undercontrol. The resultant scale thus appears to be largely a sociability scale. In a sample of 64 football players the expression scale correlated positively with the appropriate CPI variables: dominance, sociability, social presence, self-acceptance, and the extraversion (person orientation) factor. In a sample of 300 who completed both the PSI and the MMPI, contrasting MMPI profiles for groups scoring high (extraverted) and low (introverted) on the expression scale were described as energy, impulsivity, social facility, aggression, and acting out versus passivity, pessimism, social introversion, and worry. Both hypomania and social introversion were clearly related to expression. In Lanyon's (1970) study expression was only moderately related ($r = .56$) to the Maudsley Personality Inventory extraversion scale, but Mehryar, Khajavi, and Hekmat (1975) found a much closer relationship with a later version of Eysenck's extraversion scale. They administered both the PSI and the Psychoticism–Extraversion–Neuroticism Scale to more than 500 college students and factor analyzed the intercorrelations among scales. A psychological well-being factor (on which psychoticism and neuroticism were not distinguishable) and an extraversion (or expression) factor emerged.

The psychometric stature of the expression scale as an internally consistent measure of extraversion and its independence of the other dimensions assessed by the PSI have been verified in a small sample of college students (Johnson & Overall, 1973) and in a large representative sample of 800 adults (Lanyon, Johnson, & Overall, 1974). Lanyon (1978) also used the data from the latter sample to conduct an item factor analysis of the various scales, finding the strongest expression scale items to reflect outgoingness together with elements of impulsiveness, display, and aggressiveness (for males) and manic energy (for females).

MYERS–BRIGGS TYPE INDICATOR

Another measure of extraversion–introversion has been developed by Myers (1962), with the intent of capturing the definition initiated by Carl Jung (1923/1971). As explained in chapter 1, Jung conceptualized this dimension as referring to preferences for attending either to the inner world of subjectivity or to the outer world of objective events. The Myers–Briggs Type Indicator (MBTI) consists of items drawn largely from Jung's writings. There are four scales: extraversion–introversion, sensation–intuition, thinking–feeling, and judging–perceiving. Although it is not clear whether the scale is satisfactory from a Jungian point of view (see Shapiro & Alexander, 1975, pp. 51–53; Stricker & Ross, 1964) and there is little information available concerning the relationship of the MBTI to the other measures of extraversion discussed above, two recent studies (Steele & Kelly, 1976; Wakefield, Sasek, Brubaker, & Friedman, 1976) report correlations of .74 and .58, respectively, between the MBTI and Eysenck Personality Questionnaire extraversion scales. The two scales appear to be measuring the same dimension, as the canonical analysis of Wakefield et al. (1976) indicates. The latter also indicates a commonality between Eysenck's neuroticism and the MBTI thinking–judging dimension, a finding that is not supported by Steele and Kelly (1976). Carlyn (1977) has written a very positive literature review of the MBTI, in which she presents evidence of both the reliability and validity (content, predictive, and construct) of the scales, and Carlson and Levy (1973) strongly recommend the use of the Jungian typologies in general and the MBTI in particular for the study of person–environment interactions.

BENDIG'S PITTSBURGH SCALES

Perhaps one of the better brief measures of extraversion in its broadest sense was developed by Bendig (1962b). Convinced by the work of Eysenck that neuroticism and extraversion–introversion were the two major factors to be identified in personality assessment and stimulated by the work of Guilford and others, Bendig constructed the Pittsburgh Scales of Social Extraversion–Introversion and Emotionality. Drawing items from the Maudsley Personality Inventory, the GZTS introversion–extraversion (not the social activity) factor, and the MMPI social introversion scale, he used item factor analyses to construct scales of emotionality (neuroticism) and social extraversion that were internally consistent and independent of each other. The resulting extraversion scale consisted of 15 of Eysenck's items, 10 MMPI social introversion items, and 5 GZTS items. Sieveking (1973) has revised these scales so that they are now usable with both children and adults.

CLASSROOM BEHAVIOR INVENTORY

All of the other instruments discussed in this chapter are self-report inventories developed primarily for use with adults. Another tool that has received some recent attention will be particularly useful to some extraversion–introversion researchers because of its applicability to the study of younger children. Schaefer's (1971) Classroom Behavior Inventory (CBI) was developed for use with preschoolers and primary school children and is completed by the teacher or other adult observer of the child's behavior. It was designed to assess the three major dimensions of task-oriented behavior (versus distractability), hostility (versus considerateness), and extraversion–introversion, and a study of 69 second graders by Mirante and Rychman (1974) has verified the existence of this factor structure in teachers' ratings. In a study of 320 kindergarten boys Blunden, Spring, and Greenberg (1974) note the usefulness of the CBI in assessing hyperactivity (the label assigned to the first factor listed above) in young children, although correlations between teachers' ratings and observed classroom behavior were disappointingly small. Concerning the extraversion, or sociability, factor, this study showed 3 of 10 primary scales (cheerfulness, social participation, and verbal expression) to relate to it, although impulsiveness did not.

INTERPERSONAL STYLE

The most recent developments in personality assessment reflect simultaneously the interactional approach to personality research and the continued importance of the trait of extraversion-introversion. In keeping with the interpersonal or social emphasis of interactionism, two new inventories of interpersonal behavior (style) have been developed. One is described by Lorr and Youniss (1973) and the other by Nideffer (1976). The latter has the unique characteristic of also assessing cognitive processes, another emphasis of interactional psychology.

More specifically, Lorr and Youniss' Interpersonal Style Inventory (ISI) consists of 15 primary scales reflecting differences in interpersonal behavior and attitudes. When data from over 800 subjects were factor analyzed, six second-order factors emerged: extraverted, socialized, independent, structure seeking, stable, and slow tempo. Similar factors emerged in another sample of college students and in a group of prison inmates. The extraversion factor was defined by scores on the scales of directive or dominant, attention-seeking, sociable, help-seeking, and impulsive interpersonal behavior. In a sample of 75 college students, Eysenck Personality Inventory extraversion correlated with the sociable and attention-seeking interpersonal styles, and introversion correlated with the deliberate style. Stability as an interpersonal style correlated highly with Eysenck's stability, the opposite of neuroticism.

Nideffer's Test of Attentional and Interpersonal Style (TAIS) consists of 17 scales, 7 of which deal with attention and information processing and 10 of which deal with interpersonal behavior and attitudes. The cognitive–attentional variables revolve mainly around the dimensions of broad-versus-narrow attentional focus and internal-versus-external attentional focus. Correlations from 60 police applicants indicate that the TAIS extraversion scale correlates satisfactorily with the Maudsley Personality Inventory extraversion and the MMPI social introversion scales. Both of these were related to control (dominance), self-esteem, physical orientation (enjoyment of competitive athletics), intellectual expression, positive affective expression, and negative affective expression. The separate introversion scale (likes being alone, enjoys quiet thoughtful times, avoids being the center of attention) was basically unrelated to these variables, as was the behavior control (impulsiveness) scale.

The above correlations of recognized extraversion–introversion scales with various interpersonal style variables illustrate once again the value of this personality trait in interactional research, and the point is reinforced by the relationship of extraversion to the cognitive–attentional variables assessed by the TAIS. In Nideffer's study extraverts scored higher on the information-processing scale, indicating that they report processing more stimulus information than   introverts. The relationship held for both internal (broad internal attentional focus scale) and external (broad external attentional focus scale) stimuli.

CONCLUSIONS

Information from the preceding paragraphs suggests that the trait of extraversion–introversion qualifies as a person variable

TABLE 1   Recommended scales for assessing extraversion–introversion and its major components

---

Extraversion–introversion (broadly defined)
    Eysenck Personality Questionnaire extraversion scale
    16PF (or CAQ) exvia–invia factor (with 5 subscales)
    California Psychological Inventory extraversion factor (with 5 subscales)
    Bendig social extraversion scale
    Psychological Screening Inventory expression scale
    Myers-Briggs Type Indicator extraversion–introversion scale
    Interpersonal Style Inventory extroversion factor (with 5 subscales)
    Test of Attentional and Interpersonal Style extroversion scale
    Comrey Personality Scales extraversion factor

Sociability component
    16PF affectia scale
    GZTS social activity factor (with 3 subscales)
    CPI sociability scale
    MMPI extraversion, social introversion scales
    ISI sociable scale
    TAIS introversion scale

Impulsiveness component
    16PF surgency, parmia scales
    GZTS introversion–extraversion scale (with 2 subscales)
    MMPI repression, hypomania, ego-control scales
    ISI impulsive, deliberate scales
    TAIS behavior control scale

Dominance component
    16PF dominance scale
    GZTS ascendance scale
    CPI dominance scale
    ISI dominance scale
    TAIS control scale

Introspective component
    GZTS thoughtfulness scale
    MBTI extraversion–introversion scale

---

of interest to interactional personality theorists and researchers, because of its relationship to cognitive processes operative in interpersonal contexts. The evidence presented throughout this chapter should make it clear that if self-report personality inventories reflect the varieties of interpersonal behavior with any degree of accuracy, the dimension of extraversion–introversion cannot be ignored in analyzing person–environment interactions. Amazingly the potential for investigating this cluster of important person variables has gone virtually untapped. Whether one wishes to explore the variable of extraversion in its broadest sense or to utilize one or more specific aspects contained within it, there are instruments available with impressive psychometric qualities, accompanied by a wealth of information concerning their relationships with numerous other personality variables. The lists of scales presented in Table 1 should serve jointly as a summary of material discussed in this chapter and as a reference point to which the reader may return as the various scales are encountered in the following chapters.

In summary, extraversion–introversion is a personality dimension which differentiates among individuals in one or more of the following ways. These components tend to covary in individuals' behavior, but this tendency should not be overestimated.

1. Social activity: the amount of energy expended and the intensity of one's activities in social contexts, time spent in social encounters, talkativeness.
2. Social facility: social and interpersonal skill, leadership qualities, dominance, conversational skill.
3. Risk taking and adventuresomeness: spontaneity and flexibility in social behavior, contrasted with social inhibition and restraint.
4. Preference for action and objectivity in contrast to reflectiveness, introspection, and abstract–intellectual pursuits.

3

EXTRAVERTED AND INTROVERTED INTERPERSONAL ATTITUDES AND BEHAVIORS

The dimension of extraversion–introversion in combination with situational variables is a factor to be considered when discussing basic social and interpersonal processes. It is evident that many of the social processes that have received attention in social-personality research, including affiliation, attraction, attitude change, conformity, dissonance, nonverbal communication, and social learning, interact with or are affected by subjects' levels of extraversion and introversion. Investigations in areas such as these constitute the most meaningful test of the usefulness of the personality trait, either capitalizing on or negating the potential implied in the theoretical and psychometric groundwork laid in chapters 1 and 2. The material to be presented in this chapter is organized around two major themes concerning the differences between more introverted and more extraverted persons: (1) their reactions to the social environment, that is, to the behaviors of others surrounding them, and (2) the social behaviors or interpersonal interactions that they engage in or initiate.

SOCIAL EXPECTATIONS AND PRIORITIES

First of all it may be observed that introverts and extraverts have some tendency to perceive the people around them differently, to expect different things from them, and to value different aspects of their interpersonal world differently. For example, Cohen and Scaife (1973) explored the different reactions of introvert and extravert female first-year college students to their college environments. This study was done in England with education majors, who were administered the Eysenck Personality Inventory along with a self-report inventory of attitudes about their actual and ideal self and about college. The basic variable in the study was discrepancy, that is, the degree of dissimilarity one sees between herself and her ideals and the actualities of college life. In general those with higher discrepancy scores, particularly between ideal self and college experience, were most dissatisfied with college. Personality variables were important in that correlations of discrepancy and satisfaction scores were stronger for extraverts than for introverts. Extraverts with high discrepancy scores were also more likely than introverts to wish they had gone to another college.

Another important point is that, for introverts, having similar values to those on the college staff and feeling comfortable with fellow students were the most salient variables in determining their satisfaction with college life. For extraverts on the other hand satisfaction with the social aspects of college life was the most salient. Watkins (1976) corroborates this; he found that extraverts among his 235 Australian university students ascribed more importance to leisure and heterosexual activities. The social aspects of college life (important to extraverts) involve larger social activities and opportunities on campus, whereas feeling comfortable with fellow students (important to introverts) involves more individualized relationships among students. Interestingly satisfaction with academic aspects of college life was not particularly salient for either group. Apparently interactions with other students differentiate between groups better than interactions with faculty; for example, Feinberg (1972) found no overall relationship between scores on the social introversion scale of the MMPI and faculty–student contact on the university campus. The dependent variable was students' responses to the question, How many times have you spoken to professors individually outside of class this semester? There was an interaction effect in that subjects with higher grade point averages who made more faculty contacts were more extraverted, whereas students with low grade point averages who made more faculty contacts were more introverted.

We may also speculate that feeling comfortable with other students for the introverts (Cohen & Scaife, 1973) may mean being left alone or having particularly trustworthy friends to associate with during times of particular difficulty or stress, whereas for extraverts these may be the times that they most need gregarious surroundings. An earlier study by Shapiro and Alexander (1969) indicated that whereas there is no difference between introverts and extraverts (on the Myers–Briggs Type Indicator) in affiliative behavior when no stress is present, the presence of stress separates the groups so that extraverts prefer to spend a waiting period in the presence of other people whereas introverts under stress prefer to wait alone. The investigators used threat of electric shock to manipulate level of anxiety experimentally. The point of the Cohen and Scaife study is well taken, that is, that interpersonal need satisfaction is a joint function of the environmental situation and the personality type of the individual.

A study by Genthner and Moughan (1977) further indicates some of the differential expectancies of introverts and extraverts regarding the behavior of others in relation to them. Genthner and Moughan were interested in students' perceptions of a counselor. After separating subjects on the basis of the Eysenck Personality Questionnaire, each was asked to tell a listener about a dream for a period of 2 minutes and to rate the counselor, who did not interact with them but simply listened, on nine different variables. The experimental variable related to the posture of the counselor, that is, whether the counselor sat upright or leaned forward. The posture effect was not noteworthy, and it interacted with the personality variable only in one instance—extraverts rated the upright posture more threatening than did introverts. However, the personality effect was powerful, as introverts gave the listener more positive ratings on eight of the nine scales. This becomes relevant to the current discussion when we realize that the counselor was simply a silent listener, which is precisely what the introverts expected and desired, whereas extraverts did not. It appears that the silence of the listener was frustrating to the extraverts who rated them especially "not helpful" and "uninvolved." The same behavior was comforting to the introverts who rated them especially "nonthreatening" and "respectful." It may safely be assumed that there was some stress involved in the situation of disclosing a dream to a stranger and the introverts reacted characteristically by being pleased to be left alone whereas the extraverts desired affiliation and interaction in the situation.

Investigations of the reactions of extraverts and introverts, respectively, to group therapy and to transcendental meditation illustrate the same point. Boller (1974) utilized two groups, one characterized by a sensory awareness approach in which the emphasis was on emotional and physical expression among group members and the other oriented around verbal–cognitive activities with an emphasis on verbal communication among group members. Students scoring high and low on the Maudsley Personality Inventory participated in a 5-hour group led by a trained and experienced leader. At 20 different times through-out the group sessions subjects indicated their feeling tone, either positive or negative, by dropping either a red or a white poker chip into his or her individual container. The number of poker chips of each color in the container at the end of the session constituted the dependent variable. The results indicated that extraverts profited more from both groups than did introverts and more from the sensory awareness group than from the verbal-cognitive group. This is to say that extraverts enjoyed the groups more, although there is no further indication whether they actually profited in a more substantive way. Smith (1978) found introverts to benefit more, in terms of reduced anxiety, from a 6-month transcendental meditation experience. Anxiety re-duction was negatively related to the 16PF sociability scale among 50 university students who were initially high in trait anxiety. Similar results were not found for an elaborate control group that involved inactivity without meditation. Incidentally another study (Williams, Francis, & Durham, 1976) indicates that meditation training does not increase or decrease intro-version on the Psychoticism–Extraversion–Neuroticism Scale, but that male regular meditators experience a decrease in neuroticism (anxiety).

INTERPERSONAL AGREEMENT
AND DISAGREEMENT

Another interesting question is whether introverts and extraverts differ in their perceptions of and reactions to conformity pressures. There is one study that shows no social conformity differences. Snyder and Monson (1975) assigned college students to four-person discussion groups, with all persons in each group being the same sex, to discuss an issue on which there were differences of opinion among the class. The experimental condition was whether the group discussion was public or private; that is, some groups were told that their discussion was videotaped for possible class presentation. Personality variables explored were extraversion and neuroticism as measured by the Eysenck Personality Inventory and scores on the self-monitoring scale. Person effects were obvious for the latter two on measures of social conformity with highs and lows on these dimensions being virtually unaffected by experimental conditions. However, there was no main effect for extraversion, nor was the predicted interaction effect between extraversion scores and experimental conditions significant. It appears from this study that extraversion bears no relationship to social conformity in group discussions.

A special case of the operation of conformity pressures is the process of observational learning that receives such heavy emphasis in current social learning theories. This is the process of learning by watching and imitating the behaviors of others. Two studies conducted by Fouts (Fouts, 1975; Fouts & Click, 1973) show that introverted and extraverted children have different reactions to this interpersonal process. They developed their own scale to measure the personality variable, using 8 5 year olds in each group in the first study and 17 preadolescents in each group in the second. Data from the younger children indicated that introverts reproduced significantly fewer of the behaviors to which they had been exposed than extraverts, although attentiveness to the model did not differ in the two groups. They may have learned the same amount but chosen to imitate different amounts. If so, introverts were nonconformists. Among the older children in the second study conditions were arranged so that the children would be imitated by the experimenter when they made one of six possible responses. The differences between introvert and extravert groups occurred when the experimenter verbally commented on the fact that she was imitating the child at which point introverts showed a dramatic decrease in the response and maintained the low response level from that time on. Thus the introverted children appeared to avoid conformity both when asked to imitate another and when being imitated by another. Incidentally there are other recent studies that show extraverts to respond more favorably than introverts to positive social reinforcement (Gupta, 1976; Gupta & Nagpal, 1978). The studies involved verbal operant conditioning of the use of personal pronouns, a task at which introverts are superior under most conditions.

A study by Cooper and Scalise (1974) was based on the assumption and provided supportive evidence that introverts tend to expect more disagreement between their attitudes and the attitudes of those around them than do extraverts and that social conformity varies as a function of such expectancies interacting with environmental variables. The experiment involved the effects of cognitive dissonance on attitude change. Dissonance is a concept used by social psychologists to describe the state in which the person has coexisting but contradictory thoughts about a situation, accompanied by an unpleasant emotional state. They hypothesized that dissonance would be produced in a group of introverts and extraverts (assessed by the Myers–Briggs Type Indicator) by different types of informational feedback. They reasoned that introverts should experience dissonance only when made to believe that they were conforming with the attitudes of others whereas extraverts should experience dissonance only when made to believe that they were not conforming to popular attitudes. The reason is that in both cases subjects perceive their responses to be atypical for them. The results were as expected. In the experimental situation the subjects were told that a sensing device placed on the fingers could ascertain the subject's gut reaction to attitudinal questions. On the first five questions feedback from the experimenter indicated a response from the sensing device that the subject was

known to agree with, along with answers from three other hypothetical subjects, some of whom agreed and some of whom dis-
agreed with the subject's answers. However, on question number
6, which presented the critical issue of the study, the subject
received information that the other three subjects gave answers
that the subject was known to disagree with. Then half of the
subjects were told that their gut reaction to this question con-
formed to the opinion of the group whereas the other half were
told that they remained independent of the group's attitude
on this issue. The person–situation interaction was found in
that conforming introverts changed their attitude in the direction
of the group, whereas conforming extraverts did not, and that
independent extraverts changed in the direction of independence,
whereas independent introverts did not. In both cases the attitude
change was seen as an attempt to reduce dissonance. If so, dissonance production then was a function of introverts perceiving
themselves to be conforming and on the other hand extraverts
perceiving themselves to be exercising independence in the face
of group pressure. Presumably these situations would produce
dissonance only if these responses for the introvert and extravert, respectively, were atypical for them.

Further evidence along the same line is provided by Norman
and Watson (1976), that is, that interpersonal disagreement
is not seen as particularly inconsistent or unexpected by introverts compared with extraverts. However, such conditions of
imbalance or dissonance may be more arousing and emotionally
unpleasant for introverts. The combination of expected disagreement that makes one emotionally uncomfortable would be ample
reason for the introvert to prefer less complex social situations.
In their first study Norman and Watson asked 100 high and low
scorers on the Eysenck Personality Inventory to rate eight interpersonal situations (from Heider's work on balanced and un-
balanced relationships). Introverts rated interpersonal disagreement
as more unpleasant, though not more cognitively inconsistent,
than extraverts. In a second study a typical dissonance-producing
procedure (asking subjects to write an essay arguing for a position
known to be contrary to their actual belief) was found to produce more attitude change for introverts than for extraverts.
But the effect was found, as expected, only in the dissonance
condition, that involving a high degree of choice as to whether

to write the essay. We may conclude that the state of experiencing dissonance, although produced by different situations in extraverts and introverts, is a more aversive state for introverts, so that they are less tolerant of such situations. In general introverts are more anxious than extraverts about impending social comparison (Hinton & Craske, 1977; cf. chapter 4).

PERSON PERCEPTION AND INTERPERSONAL ATTRACTION

Harkins, Becker, and Stonner (1975) asked subjects classified as introverts and extraverts on the Eysenck Personality Inventory to rate 16 persons on a 21-point scale of likeability. The target persons were hypothetical and were described by one to six adjectives that could be classified as either negative or positive traits. Beyond this no indication of the content of the descriptions is offered by the authors. The results were that extraverts gave more extreme ratings than introverts; that is, extraverts rated target persons described by positive traits more likeable and those described by negative traits less likeable than did introverts. The conclusion drawn by the investigators is that extraverts are more socially responsive to others' traits, which relates to the reinforcement potential of interpersonal interactions resulting from greater need and/or greater experience in the interpersonal world.

A study that is partially at variance with these findings was conducted by Vingoe and Antonoff (1968); in this study the indication was that introverted subjects are better judges of others' traits than are extraverted subjects. The difference between the two studies lies in the fact that in the latter study subjects were actually rating people with whom they were at least fairly well acquainted rather than rating hypothetical individuals. In this study 66 first-year college women completed the California Psychological Inventory and the Eysenck Personality Inventory and rated themselves and their peers, at least those with whom they were well acquainted, on six personality variables: dominance, sociability, self-acceptance, responsibility, psychologicalmindedness, and extraversion. A total discrepancy score was assigned each person based on the difference between her ratings of the other and the other's test score. When 11 of the best judges and 10 of the worst judges were compared, the good raters were significantly more introverted than the poor raters. If we can equate the hypothetical persons presented in the study by Harkins et al. with superficial relationships, the further generalization can be made that extraverts are more socially responsive and more perceptive of traits of individuals with whom they are less well acquainted, whereas introverts gather more in-depth, accurate knowledge of persons with whom they are well acquainted.

Hendrick and Brown (1971) point out that the relationship between attraction and similarity is one of the most robust relationships in the social psychological literature; that is, attraction to another increases as a function of perceived similarity between self and other. On the other hand, however, extraversion appears to be a very highly valued trait in our culture in general. Thus it was hypothesized that the positive attraction–similarity relationship would hold for extraverts but not for introverts; for introverts opposites may attract. Subjects first completed the Maudsley Personality Inventory and were separated into introvert and extravert groups. Then, they were presented with the Maudsley Personality Inventory responses of two bogus strangers, one of whom was presented as being introverted to the same degree as the subjects in that group, the other of whom was presented as being extraverted to the same degree as the subjects in that group. It was determined that subjects perceived the similarities accurately. Subjects then rated the strangers on seven interpersonal attributes. As expected, extraverts rated the extraverted stranger as liked more, more interesting at parties, having a more ideal personality, and being preferred as a leader over the introverted stranger.

Thus the positive attraction–similarity relationship clearly held for the extraverts in this study. For the introverts, however, the results were more complex. Introverts liked the introverted and extraverted strangers equally but rated the extraverted stranger higher on being interesting at parties, having a more ideal personality, and being a preferred leader. However, when it came to the question of which was more reliable as a friend, more honest, and more ethical, extraverts rated the two equal. Introverts rated the introverted stranger higher on these characteristics. It appears that there are two patterns of social reinforcement discriminated here, particularly by introverts. One has to do with pleasant, ongoing interactions such as a person being interesting to talk with; both groups preferred the company of extraverts in this situation. The other relates to the long-term certainty and stability of a relationship, and in this case introverts preferred introverts and extraverts did not express a preference.

Similarity in extraversion–introversion is apparently not a major factor in mate selection, although perhaps it should be. A review of the literature by Vandenberg (1972) reports little evidence of assortative mating among introverts or among extraverts, and the results of two recent studies concur. H. Eysenck (1974) found no relationship among 241 couples in the general population for extraversion, a borderline correlation for psychoticism, and a significant relationship for neuroticism. Testing 102 couples, all university students, Farley and Davis (1977) found that scores of spouses on all three variables were essentially uncorrelated. The only variable upon which they found a positive correlation was the sensation-seeking scale.

However, a comprehensive study by Cattell and Nesselroade (1967) indicates that there is a difference in the similarity of their levels of extraversion–introversion between stably married couples and married couples having difficulty. Comparing 102 couples who had taken no known steps toward dissolution with 37 unstable couples who were either separated or were requesting marital counseling, they found that husband–wife correlations on the various scales of the 16PF were largely positive in the stable group and were lower and more negative in the unstable group. The correlational differences were significant in the case of three extraversion-related characteristics: outgoing, happy-go-lucky, and group dependent. Scores on the second-order extraversion factor were positively related for wives and husbands in the stable group and negatively related in the unstable group, and the difference between the two was significant. Extraversion stands out as the only variable or set of variables in the study for which such a relationship was found. Notice that the only comparison is the similarity between spouses' extraversion–introversion scores and that there is no indication of degree of extraversion or introversion being related to the stable–unstable dimension. In fact, Barton and Cattell (1972) administered a marriage-role questionnaire to 186 graduate students, scored it for 12 different dimensions or factors of marital behavior, related these scores to scores on the 16PF, and found few noteworthy relationships. Each personality factor of the 16PF served as the basis for separating subjects into high, medium, and low groups. The second-order extraversion factor was related to differences in only 1 of the 12 factors; male dominance in the relationship was related to the introversion of the subjects. In addition highly sociable subjects showed more home devotion, and three of the primary factors that are related to extraversion (dominance, enthusiasm, and venturesomeness) were positively related to degree of spouse independence and heterosexual activities.

OBSERVABLE DIFFERENCES IN SOCIAL BEHAVIOR

Whereas the first part of this chapter has emphasized the person (introvert or extravert) as an observer, with different expectations, values, and perceptions of social relationships, we now turn our attention to the person as the actor in an attempt to understand better the behavioral differences between extraverts and introverts engaged in social interactions. Such differences are perceivable by observers even though it is not always clear what behaviors one is using to judge the level of the other's extraversion or introversion. Two studies by Lippa (1976, 1978) demonstrate this. In each subjects were divided into extraverted and introverted groups on the basis of either multiple measures of friendliness (1976 study) or self-ratings of friendliness and Eysenck Personality Inventory scores (1978 study). Subjects were then asked to role play the part of a teacher giving a lesson, and naive observers rated the teachers as to how friendly and outgoing they were. Although there were other variables involved in the studies, the relevant point here is that observers tended to rate the extraverted subjects as more extraverted than the introverted subjects in both studies, even though it is clear from the first study that either personality type could successfully play either role. The correct perception of personality differences occurred in spite of the fact that extraverts and introverts did not differ on the expressive behaviors observed by the experimenters:

length of stride in walking, expansiveness of writing while demonstrating, amount of eye contact, or amount of time spent talking. So it is unknown what cues observers were utilizing in making their judgments.

Not only are extraversion–introversion differences perceptible to others, but such differences are also valued differently by the observers. Krebs and Adinolfi (1975) showed this, although they aimed their investigation primarily at an analysis of the effects of degrees of physical attractiveness on social behavior among first-year college students. Beginning with 600 students who completed sociometric ratings of their same-sex dormmates, the final sample consisted of four groups of 15 females and 15 males each, classified either as accepted, rejected, isolated (neither accepted nor rejected), and the control group whose sociometric ratings were average to positive. Subjects were administered Jackson's Personality Research Form, the SVIB–OIE and the FIRO–B Measure of Interpersonal Attitudes. These scales were factor analyzed separately for males and females, and the factors were related to the four groups described above and to physical attractiveness. For both sexes the strongest factor to emerge was called affectionate sociability, that is, personalities dominated by affiliative other-oriented needs. Accepted groups of both males and females were significantly higher in affectionate sociability than were rejected females and isolated males. The point is that a dimension something like extraversion is very important in relation to how first-year college students in the dorm are perceived by their peers. The baffling part of the study is that physical attractiveness and dating were not related to each other or to affectionate sociability, nor were there consistent differences among the four groups in physical attractiveness or dating. A weak point in the study was probably the fact that physical attractiveness was rated from high school graduation photographs.

SEXUAL BEHAVIOR

The bulk of the research on this topic has been conducted by Hans Eysenck (1970, 1971a, 1971b, 1971c, 1972a, 1973b) and is addressed in detail in a recent book (H. Eysenck, 1976b). The various studies consider sexual attitudes, sexual behaviors, sexual permissiveness, sexual perversions, and sexual disorders of both females and males, adolescents and adults. The personality variables of psychoticism and neuroticism as well as a number of other social attitudes are also included. In his book Eysenck cites the tendencies of extraverts compared with introverts to have intercourse earlier, more frequently, and with a greater variety of techniques and partners. Thus, "a happy philanderer, the extravert has considerable social facility with the opposite sex, likes and enjoys his sexual activity, is contented with it and has no worries or anxieties regarding it" (H. Eysenck, 1976b, p. 222). In contrast introverts achieve equally satisfying sex lives through more traditional monogamous relationships and engage in less premarital and extramarital sex than extraverts. It follows from Eysenck's theory that extraverts should seek stronger and more varied stimulation and have fewer sexual inhibitions. Either style may be highly satisfying or may lead to dissatisfaction and perversion when combined with elements of neuroticism (guilt, inadequacy, strong inhibitions) or psychoticism (hostility, impersonal attitudes). It is easy to see that these differences in personality within a marriage could form an important element in potential sexual incompatibility between partners.

There are two additional studies that bear on this discussion. One (Abramson, 1973) is a study of the differences between groups of college students (84 females and 75 males) who reported different frequencies of past and current masturbation. Male high masturbators were higher in self-reported (Thorne Sex Inventory) sex drive, sex interest, neuroticism, and introversion than the other males. For females the only differences between groups were in sex drive and sex interest. The author hypothesized that frequency of masturbation is a substitute form of sexual release related to lack of sociosexual contact and therefore predicted that introverts would engage in masturbation more frequently than extraverts. However, there was no correlation between frequency of masturbation and frequency of intercourse for either males or females. The other study (Eisinger, Huntsman, Lord, Merry, Polani, Tanner, Whitehouse, & Griffiths, 1972) found a group of 37 female homosexuals (members of a lesbian organization) to be high in both introversion and neuroticism compared with norms for the Eysenck

Personality Inventory. These were the only differences in a study that included medical history, complete physical examination, and anthropomorphic measurements.

INTERPERSONAL COMMUNICATION

Many of the differences that we perceive between personality groupings probably relate to visual interaction and speech differences. Inasmuch as earlier studies by Mobbs (1968) and Kendon and Cook (1969) had indicated a relationship between extraversion and eye contact, Rutter, Morley, and Graham (1972) explored this relationship further. Subjects scoring high and low on the Eysenck Personality Inventory engaged in two 4-minute spontaneous conversations about different aspects of university life. The results were mixed. Although there was no extraversion effect on the proportion of time spent in looking, the proportion of time spent in eye contact, or the mean length of looks, extraverts did initiate significantly more looks than did introverts and initiated more speech bursts than did introverts. In addition extraverts were found to engage in more frequent periods of eye contact while speaking than introverts. There appears therefore to be a speech–eye contact combination that is indicative of the more active level of interaction of the extraverts in the conversations. Earlier Ramsay (1966) had found that extraverted female college students produced longer bursts of speech and shorter periods of silence in an experimental situation than their introverted counterparts. An interesting part of this study is that it controlled for intelligence and showed ability not to be a factor in these differences. On the basis of the psycholinguistic literature the longer pauses in introvert speech were interpreted as indicating higher cognitive activity. Whether that interpretation is correct, the observable speech differences are characteristic.

The topic of self-disclosure has generated a great deal of interest recently, but apparently the personality variable of extraversion–introversion plays a very minor role in this area. More specifically, introverts and extraverts apparently do not react differentially to the self-disclosures of others to them, although extraverts may well self-disclose more in general as they speak more in social interactions. Extraversion had little effect on the outcome of three well-done studies on the subject of reactions to and reciprocation of self-disclosures. The only positive result found by Davis and Skinner (1974) was that extraversion was positively related to the amount of disclosure in a control condition only, not in the experimental conditions. Ashworth, Furman, Chaikin, and Derlega (1976) hypothesized that introverts receiving intimate self-disclosures from others would be made more anxious by those disclosures than would extraverts. The hypothesis was not supported, possibly because there was no pressure for subjects to reciprocate. The only extraversion–introversion difference in the study was that 9 of the 16 extraverts responded verbally to the experimental confederate whereas only 3 of the 16 introverts did so. Becker and Munz (1975) found no personality effects.

The results of the three studies are surprising in that they indicate that introverts are no less likely to respond with disclosures to a person who has initiated the interaction, no more likely than extraverts to be anxious in such a situation, and no more or less intimate in self-disclosures. Even at the level of personality traits, there is no relationship between the trait of extraversion, either alone or in combination with neuroticism, and scores on Jourard's Self-Disclosure Questionnaire (Gilliland, 1977). Differential relationships between anxiety variables and self-disclosure were expected for introverts and extraverts, but none were found. Similarly Tolor (1975a) found no difference between groups on their self-reported interpersonal distance from eight other social role figures. On the other hand, Strassberg and Kangas (1977) investigated the amount and intimacy of self-disclosure on a sentence completion test for 25 male and female psychiatric short-term inpatients. Males higher in social introversion on the MMPI self-disclosed more, as did females scoring lower on the hypomania (impulsiveness) scale, which is also related to introversion. Consistently patients scoring higher in anxiety also self-disclosed more. Thus among the group of inpatients the more anxious and introverted patients self-disclosed more, but it must be remembered that the disclosure consisted of an impersonal written response to a sentence stem rather than an interpersonal behavior.

Although the study of verbal self-disclosure in introverts and extraverts has been somewhat disappointing, there are fascinating differences between these two groups in terms of clarity and accuracy of nonverbal communication. Cunningham (1977) asked 26 subjects to read a standardized passage of prose after having been exposed to an affect induction technique of either elation or depression. The affect induction technique is a standardized clinical procedure in which subjects are encouraged to experience and express a given emotional feeling. Following the affect induction procedure, subjects were asked to display the appropriate emotion, either elation or depression, first with their voice and face and second with body movements as they read the passage again. The sessions were videotaped, and later each subject was asked to judge the presentation of two other subjects. Thus each subject played the role of both sender and receiver of nonverbal emotional communication.

The results indicated first of all that there were consistencies in both sending ability and receiving ability and that the two were negatively related. Second, different personality variables were associated with each. Extraversion was correlated positively with overall sending ability, including voice, face, and body communication, but was not related to receiving ability. The latter was positively related to neuroticism and sex with women being more accurate receivers than men. On the issue of receiving ability Carlson and Levy (1973) confirm that among black university students extraversion is unrelated to the perception of emotion portrayed in photographs. But with regard to sending ability Cunningham showed that extraverts experienced greater mood changes as a result of the affect induction and communicated those moods more accurately to the receivers. In terms of predicting sending ability extraversion was a much more powerful variable than either neuroticism or social desirability or even self-monitoring, each of which showed some relationship to sending ability. That extraversion would be more highly related to nonverbal communication of emotion than self-monitoring is noteworthy because self-monitoring is a personality variable that has received recent attention as a direct attempt to separate individuals who are skilled at monitoring their own reactions and in successfully making the impressions they wish to make in social situations. Extraversion and self-monitoring have been found to be positively correlated (Pilkonis, 1977a).

Although Steer (1974) failed to find differences between introverts and extraverts in speech rate during the expression of emotion, the superiority of extraverts over introverts in this area of emotional nonverbal communication has been confirmed and elaborated on in a series of studies by Buck and his colleagues, both in adults (Buck, Miller, & Caul, 1974; Buck, Savin, Miller, & Caul, 1972) and in preschool children (Buck, 1975, 1977). The methodology utilized by Buck and his colleagues has been to present subjects with color slides of various types and to ask the subjects to talk about their reactions. Unknown to the subject, his or her face but not the content of the communication is presented to observers via closed-circuit television. The observer is asked to check the category of the slide being observed and to judge the pleasantness of the subject's emotions. In the first study (Buck et al., 1972), there were slides depicting sexual scenes, scenic scenes, maternal scenes, disgusting scenes, and slides that were ambiguous or uninterpretable. In this study females but not males were able to identify the content of the slides beyond chance level and were able to judge the pleasantness though not the strength of the sender's emotion. Of seven personality variables in addition to sex included in this first study, communication accuracy was related significantly only to the extraversion of the sender, the test anxiety of the sender, the self-esteem of the observer, and the sex of the observer.

The second study (Buck et al., 1974), the method and results of which were similar to the initial study, emphasized the distinction between internalizers and externalizers. An internalizer is one whose physiological response, in terms of skin conductance and heart rate in this case, is greater in reaction to the emotional content of the slides but whose external expression is inhibited and thus does not communicate the emotion clearly to the observer. In contrast an externalizer is one who shows minimal physiological reaction but whose external expression of the emotion is marked. In the second study, when subjects were grouped into internalizer and externalizer groups on the basis of their physiological reactions and communication accuracy, it was found that externalizers were higher in extraversion and self-esteem compared with internalizers. This is further evidence that extraverts compared with introverts utilize the medium of nonverbal communication to a greater degree.

With 4–6-year-old children, Buck (1975, 1977) used slides of familiar people, that is, actual pictures of the child and friends at school, unfamiliar people, unpleasant situations, and unusual slides. At this age the sex differences found with adult subjects were no longer apparent, but the personality differences found earlier were replicated. This is noteworthy not only because of the age differences between the two samples but also because extraversion was measured in the studies of adults by self-report questionnaires and in the studies of children by teachers' ratings but nevertheless yielded the same results. In these experiments the observers were the child's mother and college students. Again sending ability was positively related to the teachers' ratings of activity, extraversion, and impulsivity, and negatively related to teachers' ratings of shyness, introversion, and solitary play. Buck's most recent (1977) study introduces the Affect Expression Rating Scale, which is a rating scale to be filled out for young children by an adult observer and is designed to differentiate between internalizers and externalizers. When factor analyzed, the first and most important of three factors is labeled expressive versus inhibited. Examination of the item loadings indicate that the dimension is virtually synonymous with extraversion versus introversion. Scores on this factor showed the expected correlations with skin conductance (negative) and communication accuracy (positive) for boys only and successfully separated externalizers from internalizers.

For whatever reason we may place more confidence in communications, verbal and otherwise, from more sociable and outgoing people. A study of attitude change by Wheeless (1974) seems to indicate so. The topic of attitudes toward the space program was selected for study on the basis of pretesting of 15 different topics, and 73 college speech students were exposed to pro and con positions on the topic camouflaged as news releases for the campus radio station. Students were given information concerning the characteristics of the source of the communication—his or her competence, sociability or friendliness, composure, extraversion or assertiveness, character, and degree of credibility. Each subject rated each communicator on those variables according to the subject's perception of the source. Significant attitude change did occur, and the variables that contributed significantly to the prediction of attitude change, in addition to the preexperiment attitudes of the subjects, were the competence and sociability of the source and to a lesser extent the extraversion or assertiveness of the source. Thus it appears that to be more friendly and assertive is to be considered more believable in the same way that to be rated more competent causes one's communication to have more impact.

MISCELLANEOUS RESEARCH TOPICS

Volunteers for Psychological Experiments

A topic that has generated some interest is concerned with personality differences of people who volunteer for psychological experiments as compared with those who do not volunteer. One recent study (Francis & Diespecker, 1973) found no differences between volunteers and nonvolunteers for a sensory isolation experiment on the Eysenck Personality Inventory or on the 16PF. However, two other studies have found differences. Burns (1974) found that students who volunteered when offered no incentive scored higher than students who volunteered after being offered an incentive and students who did not volunteer on two CPI scales, capacity for status and social presence, both of which load highly on the CPI extraversion factor. McLaughlin and Harrison (1973) provide data that further indicate that volunteers in general are higher in extraversion on the Eysenck Personality Inventory and that this difference is particularly obvious when the experiments that they are asked to volunteer for involve social interactions such as group discussions. Parenthetically subjects who were high in both extraversion and neuroticism were found to volunteer more frequently for a stress experiment involving electric shock than other groups, and this supports the idea that neurotic extraverts are less concerned about aversive situations than other personality groups.

Handwriting Characteristics

The reader who is interested in the relationship of graphology or handwriting to personality variables will be aware that extraversion–introversion is one of the personality variables that graphologists rely on most heavily in interpreting handwriting samples. Some positive evidence for this position comes from a recent study by Williams, Berg–Cross, and Berg–Cross (1977), who submitted several handwriting indexes to a factor analysis. Three factors emerged, one of which was labeled extraverted writing style, characterized by the size and the rightward slant of the handwriting and related to extraversion scores on the Eysenck Personality Questionnaire. The second factor involved slowness and size of handwriting and was related to introversion. It seems reasonable that introverts compared with extraverts might be more deliberate and attentive to detail in their handwriting. Vine (1974) points out that there must be some commonly held stereotypes in the general population about the handwriting of different personalities. Untrained introductory psychology students showed considerable agreement in judging personality from handwriting samples, and their judgments showed some accuracy on extraversion but not on neuroticism. Two additional recent studies, however, indicate no relationship between handwriting and extraversion–introversion as measured by the Eysenck Personality Inventory. The first, Rosenthal and Lines (1978), used Australian college students, who copied a passage on unlined paper. The findings show no relationship between extraversion and either letter slant or slope of line. Lester, McLaughlin, and Nosal (1977) followed a similar procedure with two samples of 68 and 43 college students. Sixteen different graphological signs including slant, size, and speed showed no consistent relationship with extraversion in either sample. There is one notable difference between the studies that showed positive effects and those that did not. In the former, handwriting was done under speed conditions, that is, with a time limitation imposed, a condition that seems to be almost inevitably present in real-life handwriting.

Hypnotic Susceptibility

Susceptibility to hypnotic influence bears some relationship to a person's general suggestibility and to ability to relax and follow external directions. According to a few recent studies extraversion is associated with such susceptibility, as measured by the Stanford Hypnotic Susceptibility Scale, which assesses subjects' reactions to a hypnotic session. Schwartz and Burdsal

(1977) found that susceptibility was associated with sociability on Cattell's Clinical Analysis Questionnaire, as well as with concrete thinking and psychasthenia (anxiety). Three studies by Gibson and his colleagues (Gibson & Corcoran, 1975; Gibson, Corcoran, & Curran, 1977; Gibson & Curran, 1974) indicate that there is an interaction between extraversion and neuroticism, with the former accounting for the majority of the variance, such that nonneurotic extraverts and neurotic introverts are more susceptible than the others.

Extrasensory Perception

Kanthamani and Rao (1972) review the literature indicating a positive relationship between ESP and extraversion and report four studies conducted with young adolescent girls and boys in English-speaking schools in India. Personality variables were measured by Cattell's High School Personality Questionnaire, and it was found that low scorers on the second-order extraversion factor had ESP scores that were consistently poorer than chance. Extraverts, however, scored significantly higher than chance in three of the four studies. Randall (1974) used the Junior Eysenck Personality Inventory with 13–14 year olds in Britain and came up with somewhat more complicated results: nonneurotic introverts and neurotic extraverts were superior.

OBSERVATIONS FROM AN INTERACTIONAL PERSPECTIVE

Much of the research presented in this chapter is commendable for its explicit or implicit interactional flavor. In the most clearcut cases, subjects are divided into groups on the basis of one or more personality variables and exposed to differing experimental situations; then the effects of the person variable alone, the environment variable alone, and the combination of the two are analyzed. In many cases the interaction effect is statistically significant and psychologically meaningful. The implication is clear that the personality traits do not have the same effect on behavior regardless of situational differences but also that situational forces do not operate independently of personality differences. These results are illustrative of the potential use of extraversion–introversion in social-personality research, but they represent only a beginning in applying interactional research designs to important areas of social and interpersonal behavior. For example, the attribution process by which people ascribe characteristics to self, others, and situations has not been mentioned in relation to extraversion–introversion in the current literature. The same may be said for research on the situational elicitation and control of aggression, interpersonal conflict and cooperation, and complex group behavior, to name a few. Research of an interactional nature conducted in a variety of areas is necessary in order to illuminate the nature and power of person-environment interactions and in order to test the limits and potential of extraversion–introversion as a useful person variable.

Most of the available interactional research addresses the question of codeterminant effects of person and environment on behavior. The assumed reciprocal effect of behavioral experiences on the personality of the actor (another form of interactionism discussed in chapter 1) has received minimal attention in current research on extraversion–introversion, with the exception of some research on the effects of therapy on personality. Such research is needed to complete the picture. For example, Fouts (1975) found introverted children, in contrast to extraverts, to react to the realization that they were being imitated by stopping the imitated response. What effect did that realization and behavior change have on the level of introversion of the child? Surely there is some reciprocal effect, which would be amplified by a series of consistent experiences. The most likely effect is to strengthen or maintain the already existing tendency. In this case withdrawal from social interaction (being imitated) probably strengthens the introverted tendency that produced the reaction in the first place. But this general rule of self-perpetuation of personal tendencies would have many exceptions. The introverts in Hendrick and Brown's (1971) study who stated a preference for being with extraverts at parties may be moved, if their preferences are actualized, toward extraversion as a result of the consequent experiences with the extraverted friend. The point is that person variables are not static qualities. Research on the conditions under which they are maintained or changed is important but scarce.

4

EXTRAVERSION-
INTROVERSION
AND OTHER IMPORTANT
PERSONALITY TRAITS

The content of this chapter differs from that of chapter 3 in that the preceding chapter focused on behaviors, thoughts, and emotions actually exhibited in social situations or in laboratory situations that constituted social analogues. The emphasis there was upon attempting to discern the different interpersonal styles of introverts and extraverts as actually acted upon in interpersonal situations. This chapter, on the other hand, focuses upon self-reported traits, characteristics, or attributes as assessed by questionnaire or some similar method. This focus gives us an opportunity to look at the differing cognitions, emotions, and behaviors exhibited by introverts and extraverts, primarily in the interpersonal sphere, as perceived by the persons themselves as they respond to questionnaire items.

Chapter 2 focused upon the central place held by the dimension of extraversion-introversion within the total personality sphere, that is, as measured by global personality instruments measuring many personality traits simultaneously. Most of the personality variables discussed in this chapter have risen to a place of importance because of their usefulness to particular research groups investigating particular personality domains and thus have emerged in isolation, as it were, rather than as part of a systematic attempt to test personality in general. As a result single questionnaire measures of these traits are not typically embedded in larger global assessment batteries.

This chapter then should serve at least two purposes at once. One is to expand our understanding of the dimension of extraversion–introversion by noting its relationship to other variables that have proven themselves to be important to personality researchers working on specific topics of interest. The second purpose, perhaps equally or more important to the reader, is the understanding to be gained about the various concepts by noting their relationship to extraversion–introversion. Because of the nature of the process by which these variables have attained a place of importance in personality research, it is usually not clear how such a variable relates to other more traditional personality traits as measured by global personality batteries. Relating these variables to extraversion–introversion, which as chapter 2 related must rank among the top few personality dimensions in delimiting the differences between personalities of various types, helps us to understand how a newly created personality trait relates to the larger body of personality traits that have been studied heretofore. Semantics and theoretical discussions may imply the answer to these questions, but the questions are actually empirical ones. The purpose of the present chapter is to review the evidence at hand. Further insight on these traits is to be gained by considering their relationship to neuroticism, which is also assessed by Eysenck's questionnaires. This is the other most commonly agreed upon major dimension in global personality assessment and differentiates among people on the basis of their anxiety proneness, emotional reactivity or instability, and tendencies toward anxiety-related disorders. Scores are frequently available on both extraversion and neuroticism, and in some studies subjects are divided into the four possible combinations of neurotic extraverts, neurotic introverts, stable extraverts, and stable introverts. It is often useful to view scores on other personality traits as representing an interaction between these two dimensions.

INTERNAL AND EXTERNAL CONTROL
OF REINFORCEMENT

One of the most popular concepts in current personality research is locus of control, a personality variable that has to do with the beliefs that one holds about what factors are dominant in controlling important outcomes in life. More specifically the concept involves persons' perceptions of whether the reinforcements they receive are dependent upon or independent of their own actions and behaviors. A person with an internal locus of control is one who believes that reinforcements are consequences of one's own behavior, that whether the consequences are positive, negative, or neutral, they are determined primarily by the person's actions themselves. This carries the implication that one perceives oneself as skilled in manipulating the environment in order to attain desired consequences. An external locus of control describes the opposite orientation. Such a person believes that he or she is not in control of the consequences and outcomes in life, that there are important external forces that determine these outcomes and over which control is difficult or impossible. The distinction then is basically between internality, the belief that achievement or lack thereof is dependent on ability, initiative, motivation, persistence, skill, and so on, and externality, the belief that achievement is more dependent on factors such as luck or chance or is based rather on the actions of other important people in the environment. The internal–external locus of control dimension is conceptualized as a continuum and like other personality traits may be highly situation specific or may show considerable generality across the situations in one's life.

The similar sounding names of internal–external locus of control and extraversion–introversion have unfortunately led to semantic confusion concerning the relationship between the two variables. Actually the apparent similarity between the two is very shallow, and the conceptual or theoretical foundation for postulating a relationship between the two is very weak. Likewise the data that have been collected indicate that if there is a relationship at all between locus of control and extraversion, it is a highly complex one. The dimensions are clearly not interchangeable despite the similar-sounding names, and the student of personality would do well to distinguish clearly between the two.

Platt, Pomeranz, and Eisenman (1971) administered Rotter's Internal–External Control Scale, which is the most widely used measure of locus of control, along with the Eysenck Personality Inventory and the MMPI to over 1,100 first-year college students and found locus of control to be unrelated to all measures of introversion and extraversion administered. They did find a correlation between externality and neuroticism, indicating that individuals with a more external locus of control tend to be more anxious than those with an internal locus of control, a finding that has been echoed by a number of other studies. Shriberg (1972) found precisely the same results with the Eysenck Personality Inventory and Rotter's scale using a select sample of 70 female speech therapy students.

Considerable effort has been devoted to determining more specifically what is measured by Rotter's Internal–External Control Scale and to the multidimensional nature of the concept of locus of control. One approach is to divide Rotter's items into three categories dealing with disbelief in luck or chance, belief in the modifiability of political systems, and belief in individual responsibility for failure. Joubert (1978) found that none of the above were related to extraversion scores on the Eysenck Personality Inventory in a sample of college students. Schwartz (1973) administered three different measures of each of six different personality traits to 100 college students in order to determine the degree of agreement among various measures of the same trait and the interrelationships among the traits. The six traits measured were locus of control, extraversion, neuroticism, cultural estrangement, guilt, and social desirability. Each was assessed by an appropriate scale of the 16PF and of Gough's Adjective Check List as well as by a specially designed measure of each trait (Rotter's Internal–External Control Scale and Eysenck's Maudsley Personality Inventory). The 16PF measures of locus of control and extraversion were the autonomy and the sociability scales, respectively. The Adjective Check List measures of locus of control and extraversion were the self-confidence and intraception scales, respectively. Despite the obvious difficulty in selecting equivalent scales to measure each of these traits, the author concluded that there was sufficient evidence to indicate the convergent and discriminant validity of all the traits except guilt and to indicate the relative independence of the traits from one another. More specifically there was a small positive correlation between Rotter's locus of control scale and Eysenck's extraversion scale but not with the other measures of extraversion. Nor was Eysenck's extraversion scale correlated with the other two measures of locus of control. Interestingly the 16PF sociability scale was not highly correlated with the other two scales of extraversion used in the study.

In dealing with locus of control it is important to remember, as noted by Collins, Martin, Ashmore, and Ross (1973), that the difference between the two orientations is a difference in beliefs about or perceptions of the relative importance of internal as opposed to external factors, and there is really no implication that the beliefs accurately reflect the causes of one's behavior. It might be argued that the extraversion–introversion dimension reflects an actual rather than a perceived difference in the degree to which one's behavior is controlled by internal and external factors. The extravert may be more keenly attuned to social and environmental influences whereas the introvert may be more attuned to internal, private experiences; the result is a situation in which the environment is more powerful in controlling the behavior of the extravert than that of the introvert. The principal evidence supporting this speculation lies in data relating to the impulsivity subcomponent of extraversion in which the extravert reacts more impulsively to changing environmental conditions but the introvert remains more internally controlled by long-range plans and intentions. However, it is probably more accurate to conceptualize extraverts and introverts as being affected differently by different environmental conditions and likewise by internal conditions rather than seeing one as more environmentally controlled than the other.

Collins et al. (1973) discussed these and other similar issues in detail in connection with what they termed the "internal–external metaphor" in theories of personality. In their data collection, a 63-item questionnaire was administered to 163 subjects, factor analyzed, and related to scores on the Eysenck

Personality Inventory, Rotter's Internal–External Control Scale, and others. The four factors that emerged from their 63-item questionnaire were assumed to represent the dimensions covered by the internal–external metaphor. The first factor was labeled other direction and reflects persons' perceptions of their own behavior as being too much in conformity to social expectations, associated with low self-esteem. Rotter's externals and Eysenck's introverts both tended to score high on this scale. The second factor was labeled inner direction, indicating persons' beliefs that their behavior is a function of their own personal convictions and attitudes rather than social pressure. Scores on this factor tended to be related to Rotter's internality but not to introversion. The third factor is the one that showed the strongest relationship to extraversion but was not related to locus of control. The factor involves the element of impulsiveness, labeled lack of constraints, and represents impulsiveness in the sense of spontaneity, flexibility and freedom from inhibitions. The fourth factor was labeled transsituational predictibility of behavior, reflecting a person's belief that the behavior of friends, the behavior of other people in general, most behavior, and his or her own behavior are predictable across situations. This factor was correlated with Rotter's internality but not with extraversion. The correlation between Rotter's and Eysenck's scales was not significant.

The only common element then between locus of control and extraversion indicated by this study is that both externals and introverts tend to see themselves as too other directed or too socially conforming, apparently for the purpose of attaining social approval. Note that this common element is shared by introverts and externals, a reversal of what would be expected by implying similarities from the names of the variables and contrary to the original predictions of Collins et al. Eliot and Hardy (1977) note the importance of the common element described above and suggest that extraversion on the Myers–Briggs Type Indicator reflects a feeling of ease concerning interpersonal contact, a feeling that persons with an internal locus of control should share because of their confidence in dealing with the environment. They predicted and found internally oriented college students to be more extraverted than externals. If this reasoning is sound, it is not clear why Eysenck's extraversion factor should not produce similar results.

In addition, whereas the analysis of variance procedure of Collins et al. (1973) did not show the four factors to interact in relation to extraversion scores, there were complex interactions for locus of control. The interactions may be simplified by saying that the most internally oriented (locus of control) individuals were those who scored toward the internal end of each of the four factors, whereas Rotter's most external individuals scored toward the external end on all four factors. Actually the authors interpret their data as suggesting that there are two independent types of internals, one of whom believes that the world is predictable and does not believe that he is other directed and the other of whom believes that he is inner directed but feels constrained and inflexible. Neither of these types relates clearly to the introvert or the extravert.

A study designed in our own laboratory (McWithey, 1978) zeroes in further on some of the issues raised here. In this study locus of control was measured among 71 undergraduate students by Rotter's Internal–External Control Scale and by another locus of control scale (Levinson's), which provides a separate score for internality and two scores for externality. Externality is subdivided into a chance scale and a powerful-others scale, indicating a division between two possible sources of external control of behavior. The Eysenck Personality Inventory scales of neuroticism and extraversion were used along with sociability and impulsivity subscales consisting of items from the Eysenck Personality Questionnaire. Following the findings of S. Eysenck and Eysenck (1977b), impulsiveness was further subdivided into four factors: narrow impulsiveness (acting on impulse), risk taking, liveliness, and nonplanning, and there was a total impulsiveness score. In the correlational analysis of these data, none of the locus of control variables correlated significantly with either extraversion or sociability. However, three of the four scales showed a correlation between externality and neuroticism.

The only impulsiveness variable that was clearly unrelated to locus of control scores was liveliness, which along with risk taking is the aspect of impulsiveness most clearly related to extraversion. The other impulsiveness scales were generally related positively to externality as measured both by the Rotter scale and by the powerful-others subscale. These relationships were strongest for narrow impulsiveness and total impulsiveness. Subjects were also separated into four extraversion–neuroticism groups on the basis of median splits on these variables, and analyses of variance were computed using the locus of control scores as dependent variables. There were 16 subjects in each group. Consistent with the correlational analysis, there were main effects of neuroticism for three of the four locus of control variables, and there were no significant extraversion effects. It was anticipated that neuroticism and extraversion might interact to produce effects on these variables, but there were no significant interaction effects.

It is abundantly clear then from these studies that an external locus of control is more closely associated with anxiety or neuroticism than with extraversion and is clearly not associated with sociability. It does appear, however, that there may be some complex link between the impulsivity component of extraversion and locus of control, although it may well be that different aspects of impulsiveness are related to each. The relationship between externality and impulsivity or more specifically between powerful-other externality and impulsivity found by McWithey is consistent with the laboratory studies (see Geen, 1976) that indicate that external individuals placed in a skill (intellectual) situation often show atypical, erratic, and unpredictable (impulsive) behaviors, apparently because they tend to view the situation as being a chance- or luck-oriented task rather than a skill task. Thus in that particular setting one might make similar predictions concerning impulsive behavior for both extraverted individuals and individuals with an external locus of control and especially for one who shares those characteristics. Now that it is clear that the dimensions of internal–external locus of control and extraversion–introversion are basically independent dimensions, perhaps fruitful research combining the two person variables with predictions made concerning behavior in specific situational contexts will be forthcoming.

MISCELLANEOUS INTERPERSONAL VARIABLES

Next to be considered is a set of variables that relate specifically to interpersonal relationships and for whom the relationship to extraversion and introversion should be quite obvious. Although the research on most of these is quite scanty, the relationships found are noteworthy. For example, considering Sheldon's three-dimensional classification system for temperament types and physique types, it would be a clear-cut expectation that introversion would be associated with cerebrotonia, which is the intellectual, meditative, shy temperament typically associated with thin body build. Likewise extraversion would be associated with both viscerotonia, the sociable, happy-go-lucky individual who tends to be fat in body build, and somatotonia, the muscular, athletic, active type. Lester (1976c) found these expectations to be borne out for both cerebrotonia and somatotonia but not for vicerotonia. The study involved 44 college students with extraversion measured by the Eysenck Personality Inventory. Lester (1974) had suggested that viscerotonia represents the sociability component of extraversion whereas somatotonia represents the impulsiveness component. Unfortunately Lester (1976c) does not provide the relevant information with which to evaluate that suggestion.

In other isolated findings Averett and McManis (1977) and Vestewig and Moss (1976) each found extraversion to relate strongly to self-report measures of assertiveness. However, Vestewig and Moss found that in a projective measure in which five scenarios were presented to subjects who then indicated their five most likely responses in order of preference, extraversion and assertiveness were related only for males and only for two of the five scenes. The situations presented involved a professor giving a student a bad grade, seeing another waited on out of turn in a restaurant, being confronted with a noisy group in a library, being confronted by an overly aggressive salesman, and having to sit with a noisy group in the cafeteria. Although in totaling responses to the five scenes extraverts were more assertive than introverts (for males only), the only specific situations in which the correlation between extraversion and assertiveness was significant was in the library and in the case of the salesman. There was some tendency for neuroticism to be negatively related to assertiveness. Dana and Cocking (1969) found extraversion to relate to a measure of interpersonal dominance compared with submission but not to relate to a measure of interpersonal affection opposed to hostility.

These two dimensions have been widely recognized as the most important variables in interpersonal behavior and occupy an important role in Carson's interactional theory of personality (see chapter 1). Another interpersonal scale designed to assess empathy was found to relate positively to both males' and females' extraversion scores in a sample of 435 social science students. Empathy was negatively correlated with both neuroticism and psychoticism (Hekmat, Khajavi, & Mehryar, 1974). Vandenberg and Price (1978) also found extraversion and empathy on the Comrey Personality Scales to be related.

SENSATION SEEKING

An interpersonal variable that has been researched more thoroughly in its relationship to extraversion is sensation seeking. There are four subcomponents that elaborate the meaning of the construct: thrill and adventure seeking, disinhibition, experience seeking, and boredom susceptibility. The last word on the relationship between extraversion and sensation seeking seems to have been voiced by Zuckerman, Bone, Neary, Mangelsdorff, and Brustman (1972) when they reviewed previous literature and presented original data of their own. In one study the Eysenck Personality Inventory extraversion scale was positively related to all subcomponents of the sensation-seeking scale except boredom susceptibility. In another study two of the four scales, disinhibition and boredom susceptibility, were negatively related to the MMPI social introversion scale, and all were positively related to hypomania (impulsiveness). In still another, sensation seeking was positively related to three of the five 16PF extraversion scales (dominance, surgency, and adventurousness) although not to sociability or group dependence.

The authors' conclusion from these data and from the review of earlier studies was that sensation seeking is related to an uninhibited, nonconforming, impulsive, dominant type of extraversion but not to sociability. A more recent study by Farley (1977) may also support this conclusion. He administered two single-item self-ratings ("outgoing" and "need for stimulation and excitement") to groups of ninth graders and college students and found them to be correlated only for college males. An informative study by Vestewig (1977) utilized

178 college students involved in a complicated laboratory gambling task. As expected, extraverts chose high-risk alternatives more often than introverts in all conditions and also changed their risk levels more often than introverts as gambling conditions changed. Vestewig takes this as support for the formulation that asserts that extraverts are stimulation seekers relative to introverts and notes that extraversion as measured by the Eysenck Personality Inventory is one of the few personality dimensions that has been shown to relate consistently to laboratory measures of risk taking.

FIELD DEPENDENCE

The dimension of field dependence versus field independence originated in research on perceptual processes and has been applied to the personality realm. Perceptually, field-dependent individuals are those who are dependent or reliant on external cues to an extreme degree whereas field-independent individuals are able to rely at least partially on internal cues in their perceptual processes. A good example of the difference between the two may be seen in their performance on a visual rod-and-frame test, in which they are required to place a bar or rod in an upright, vertical position within a rectangular frame that may be rotated to varying degrees of slant. The task is performed in a dark room in which other sources of visual reference to the vertical are unavailable. Field-dependent individuals have difficulty overcoming the slant of the frame in attempting to place the rod in a vertical position, whereas field-independent individuals have more success at the task. It appears that field-independent individuals use among other things their own bodily position for a reference point in placing the rod in a vertical position. Another task at which field-dependent individuals have difficulty is finding embedded figures within a complex visual display. Field-independent individuals do not find this task so difficult.

The relevance of this variable for personality research lies in the generalization that may be made on the assumption that field-dependent people also are more oriented to environmental cues in the social realm. Witkin and Goodenough (1977) hold that field-dependent individuals make greater use of external

social referents in an ambiguous situation, are more attentive
to social cues, have an interpersonal orientation, and are more
socially skilled than field-independent persons, who in turn
have greater cognitive analysis skills. On the basis of the foregoing description field-dependent individuals should clearly
be extraverted and field-independent persons should be introverted. Lester (1974) reaches the same conclusion based on
a common physiological element in the two personality traits.
However, there is only one recent study involving a small sample
of 35 female college students that supports the hypothesized
relationship. The two tests used were the Group Embedded
Figures Test and the Eysenck Personality Inventory extraversion scale (Loo, 1976). Later, however, Loo and Townsend
(1977) clarified the relationship by showing that in three small
samples field dependence was unrelated to the sociability items of
Eysenck's scale, unrelated to sensation-seeking items, but associated in two of the three samples with fast decision time as
measured by five items on the extraversion scale. One study
of an unusual population, abnormal offenders (Blackburn, 1972b),
found the opposite to be true: 15 extreme field-dependent individuals were more introverted on the MMPI social introversion
scale, but not on the Eysenck Personality Inventory, than 15
extreme field-independent subjects. Division of subjects into
groups was based on the Group Embedded Figures Test.

Numerous studies have shown no relationship between the
two variables. Such was the case with Cegalis and Leen (1977)
using the Myers–Briggs Type Indicator; Ghuman (1977), who
administered Cattell's Children's Personality Questionnaire to
11 and 12 year olds; Lester (1976c), in three separate studies
utilizing small groups of college students; and Mayo and Bell
(1972). Likewise Fine (1972) presents data from seven different samples, all of which indicate no relationship between
field dependence and extraversion. Eysenck's extraversion scale
was used in some of the samples and the MMPI social introversion scale in others. Having demonstrated that field dependence
and extraversion–introversion are unrelated, Fine considered
the possible interaction of the two dimensions as related to
mental health and adjustment. He suggested that the combination of field dependence and introversion was an unhealthy
combination because the two characteristics are incongruent

and work at cross purposes. The result would be anxiety and neurotic tendencies. The hypothesis was tested by taking subjects in each of the seven samples and dividing them into four possible field dependence–field independence, extraversion–introversion categories. In six of the seven samples, subjects scoring high on the neuroticism scale of the Maudsley Personality Inventory, the anxiety factor of the 16PF, or the three neurotic scales of the MMPI were overrepresented in the quadrant characterized by field dependence and introversion. A further study by Doyle (1976a) also supports the hypothesis. Using the Eysenck Personality Inventory and the rod-and-frame test, Doyle identified 16 field-dependent extraverts and 5 field-dependent introverts and found that the latter had significantly higher neuroticism scores and significantly lower scores on three of the scales of the Personal Orientation Inventory, a measure of self-actualization.

REPRESSION–SENSITIZATION

One of the most robust findings in the current literature on personality traits is that the extraversion–introversion dimension is correlated with the repression–sensitization dimension: introverts tend to be sensitizers, and extraverts tend to be repressors. The basic idea behind the repression–sensitization scale is that individuals may be differentiated from one another on the basis of typical defense mechanisms or coping strategies that they use in dealing with stress and negative emotion. Repressors, as the name implies, tend to deny or at least prefer not to verbalize adjustment problems and emotional experiences. As a result, for example, they tend to tolerate greater amounts of pain at least for short periods without comment and to present themselves in socially desirable ways. Sensitizers on the other hand tend to be very much aware of their negative emotions, stress, problems, and so on and even to exaggerate these. They are more likely to use intellectual defense mechanisms such as isolation, intellectualization, and rationalization rather than to repress or deny problems. It is unclear whether sensitizers actually have more adjustment problems, anxiety, and depression than do repressors, but it is clear that they admit them more freely. Sensitizers are less likely to devalue themselves for having emotional experiences, whereas repressors may see such experiences as a sign of weakness. The interested reader is referred to Geen (1976) for an up-to-date review of the literature on this subject.

Data presented some time ago by Byrne (1964), who created the Repression–Sensitization Scale, are noteworthy because of the variety of scales of extraversion found to be related to this variable. He found that MMPI social introversion and sensitization correlated almost perfectly. Likewise Guilford's thinking-introversion and social-introversion scales were associated with sensitization. Consistently the CPI extraversion factor, the Myers–Briggs Type Indicator, and Guilford's rhathymia (impulsiveness) scale were associated with repression. Already it is clear that sociability, impulsiveness, and reflectiveness are all related to repression–sensitization. Cohen and Oziel (1972) found that a group of 20 extreme repressors were significantly higher on extraversion as measured by the Maudsley Personality Inventory than a group of 20 extreme sensitizers. Lester (1976c) and Dana and Cocking (1969) also found extraversion to be associated with repression. Only Shriberg (1972) found the two variables to be unrelated among a group of female college students.

The concepts of sensitization and introversion are highly compatible concepts involving awareness of and reflection on internal, emotional, and intuitive experiences. But there is one major difference between sensitization and introversion: the former is consistently associated with anxiety and neuroticism. Sensitizers are higher in self-reported anxiety whereas introverts do not consistently score higher on anxiety scales. It may be that sensitizers would be more accurately characterized as neurotic introverts and repressors as stable extraverts, but there is currently little evidence available with which to evaluate that hypothesis. Colson (1972) did find that his correlation between sensitization and introversion in a group of suicidal graduate students was largely accounted for (according to partial correlations) by the common variance shared with neuroticism.

Considering the sociable, other-oriented, and impulsive extravert as a repressor who either by choice or ability is relatively unaware of his or her own negative emotions provides a further perspective toward understanding extraversion. There may be an implication here that the lack of restraint and lack of social inhibition of the extravert may be as much a matter of choosing not to attend to those internal stimuli as a matter of not having learned them. Incidentally we must be careful to distinguish between the meaning of the term repression as used in connection with the repression–sensitization scale and the meaning of the term as used in connection with the repression scale of the MMPI as discussed in chapter 2. To be repressive in the latter sense indicates an overcontrol of one's behavior that is the opposite of impulsiveness and as such is a characteristic of the introvert. To be repressive in the sense of the repression–sensitization scale is an extraverted characteristic dealing not with overcontrol of behavior but rather with inattentiveness to internal emotional stimuli.

Bauer and Achenbach (1976) deal with the dimension under consideration by adding a third element, self-image disparity. The investigators took 20 male freshmen and 20 male seniors at Yale University, administered the repression–sensitization scale and Giedt and Downing's MMPI extraversion scale, and assessed self-image disparity by administering 30 self-referenced statements referring to both the real and the ideal self. The term self-image disparity refers to the difference between how individuals see themselves currently and how they prefer to be. From the correlations among extraversion, repression–sensitization, and self-image disparity in the two groups who were assumed to be at different developmental levels, the authors concluded that the three variables actually represent a single dimension. They feel that the concept of self-image disparity accounts for the differences between repression–sensitization and extraversion–introversion. So interpreted, the common element among all three dimensions would be a sensitivity and willingness to acknowledge differences between one's actual and ideal self associated with a high motivation to improve oneself. If so, that description would apply to sensitizers, introverts, and individuals with high self-image disparity and the opposite description would apply to extraverts and repressors.

A study by Miller and Magaro (1977) provides evidence concerning several of the variables discussed in this chapter. The perspective of the study was to identify four different types of personalities based on various specified combinations of scores on a number of personality inventories. Among the scales used in two different studies were the Sensation Seeking Scale, the Repression–Sensitization Scale, the Internal–External Locus of Control Scale, the MMPI social introversion scale, the Group Embedded Figures Test (field dependence), the Eysenck Personality Inventory, and two measures of self-esteem. The two samples consisted of 107 and 130 college students, respectively. The data were analyzed by cluster analysis and examined to determine whether the clusters that emerged were similar to the theoretical clusters previously identified. It may be worth noting in passing that two of the clusters, one labeled the hysteric style and the other the character disorder style, involved extraversion in combination with some other variables, whereas a third, labeled the depressive style, was associated with introversion in combination with other variables. There was theorized to be a fourth cluster, the compulsive style, which should have introversion as a major element but for which the results were not clear-cut.

More relevant to the current discussion, however, are observations concerning the co-occurrence of extraversion and other variables discussed in this chapter in the various clusters identified. There were four clusters identified in Study 1 and five clusters identified in Study 2, allowing nine clusters in which to observe the association of extraversion with other variables. The most evident relationship in these data is between extraversion and sensation seeking, in which the placement in clusters was congruent in eight of the nine cases. In other words, if high extraversion scores emerged as part of a cluster, high sensation-seeking scores did also. When introversion was part of a cluster, low sensation-seeking scores were apparent in defining the cluster. The next most obvious variable associated with extraversion was the repression–sensitization scale with extraversion and repression occurring together or sensitization and introversion occurring together in four of the nine possible clusters. Consistent with material presented earlier in the chapter, there was little congruence between extraversion and locus of control and between extraversion and field dependence. The same is true for the variables of dogmatism, self-esteem, and anxiety, which are discussed next.

SOCIAL SELF-ESTEEM, SOCIAL ANXIETY, AND SHYNESS

Detailed study of the factor analytic studies presented in chapter 2 indicate that the extraversion factor and the anxiety (neuroticism) factor running through most personality batteries are essentially independent of each other. However, when there is an exception because of the testing of a special population or because the scales utilized are not carefully constructed in such a way as to maintain the orthogonality of extraversion and neuroticism, the tendency is toward a negative correlation between the two. When introverts have adjustment problems, they are more likely to be anxiety-related disorders; in fact the typical conceptualization of a neurotic is what Eysenck would describe as a neurotic introvert. Actually the relationship between introversion and anxiety may be seen more clearly when examining variables that are correlated with anxiety, such as self-esteem or sensitization, than when investigating the anxiety-introversion relationship directly.

Considering self-esteem, one should recall the study by Bauer and Achenbach (1976), which equated the repression–sensitization, the extraversion–introversion, and the self-image disparity dimensions as being one and the same. Other studies show relationships tending in that same direction, although the findings are not nearly as strong as that language would imply. For example, Bown and Richek (1969) tested a group of about 150 elementary and secondary education students, all female, with the Myers-Briggs Type Indicator and with a self-report inventory of self-perception. Introverts were found to have significantly lower scores on acceptance, valuing, and liking of self as well as of others. In interpreting studies such as this the Bauer and Achenbach perspective reminds us that self-image disparity is not necessarily unhealthy because the other extreme, that associated with extraversion, is one of denying self–ideal discrepancies, that is, repression.

Tolor (1975b) used a very unusual method for assessing self-esteem. In his study college students placed gummed labels representing either themselves or another social figure on a page on which the only reference point was another label representing either self or another social figure placed at the midpoint of the paper on the left-hand side of the page. Placement of self spatially above others on the page was taken as an indicant of self-esteem, and the procedure was repeated 16 times with different combinations of figures. Out of 80 original subjects 13 who showed a clear tendency to place self above others were found to be significantly more extraverted (Eysenck Personality Inventory) than 22 subjects whose placements indicated low self-esteem. From these two studies it appears that introverts tend to rate both themselves and others lower but to rate themselves even lower than others compared with extraverts. Lester (1976b) administered a measure of Sheldon's three temperament types to 54 undergraduates and then asked them to describe their real and ideal selves. The cerebrotonic temperament type is the one corresponding to introversion and was the least preferred of the temperament types. Both females and males rated their ideal selves as less cerebrotonic (introverted) than their actual selves. It appears that introverted college students prefer to be less introverted.

However, self-esteem is not unidimensional and involves both a personal dimension and a social dimension, only the latter of which is related clearly to extraversion–introversion. Bagley and Evan-Wong (1975) factor analyzed a popular self-esteem inventory after administering it to nearly 300 subjects, 14–15 years old. They found two factors, the first labeled unhappiness and poor self-esteem and the second labeled social confidence and extraversion. They found that these two factors were essentially independent of one another and that the first was related to neuroticism as measured by the Eysenck Personality Inventory but not to introversion, whereas the second was related to extraversion but not to neuroticism. Thus, similar to the research with repression–sensitization, it appears that subjects classified as both introverted and neurotic would have the lowest self-esteem scores, having both poor personal self-esteem and low social confidence. Stable extraverts would have high self-esteem scores. The relation of self-esteem to extraversion would be greater when using measures of self-esteem that tap primarily social confidence and would be less when using measures of self-esteem that tap primarily personal anxieties.

The same picture emerges from studies of anxiety. There is

little evidence of a relationship between introversion and anxiety when general measures of anxiety are used. For example, Bull and Strongman (1971) administered the Manifest Anxiety Scale and Cattell's Anxiety Scale Questionnaire to 85 college students and found no relationship between those scales and Eysenck Personality Inventory extraversion–introversion scores. However, when measures of social anxiety are used, the findings are different. Breen, Endler, Prociuk, and Okada (1978) related the scales of the CPI to scores on the Situation Response Inventory of General Trait Anxiousness. The latter is a measure of trait anxiety that yields four fairly independent scores for different types of potentially anxiety-arousing situations: interpersonal, physical danger, ambiguous, and innocuous. The CPI sociability scale was correlated negatively only with interpersonal trait anxiety and anxiety aroused in ambiguous situations, which indicates that less sociable persons have higher anxiety in those areas. However, the opposite was true for physical danger trait anxiety, which was positively related to sociability. The subjects were 278 senior, female nursing students.

The relationship between introversion and social anxiety is so strong that Patterson and Strauss (1972) had difficulty separating the two, using Bendig's social extraversion scale, their own interpersonal anxiety scale, and the social avoidance and distress scale. Actually the situation is more complicated. Gilliland (1977), in a study conducted in our laboratory, factor analyzed scores from the Eysenck Personality Inventory extraversion and neuroticism scales, the social avoidance and distress scale, the fear of negative evaluation scale, the sensitivity to rejection scale, and affiliative tendency scale. The factor analysis revealed two clear-cut factors of social anxiety, one related to neuroticism and the other related to introversion. The factor related to neuroticism only is probably best described as a need for social approval or a fear of losing social approval and was defined largely by scores on the fear of negative evaluation and fear of social rejection scales. The social anxiety factor related to introversion but not to neuroticism is adequately labeled social avoidance and distress and involves actual or desired avoidance or escape from anxious social situations accompanied by emotional tension and discomfort when avoidance is not possible. These two factors corroborate the thinking of Watson and Friend (1969), who pioneered in the area of social anxiety with their construction of the social avoidance and distress and the fear of negative evaluation scales. Again, combining these two types of social anxiety would lead to the conclusion that neurotic introverts are the most socially anxious whereas stable extraverts are the least.

Pilkonis (1977a, 1977b) has conducted an intensive and informative study of shyness. The study consisted of asking 263 college students whether they perceived themselves to be shy persons. The 41% who responded affirmatively were then compared with the others on various personality variables and then the group of 100 shy persons were investigated in more detail to identify different clusters that may exist within that sample. Instruments used were the Stanford Shyness Survey, the self-consciousness scale, the self-monitoring scale, the Eysenck Personality Inventory (scored also for sociability), and an introversion–extraversion rating scale focusing on whether thoughts and interests were directed inward or outward. An initial validity check indicated that those who called themselves shy persons were in fact more introverted on both measures, less sociable, more neurotic, more socially anxious, and higher in public self-consciousness, although not in private self-consciousness. The distinction between public and private self-consciousness arose from the research of Fenigstein, Scheier, and Buss (1975). They developed a 38-item scale to measure the trait of self-consciousness. Factor analyses of correlations from nine different samples consistently produced three factors, private and public self-consciousness and social anxiety. The first involves one's awareness of inner thoughts and feelings, and the second involves awareness of oneself as a social object. The three factors are intercorrelated except in the case of private self-consciousness and social anxiety. Pilkonis's data indicate no relationship between extraversion or sociability and either type of self-consciousness, although introversion was associated with social anxiety.

The main thrust of Pilkonis's studies was to determine if there are different kinds of shy persons. Thus a cluster analysis of those who called themselves shy was performed, and the indication was that there are two major groups. There are the publicly shy, who focus on their behavioral deficits, and the privately shy, who focus on their subjective discomfort. The publicly shy are publicly self-conscious, are concerned about their lack of skill, and fear embarrassment in social situations. The privately shy are anxious in the sense of being internally aroused and uncomfortable in social situations. Apparently the two groups are equally introverted on Eysenck's scale.

It is worth noting in this context that extraversion shows a consistent positive relationship with self-actualization as measured by the Personal Orientation Inventory. An early finding by Knapp (1965) has recently been replicated by Doyle (1976b). In the latter study, which involved 150 university students, neuroticism scores as measured by the Eysenck Personality Inventory were consistently negatively related to self-actualization scores whereas extraversion was consistently positively related to the 12 Personal Orientation Inventory scales, even though not all correlations were significant. The strongest relationship was for spontaneity, which should come as no surprise.

SOCIAL ATTITUDES: CONSERVATISM AND DOGMATISM

An area that has received considerable study, possibly because of Eysenck's interest in it, is the relationship of introversion and extraversion to various social attitudes, including variables such as dogmatism, conservatism, radicalism, toughmindedness, and authoritarianism. In connection with the study of the effects of genetics on personality traits, Eaves and Eysenck (1974) administered a 60-item Public Opinion Inventory to a large sample of twin pairs. The two major social attitude variables measured were radicalism and toughmindedness, and it was found that there was a positive correlation between extraversion and toughmindedness but no correlation with radicalism. Toughmindedness has to do with displaying practical, selfish, and expedient attitudes in contrast to idealistic attitudes that on some test batteries would be labeled psychologicalmindedness. The variables involved here are further spelled out in a study by Wilson and Brazendale (1973), in which six different factors of Wilson's Conservatism Scale were related to extraversion in a sample of 97 female student teachers. Extraversion scores were associated with the social attitudes of liberalism as opposed to conservatism, realism, which is similar to toughmindedness, hedonism, and an absence of religion–puritanism. Thus in comparison with the introverts these attitudes describe the extravert as liberal in the sense of not being adverse to novelty and change, realistic and practical in attitude, and relatively free from religious beliefs and sexual inhibitions. The two factors unrelated to extraversion–introversion were militarism–punitiveness and ethnocentrism. In contrast neuroticism was correlated only with the intolerance involved in ethnocentric attitudes. Similarly Nias (1973a) found both adults and college students to show positive correlations between liberalism, particularly hedonism, and extraversion. This study attempted further to relate attitudes and personality to opposition to the Common Market in England but found no such relationships. Pearson and Sheffield (1976) were unable to replicate earlier findings in samples of female student nurses, female psychiatric patients, and 13 and 14 year olds. They found no relationship between conservatism scores and Eysenck's personality variables. However, when Nias (1973b) administered a children's version of the Wilson Conservatism Scale and the Junior Eysenck Personality Inventory to more than 400 children 11-12 years of age, he found extraversion to be correlated with two of four factors emerging from the children's responses. Extraversion was related to positive attitudes about sexuality and to positive attitudes about religion. Thus as in the adult studies introverts were more conservative. In a slightly different frame Cohen and Harris (1972) administered a School Environment Preference Schedule, which measured what they called bureaucratic orientation, similar to authoritarianism. Among their sample of 86 10-11 year olds, extraversion as measured by the Junior Maudsley Personality Inventory was related to bureaucratic orientation and to dogmatism as measured by Rokeach's scale but not with the conservatism scale used in studies described above. Furthermore the relationship held only for boys.

To the extent that there is agreement among these studies, there is further insight to be gained concerning the differences between introverts and extraverts. Extraverts in general are more liberal in their attitudes toward the pleasures of life (hedonism—and a large number of the items on these scales refer to sexual pleasures), more liberal and less puritanical in their attitudes toward religion, more pragmatic or even selfish, but not more prejudiced or punitive in their thinking about others. The most clear-cut findings come from English adult males, and the differences are not so obvious in females or children and may not apply cross-culturally. With regard to religious attitudes, for example, McClain (1978) administered several scales to U.S. college students, including the 16PF, the Edward's Personal Preference Schedule, and the CPI, along with Allport's Religious Orientation Inventory, a scale designed to assess depth and type of religious attitude. McClain factor analyzed the combination of these scales and found eight factors to describe the responses. Among the factors were self-control versus impulsiveness, social ascendency, and affiliation. Social ascendency was clearly defined by both the CPI and the 16PF extraversion scales as well as the dominance scale of the Edward's Personal Preference Schedule. Clearly this was an extraversion factor and was found to be unrelated to religious attitudes.

Rokeach's Dogmatism Scale is a variable that is related to the social attitude variables discussed above and that has received considerable attention in North American psychology. As noted above Cohen and Harris (1972) found dogmatism to be positively correlated with extraversion in their sample of male 10 and 11 year olds. Dogmatism is a cognitive style that represents an oversimplification of complex information presented to an individual, presumably in an attempt to maintain a sense of order and security in dealing with that information. Thus dogmatic social attitudes would be those involving relatively concrete, simplistic, rigid categories to which relatively simple rules of interpretation are applied. One may be dogmatic either in liberal beliefs or in conservative beliefs, and although dogmatism is more typically associated with prejudiced, right-wing conservative social attitudes, this relationship is not a necessary one. Rokeach's Dogmatism Scale attempts to assess dogmatism of the left as well as dogmatism of the right. Smithers and Lobley (1978) make the interesting suggestion that dogmatism may be involved in both extreme introversion and extreme extraversion rather than being related linearly to that dimension. In three large samples of English college students, scores on the Rokeach Dogmatism Scale and the Eysenck Personality Inventory extraversion scale were not correlated overall, nor was extraversion correlated noticeably with toughmindedness. However, when factor analyses were performed, dogmatism loaded sometimes with an introversion factor and sometimes with an extraversion factor. The interpretation that dogmatism may be associated with extremes of either certainly needs further study but is an interesting possibility. It may be that introverts deal with external, social sources of information such as social pressure in a relatively dogmatic way, oversimplify the information at hand because of its threat potential, and thus render themselves unable to deal with complex social information in an appropriate or self-assuring manner. On the other hand, extraverts seem to have the same problem with internal information. Consistent with our discussion of the correlation between repression and extraversion, extraverts may oversimplify internal sources of information such as emotions and intuitions. Thus each type of personality is more confident in dealing with the infromation that he or she treats in a more complex manner, that is, external information for the extravert and internal information for the introvert.

Finally a study by Simmons (1976) may point in an important future direction for personality research. Rokeach has gone beyond the concept of dogmatism to propose a value orientation approach to personality, and Simmons has constructed a value survey, which consists of 100 statements rated on a 7-point scale as to "value to me." In this study about 200 college students showed numerous positive correlations of their value survey statements with their extraversion scores. Correlations with neuroticism scores were practically nonexistent. On the basis of the findings extraversion may be interpreted as (1) value affirming rather than value eschewing; (2) valuing open, warm, and loyal social relationships, especially in terms of entertaining others and spending time with others; (3) valuing vibrancy, vitality, vigor, and viability in daily living, especially in terms of seeking adventure and excitement; (4) valuing the search for individuality with integrity; and (5) valuing participation in the business life of the community.

SUMMARY: MEANING OF EXTRAVERSION-INTROVERSION

At the end of chapter 2 the conclusion was drawn that there are four related but nonidentical dimensions tapped by the various

measures of extraversion: social activity, social facility, impulsiveness (adventurousness and risk taking), and nonintrospective
tendencies. The material in chapters 3 and 4 has generally supported the assumption of these differences between more extraverted and more introverted people, has provided more detail
about each, and has often shown their interaction with situational variables. Concerning sociability, extraverts have been
seen to value, enjoy, and engage in a wide range of social and
affiliative activities and to be socially confident. In contrast
introverts value privacy and close friendships more highly, have
lower social self-esteem, expect interpersonal disagreements,
and perceive themselves to be too other directed. Their negative
expectations about ongoing or impending social interaction
lead to either social avoidance or feelings of distress and discomfort or both.

Concerning impulsivity, studies of sensation seeking and
risk taking confirm differences on this dimension. Clearly introverts exercise a higher degree of control or inhibition of their
behavior than do extraverts. The same was shown to be true
of the behavioral (nonverbal) expression of emotion: extraverts
are more expressive. But the pattern is reversed for the internal
experience of emotion and the verbal expression thereof: extraverts exert repressive control over the intensity of their emotional
experience, whereas introverts are more in touch with their
emotions, although they do not display them outwardly. Thus
the more extraverted person is emotionally inhibited but behaviorally expressive, whereas the more introverted person is
behaviorally inhibited but experiences a greater depth and variety
of emotion. This is an important manifestation of the difference
in introspectiveness and reflectiveness between the two.

5

EDUCATIONAL AND VOCATIONAL ACHIEVEMENTS OF EXTRAVERTS AND INTROVERTS

The content of the next three chapters brings the study of extraversion–introversion out of the laboratory and into the realm of applied psychology. Consideration is given to the relationship between personality and behavior at school and at work and to the day-by-day decision making, behavior patterns, and the modes of adjustment that constitute one's life-style. This chapter deals with achievement, chapter 6 with maladjustment, and chapter 7 with personal and social behavior patterns that may become problematic, such as the use of alcohol. In most cases the behavior in question is studied in natural settings where precise experimental control is impossible and where multiple causal factors are operating; thus it is unrealistic to expect a single personality dimension such as extraversion–introversion to account for large portions of the variance. Consider, for example, the many causes of a person's choice of a career in engineering: ability, exposure, encouragement from parents and friends, monetary considerations in advanced training, and so on. If there were 10 such factors of relatively equal importance, none would account for more than 10% of the variance, and that estimate is probably generous. Therefore, in this research the search is for variables the effects of which are consistent in various studies, although the effect may not be strong in any of the studies. Such research is of both theoretical and applied interest in testing the limits of the application of the personality trait and in testing the direction and magnitude of its effects.

ACADEMIC PERFORMANCE

Age and Personality

There is one particularly robust finding that appears consistently in the study of introversion and extraversion. In the educational realm extraverts are superior to introverts in the preschool and primary school ages, up until perhaps 12-15 years of age. Then a transition occurs, and beyond that level introverts are superior to extraverts. Although the correlation between extraversion and achievement is not large on either side of the transition period, the relationship is consistently positive before age 12 or 13 and consistently negative after age 15 or 16. Literature reviews by Entwistle (1972) and by Anthony (1973) each support this conclusion, and results of more recent studies are also consistent with this finding. Entwistle found extraverts, particularly stable extraverts, to be superior to introverts up until age 13 in studies using Eysenck's scale and until age 12 or 14 in studies using the Cattell scales, all in Great Britain. Research using both scales show introverts to be superior beyond that age level. Although the majority of studies in the United States have been of the older age groups, the same trend appears.

Although throughout this literature there is general agreement among authors as to the age effect described above, there are differences in opinion as to the interpretation of how the age effect occurs. Entwistle discusses the difference in terms of different responses to social motivation on the part of introverts and extraverts and indicates that the introvert is a late developer educationally because the social motivations so important in early school years are not as important to the introverted as to the extraverted child. However, at more advanced levels of education social motivation takes second place to individual or intrinsic motivation in the educational process at which point the introvert is best suited to educational attainment. It is true that good study habits, including self-discipline, consistency, and perseverance, are related to introversion and are an important factor in academic success at the later grade levels.

Anthony's interpretation of these same findings is a bit different. He also reviews studies that indicated that developmental changes in the level of extraversion parallel the age trends outlined above. In addition, he cites cross-sectional studies that indicate that extraversion increases in the general population until about age 14 and then begins to decline from that point throughout the life-span. On the other hand, the development of ability follows a linear progression, increasing until the 20s before leveling off. Anthony feels that plotting these two curves together provides an explanation for the transition in superiority between introverts and extraverts in the educational realm He makes the (dubious) assumption that one who is a late developer in reaching a peak in extraversion would also be a late developer in attaining a peak of ability. The superiority of the extraverted child arises from the fact that he or she is an early developer both in terms of personality and ability; as long as both lines are increasing in parallel fashion, say up to age 13, there is a positive relationship between extraversion and ability. At that point, however, extraversion reaches a peak and begins to decline whereas ability continues to increase so that beyond the age of 13 or 14 the person who is more advanced in both personality and ability is progressively becoming more able and less extraverted, thus the negative correlation between extraversion and ability beyond age 14. Although this explanation seems less likely, it does bring to our attention the important fact that we cannot simply assume that the same individuals who are introverted at age 9 and performing more poorly are the ones who are also more introverted at age 16 and performing better. Anthony is suggesting in fact that those who are introverted at an earlier age and performing more poorly are the ones who are more extraverted at the age of 16 (because they reach their peak later) and continuing to perform poorly. Thus, whereas one position holds that the level of extraversion and introversion remains the same and the academic performance changes, the other position assumes that the level of performance stays the same and the degree of extraversion–introversion changes.

A recent report indicates that both changes are occurring simultaneously. Anthony (1977) reports an analysis of longitudinal data collected in 1969 by Rushton. A large number of children (266) were tested at age 10–11 and again at age 15–16 with intelligence, math, and English tests and with Cattell's personality test. As expected, correlations of extraversion with the intellectual and academic variables changed from positive to negative as a function of time, especially for English. Correlations with change scores from the first to the second testing indicated that the students who were more capable initially became relatively more introverted with age; in addition, the students who were more introverted initially became relatively more capable with age. And the seemingly contrasting relationships were similar in magnitude. Whatever the explanation the age by personality effect is an agreed-upon finding in the study of educational processes.

Younger Children

One study of preschool and first-grade children (Stedman & Adams, 1972) indicates a strong superiority of extraverted over introverted children. The subjects in the study were disadvantaged Mexican–American children, who were tested for personality and achievement differences at the beginning of a preschool Headstart program and tested again at the end of the first grade with the Metropolitan Achievement Test. Seventy-six children were involved in the study. The personality measure used was Schaeffer's Classroom Behavior Inventory, which involves teacher ratings of a number of child attributes and is scored for positive social behavior, extraversion–introversion, and positive task orientation. The extraversion score includes amount of verbal expressiveness, gregariousness, absence of social withdrawal, and absence of self-consciousness. Of all the measures taken at the beginning of the Headstart program, extraversion was the best predictor of achievement at the end of the first grade, showing a strong positive relationship to the three Metropolitan Achievement Test subareas of word knowledge, reading achievement, and math achievement. If these results apply to the general population of preschool and first-grade children as well as to disadvantaged children, the greatest superiority of extraverts over introverts occurs at the earliest ages.

In a thorough study of the reading achievements of 8 year olds, Elliott (1972) determined that the positive relationship between extraversion and reading achievement at this age level was not a function of either chronological age differences among the 8 year olds or mental age (IQ) differences. With these two factors eliminated, the explanation of the superiority of extraverts over introverts must lie within the interaction between personality and educational practices. Elliott's conclusions were drawn on the basis of relating extraversion to reading achievement in three restricted samples, one based on similarity of chronological age between 8 years, 6 months, and 8 years, 11 months; another based on similarity of mental age or IQ; and a third based on similarity of reading age. With each of the three held constant, extraversion could be related to the other two in each sample and thus clarify the relationship. The high positive relationship of extraversion to reading age remained even when chronological age and IQ were controlled for, but the reverse was not true. Therefore, the reading superiority of extraverts was not a function of either chronological age or IQ differences.

In another study of younger students (Jensen, 1973) the correlations between extraversion and both intelligence and achievement were consistently small but positive. White, black, and Mexican–American students in the fourth through the eighth grades in California were given a battery of tests, including the Junior Eysenck Personality Inventory, at the beginning of the school year and tested by the Stanford Achievement Test at the end of the school year. In this particular study, the strongest relationships occurred at the sixth-grade level.

Barton, Bartsch, and Cattell (1974) collected data that appear to apply to the beginning of the transition period. Using Cattell's High School Personality Questionnaire, which was scored for both anxiety and extraversion, large samples of both sixth and seventh graders were administered intelligence and achievement tests at 6-month intervals over a 12-month period. The only findings relating to extraversion that are reported in the article indicate a change over time in the relationship between extraversion and social studies grades. Initially, extraverts scored higher than introverts, but at 6 months and 1 year later were equal to introverts in social studies scores. Over this time-span all subjects improved, but introverts improved more than extraverts. Interestingly both extremes, introverts and extraverts, scored higher than did a group of ambiverts. It appears that the subjects in this study were undergoing the transition, the quality of which appears to be that introverts were catching up so that they were equal to the extraverts by the time they reached the end of the seventh grade. Apparently, however, these results apply only to social studies.

Older Students

Insight into some of the variables that are important in these age changes come from a detailed longitudinal study of 345 boys, covering the ages of 11–15 (Banks & Finlayson, 1973). School examination performance was studied in relation to Junior Eysenck Personality Inventory scores. In general, introverts performed better, especially in two schools where ability and aspiration levels were higher. And the relationship between introversion and performance increased with age, particularly for students with higher neuroticism scores. Results were also strengthened when extreme over- and underachievers were considered. There were two clusters of variables in the study that were related to successful academic performance. One centered around achievement motivation, whereas introversion was an important element of the other. Included with introversion were (1) intellectual curiosity, (2) homework orientation, (3) parental warmth and support, combined with (4) dependence and conformity on the part of the boy, and (5) a slower development of interest in girls.

Apparently the transition period occurs over a fairly lengthy period of time and is seen most clearly in the basic sciences. A study by Seddon (1975) used 741 15–19-year-old chemistry students at various educational levels. Employing multiple regression analysis, he found that extraversion–introversion was not related to IQ but was related to achievement in chemistry. For the sample as a whole there was a negative correlation of extraversion with chemistry achievement, an indication that for these students the transition had already occurred. More important, however, there was an interaction between extraversion and age that indicated that the negative correlations of extraversion with performance increased at each age level so that the prediction of the superiority of introverts over extraverts continued to increase with each year of experience. A few weeks after the above data were collected, the same subjects were exposed to a nine-session self-instructional chemistry program (Seddon, 1977). According to pre- and posttreatment scores on a background chemistry test, there was an interaction as in the earlier data between extraversion and chronological age.

Goh and Moore (1978) found generally negative correlations between extraversion and grade point average among 78 university students, 48 vocational technical institute students, and 49 high school students in the United States. There were no differences between groups on Eysenck Personality Questionnaire extraversion scores, indicating that differential correlations were not the result of different levels of extraversion at the three educational levels. The negative correlation between extraversion and achievement was significant only at the university level and was much higher for a group of science students than for social studies students.

One study conducted with black Ugandans (Honess & Kline, 1974) and another with South Africans (Orpen, 1976) seem to pinpoint the transition point at a slightly later age. With black rural Ugandans aged 14, 15, and 17, the only relationships between extraversion and achievement occurred in the younger girls, for whom there were positive correlations with three of the five academic subjects used. Orpen's comparison was between rural South African blacks and Afrikaans-speaking rural whites. The results were the same for both groups. In a group of 14 year olds of both races the correlation between extraversion and achievement was positive, whereas in a group of similar students of both races at the college level the relationship between extraversion and achievement was negative. In both cases achievement was based on performance on regular year-end examinations.

In general, however, studies conducted in other cultures indicate that either the transition to introvert superiority occurs

considerably later or that there is simply no relationship between extraversion–introversion and scholastic performance
in those cultures. Paramesh (1976) found no relationship between
extraversion or neuroticism (Eysenck Personality Inventory)
and performance in seven different subject areas among 155
high school boys in India, and Mehryar, Khajavi, Razavieh, and
Hosseini (1973) found no relationship between college achievement and extraversion in Iran. They correlated an Iranian version
of the Eysenck Personality Inventory as well as a psychoticism
scale with college entrance exams. Only a small positive relationship of extraversion with IQ and no relationship between extraversion and either math or natural science scores were found
for either females or males. To my knowledge this is the only
study involving psychoticism, and this study found it to be a
powerful variable that correlated negatively with achievement
in Iranian university students.

Other minor related findings include a study by Griffiths
and Crocker (1976), who found only a slight tendency for introverts in Newfoundland to make better grades in first-year college
chemistry. Actually these investigators were attempting to relate
personality differences to different teaching methods but found
no interaction between individualized and conventional approaches to teaching chemistry to first-year college students.
Mann and Rizzo (1972) explored the relationship of extraversion as measured by the 16PF to a specially designed scale for
the prediction of collegiate academic success. The scale is the
achiever personality scale of the Opinion, Attitude and Interest
Survey. According to the authors this achiever personality scale
correlates .35 with college grade point average even though it
does not correlate with the usual high school predictors of
academic success in college. The findings from this study were
that the extraversion scale of the 16PF correlates negatively
with the achiever personality scale with subjects consisting of
480 male freshmen. Mehryar, Hekmat, and Khajavi (1975) asked
U.S. university students, "Do you regard yourself as an aca-
demically successful student?" The group that answered the
question yes was compared with the group that answered the
question no on the Psychoticism–Extraversion–Neuroticism
Scale and on Lanyon's Psychological Screening Inventory. In this
study there were no differences between groups on extraversion

(expression) for either scale. Hogan (1976) found a small positive correlation between subjective introversion and self-estimated IQ scores among 167 college students.

Organ (1975) pinpointed some of the study habit differences between introverts and extraverts that may be connected with their different achievement at advanced educational levels. Subjects were 50 graduate business students in each of three classes who were given an opportunity in the course to earn bonus points with high scores on pop quizzes. There was a negative correlation between extraversion and bonus points earned that was not accounted for by aptitude differences; this implies that introverts have more consistent study habits and respond more appropriately to the reinforcement contingencies in the college environment.

TEACHING STRATEGIES AND PERSONALITY

There is an immense body of literature beyond the scope of the present discussion that involves laboratory studies of the cognitive and intellectual performance of introverts and extraverts and that relates primarily to Eysenck's theory of the biological differences between introverts and extraverts. It is not clear at this point what direct implications may be drawn from this laboratory research to apply to the educational process per se or to the understanding of the differences between introverts and extraverts in the classroom, but at some point these implications will likely be clarified and applied to the understanding of academic differences. The interested reader is referred to the recent work of M. W. Eysenck (1976, 1977).

A few studies involving actual classroom learning experiences of introverted and extraverted students have been conducted, such as a pair of studies by Leith (1973) and Trown and Leith (1975). Leith briefly describes four studies that indicate that adolescent introverts do better if there is more guidance, prompting, and structure, whereas extraverts do better in more ambiguous, exploratory atmospheres. He utilized a 5-week programmed instruction course to teach elementary meteorology (rainfall) to adolescents, whereas Trown and Leith (1975) developed a special 12-week mathematics section to be implemented by the teachers of fifth-grade classes. Students were divided into high- and low-neuroticism and high- and low-extraversion groups based on the H. B. Personality Inventory. The differences between the teaching strategies were complex but applied the same basic differences found useful in earlier studies. Some teaching strategies were described as exploratory, inductive, and large-step, and the others as supportive, deductive, and small-step. The results of the first study replicated the extraversion–introversion difference found in the earlier studies. Introverts did better on the highly structured program whereas extraverts did better with the less supportive approach. Only an effect for neuroticism was found in the second study, in which the exploratory strategy was facilitative for low-anxiety subjects but debilitative for high-anxiety subjects. Interestingly neither teaching strategy was shown to be superior overall. Thus the important implication is that teaching strategy must be matched by personality type in order to be maximally effective. But the question of which personality variables are relevant to the interaction remains an open question. In adolescents, who are near the age transition point discussed above, it appears that introverts may need more structure whereas extraverts need less.

These findings are mirrored in a study by Shadbolt (1978) using first-year university students. In a first experiment 211 students were taught introductory genetics with the aid of a programmed text, and in a second 145 students of the history of education served as subjects. Personality was measured by the H. B. Personality Inventory and by the Eysenck Personality Inventory, respectively. In both experiments students were exposed to either a structured–deductive or an unstructured–inductive teaching approach. Based on posttest assessments, there were an interactive effect of extraversion and teaching strategy in Experiment 1 and an interaction between neuroticism and strategy in Experiment 2. In the first case introverts performed better with a structured approach, and in the second neurotics performed better with a structured approach. Minimal results showing the same tendency are reported by Rowell and Renner (1975), who examined the performance of masters-level education students in Australia in four different courses. Unexpectedly for the authors scores on the Eysenck Personality Inventory were unrelated to a preference for written essay work versus formal examinations and also unrelated to performance. Extraverts outperformed introverts in only one course, educational sociology, and the authors surmised that this may have been the result of a lower degree of class structure in that course.

Other attempts to relate personality differences to instructional variables have not met with similar success. Robertson (1978) was interested in attention deployment in grammar school students; attention deployment was defined as whether they chose to study only one or more than one topic simultaneously in a programmed study of probability theory. No relationship to Eysenck Personality Inventory scores was found. Power (1977) likewise could find no effect of extraversion and rate of interaction with teacher on several indices of achievement in eighth-grade science classes.

In conclusion the results reported provide a fairly consistent picture of the relationship of the extraversion–introversion personality variable to academic performance. In the lower grades extraverts perform better than introverts. There are nonsignificant differences between the groups in the early teen-age years, and in late high school (and university) introverts perform better than extraverts. Although the interpretation remains unclear, it appears that these differences are not accounted for by differences in intelligence, and differences in neuroticism or anxiety do not interact consistently with the extraversion–introversion variable in such a way as to explain the differences between groups. Differences on the psychoticism variable may be important, and further studies are in order here. As Entwistle (1972) points out, there are a number of variables that may enter into this transition that have not yet been fully explored, not the least of which is the continuing selectivity that occurs in samples as the researcher moves from primary grades to university. The population covered by a random sample of third graders is clearly not the same population as a random sample of university students who differ on many variables related to academic specialization and vocational goals. More longitudinal studies in which the same subjects are tested year after year for a period of 6 or 8 years through the transition period would seem to be essential in clarifying the relationships involved.

VOCATIONAL PREFERENCES

The personality dimension of extraversion–introversion is a major variable in the study of vocational behavior. Costa, Fozard, and McCrae (1977) administered the Strong Vocational Interest Blank to more than 1,000 adult males, factor analyzed the scale, and extracted five factors of vocational interests. The factor accounting for the most variance was labeled person-versus-task orientation. The most person-oriented vocations were community recreation administrator, YMCA secretary, chamber of commerce executive, credit manager, business administrator, rehabilitation counselor, social worker, and social science teacher. The most task-oriented professions were architect, physicist, mathematician, engineer, artist, chemist, and dentist. These subjects were also given the 16PF, the scales of which were related to the five vocational factors extracted. The primary extraversion scales on the 16PF related clearly to the person-versus-task orientation factor on the SVIB. That is, those subjects preferring person-oriented vocations also rated themselves as being outgoing, happy-go-lucky, venturesome, and group oriented, whereas subjects preferring task-oriented vocations scored low on those variables. These are four of the five 16PF scales that define the second-order extraversion factor.

Similar results have been found with the California Psychological Inventory, which was administered along with the SVIB by Johnson, Flammer, and Nelson (1975) to 359 male college freshmen. The CPI was factor analyzed, with extraversion being the second of five factors extracted. This factor reflected primarily high scores on the dominance, sociability, and sense of well-being scales and was clearly the most important of the five factors extracted in terms of relationship to occupational scales. Extraverts preferred the occupations of YMCA staff member, personnel director, public administrator, rehabilitation counselor, social worker, school superintendent, and minister. Introverts preferred dentist, architect, physicist, chemist, engineer, carpenter, farmer, and printer. Interest in business and sales was not related to either.

The relevance of this personality dimension is further underscored by the usefulness of the Occupational Introversion–Extraversion Scale (Johansson, 1970), consisting of a recombination of items of the SVIB. This scale correlates satisfactorily with other extraversion scales (Goodyear & Frank, 1977; Johnson, Nelson, Nolting, Roth, & Taylor, 1975). Johnson et al. found that extraversion scores on this scale were associated with vocational scales tapping physically active, outgoing, and administrative interests, and Goodyear and Frank (1977) found introversion to be related to the vocations of engineer, physicist, mathematician, and farmer. In contrast extraversion was related to YMCA secretary, chamber of commerce executive, and community recreation leader. In addition these authors found physical science, biological science, and engineering majors in college to be more introverted than business administration majors.

Interestingly each of these studies involved males and none utilized Eysenck's scale of extraversion–introversion. However, an older study by Bendig (1963) administered the Maudsley Personality Inventory and the SVIB to both male and female first-year college students in 1959. Social introverts of both sexes indicated more of an interest in architect, physicist, engineer, and chemist. However, extravert women and men had different interests, extravert men preferring social service occupations and extravert women preferring sales occupations. Although these results with males are consistent with later studies, it is unlikely that the same results would occur again with female students 20 years later.

Holland's (1973) theory of vocational choices, in which he delineates six vocational personality types, does not utilize a single extraversion–introversion dimension, but several authors have noted some obvious semantic similarities. At face value it appears from Holland's descriptions that extraversion is included in both the social and enterprising personality types whereas introversion relates primarily to the investigative personality type but is also involved in the conventional and realistic personality types. His sixth type, the artistic, is not clearly related. A word of caution is in order in taking these descriptions at face value because of the results of Ward, Cunningham, and Wakefield (1976). They administered Holland's Vocational Preference Inventory to 425 college students and found that neither the social nor the investigative scales showed the expected relationship with the 16PF scales known to be related to extraversion–introversion. However, these investigators used primarily females as subjects whereas most of the work that has been done on vocational interests involves primarily male populations. Good correlational studies among established measures of extraversion and Holland's six vocational personality types are in order. Nevertheless the point is that when one talks about vocational interests, this personality variable receives frequent attention. Parenthetically the reader with special interests in this area will be aware of the recent studies indicating, on the one hand, an important genetic influence on vocational types (Grotevant, Scarr, & Weinberg, 1977; Roberts & Johansson, 1974) and, on the other, important paternal effects (DeWinne, Overton, & Schneider, 1978). Inasmuch as extraversion-introversion is an important dimension in these types, the information on hereditary influences in chapter 8 will be of particular interest.

The studies just described have approached vocational choices solely from the standpoint of preferences and interests without dealing explicitly with the influence of ability or educational achievement. However, it should be clear from the content presented earlier in the chapter that introverts have a tendency to achieve higher educational and professional training levels than extraverts because of their superiority at advanced educational levels. Such differences undoubtedly influence preferences for occupations for which advanced degrees are required. At the same time academic excellence in these professional areas (e.g., physics) may depend on one's interest, toleration, or fascination with the subject matter. Finally individuals who become interested in various occupational and academic pursuits may experience personality changes as a result.

An area of potential research that has not been tapped has to do with specializations and chosen activities within a given profession. For example, one's practice of professional psychology may be highly person oriented as in clinical psychology or highly research oriented or highly administrative in nature or various combinations of the three. Therefore, whatever one's profession, there may be vast differences in the actual daily work routine, the selection of which may be explainable on the basis of personality patterns.

Consideration of the major fields of study chosen by college students is quite relevant to the present discussion because they represent actual vocation-related decisions rather than simple statements of preference. Kokosh (1976) investigated personality differences on the MMPI between groups of college graduates who majored in either sociology and history or physics and zoology. Sociology and history majors were found to have higher hypomania (impulsiveness) scores and lower social introversion scores than physics and zoology majors. Recall that Goodyear and Frank (1977) also found physical science, biological science, and engineering majors to be more introverted than business administration majors. In India (Kanekar & Mukerjee, 1972) 40 students in the arts (including social sciences) were less intelligent, more extraverted, and more neurotic on the Eysenck Personality Inventory than a similar number of graduate students in science. (The authors were expecting season-of-birth effects on personality but found none.) But in the same country Shanthamani and Hafeez (1973) found opposite differences, that is, managers more introverted and engineers more extraverted. This study used a newly developed scale of extraversion–introversion, the validity of which was poorly documented. And when Horn, Turner, and Davis (1975) tested groups of college students majoring in social science as opposed to engineering, they found no differences on Maudsley Personality Inventory extraversion scores. Similar results were found with a group of high school seniors expressing interest in either social science or engineering degrees.

In summary the information relating to introverts' vocational choices seems clearer than that for extraverts. Because of aptitude differences, college achievement differences, and/or vocational interests, introverts are more likely to end up in the task-oriented, technical professions than are extraverts. Some authors have interpreted this as an orientation toward things, but probably that is too simple. The orientation seems to be toward ideas, often abstract ideas, and structured, detailed work as opposed to the less well-ordered and perhaps more practical person-oriented occupations.

One of the reasons that the picture is clearer for introverts than for extraverts, as suggested by Pillai (1975), may be that introverts are more consistent in stating their occupational interests, values, and aspirations than are extraverts. His subjects were more than 400 high school students in India who completed an occupational values questionnaire and an occupational aspirations questionnaire separately. Disparity between the two was related to both extraversion and neuroticism. The author explains that more introverted students both value and aspire to traditional, high-status, professional vocations. More extraverted students state more liberal, less socially conforming values, but their actual aspirations are governed more by immediate status and monetary considerations.

MISCELLANEOUS VOCATIONAL STUDIES

The global studies of the SVIB reviewed earlier indicate a moderate preference of introverts for the profession of artist. These findings are corroborated in a recent study by Gotz and Gotz (1973), who administered the Maudsley Personality Inventory to students at an art academy. Art teachers were asked to nominate the young adult students with whom they had worked for a minimum of 2 years for inclusion in either the gifted or the ungifted category. Fifty of each were utilized in the study. In addition, 15 of the 50 gifted students were designated highly gifted. The findings indicated that the gifted students were significantly more introverted and more neurotic than the ungifted students and than standard norms. There was no difference between the ungifted students and standard normative data on introversion and neuroticism. Furthermore, the 15 highly gifted students were significantly more introverted and neurotic than the remaining 35 gifted students. Therefore the relationship of introversion to the degree of creativity among professional art students is clear. Parenthetically a number of minor findings may be noteworthy to the reader with special interest in the area of creativity. Leith (1972) administered a measure of creativity to 9–13-year-old German children and found that introverts scored better than extraverts under normal testing conditions (moderate stress) but that the findings were reversed when they were tested under reduced-stress conditions. Two studies were unsuccessful in finding relationships between personality variables on Cattell's High School Personality Questionnaire and music aptitude and achievement in seventh and ninth graders (Schleuter, 1972; Thayer, 1972). Extraversion has been found to relate to creativity of attitudes (Bascuas & Eisenman, 1972) and to the ability to form clear and controllable mental images (Euse & Haney, 1975). On the other hand, introverts produce more fantasy in their story telling in response to projective tests (Palmiere, 1972), show a preference for abstraction in visual displays (Jamison, 1972), and prefer romantic to classical art (Rosenbluh, Owens, & Pohler, 1972).

The relationship between interest in the ministry as a vocation and extraversion has been found to be a slight positive one in the global studies mentioned above, which would seem in many respects to fit the person orientation of extraverts as opposed to introverts. However, the picture is more complicated as shown in a literature review by Nauss (1973). The studies of theological students and ministers reviewed indicate that ministers actually combine one aspect of extraversion, that is, friendliness, dominance, and sociability, with one aspect of introversion, that is, reflectiveness, introspection, and seriousness. According to Nauss the profile resulting from the combination of these characteristics plus other more minor attributes describes the ministerial personality. It is amazing that this is the first mention in the research reviewed in this chapter of the subcomponents of extraversion–introversion. Along the same line Carlson and Levy (1973) reasoned that persons classified as intuitive extraverts on the Myers–Briggs Type Indicator should be much more likely to be involved in volunteer social service activities than other personality types. In this context extraversion is described as an empathic responsiveness to others, and intuition is described as an openness to others' possibilities. They provided striking supportive evidence from a group of 10 black university students who were doing volunteer work in a halfway house for disturbed adolescents, 7 of whom scored in the predicted category. Only 1 of 10 students in a control group was an intuitive extravert. Dorr, Cowen, Sandler, and Pratt (1973) did not find extraversion differences on the OIE or on a larger extraversion factor derived from factor analysis of several measures between adult nonprofessional mental health workers and controls. The workers (females) had been hired to work with children in a school mental health program.

Finally in two isolated studies Lester (1976a) found no differences between white male police officers and standard extraversion norms (consistent with SVIB studies reported earlier), and Exner, Wylie, Leura, and Parrill (1977) found no difference between prostitutes as a group and normals. The personality profiles of five groups of prostitutes, assumed to represent a hierarchy in terms of status within the profession, were compared with control groups matched on age, marital status, education, and father's occupational status. The five groups were 25 call girls, 25 in-house prostitutes, 10 basic streetwalkers, 10 day-time streetwalking housewives, and 10 streetwalkers who were also addicted to drugs. Each subject was paid $25 for 3 hours of personality assessment with a female experimenter. Both the MMPI and the Rorschach inkblot test were administered. The general conclusions were that the basic streetwalkers seemed more immature and dependent than their controls and more so than their higher class associates. The streetwalking addicts and the streetwalking housewives showed more signs of psychopathology. On the social introversion scale two of the three groups of streetwalkers were more socially introverted than their normal controls and the higher status callgirls and in-house prostitutes. The housewife streetwalkers were more socially introverted than their more successful colleagues but not more introverted than their normal controls. The more successful prostitutes were no more introverted than their respective control groups.

WORK BEHAVIOR

There are a few recent studies of the relationship of extraversion–introversion to specific behaviors on the job, from repetitive factory work to the work of managers of large companies. At the managerial level, for example, Kirton and Mulligan (1973) found attitudes toward organizational change to be related to a combination of neuroticism and extraversion. Subjects were 258 managers from eight companies with at least 1,000 employees each. The four extraversion-by-neuroticism groupings were compared and the finding was that the two personality variables interacted, although there was no effect of either taken separately. Subjects scoring high on both the neuroticism and extraversion scales and subjects scoring low on both scales (neurotic extraverts and stable introverts) had more positive attitudes toward change in managerial practices in general, more positive attitudes toward specific, innovative appraisal schemes or promotion policies being introduced, and the lowest level of discontent with the institution and with superiors. On the other hand, Marsteller and Slocum (1972) found minimal relationships among measures of need satisfaction patterned after Maslow's hierarchy of needs and personaltiy attributes measured by the Bernreuter Personality Inventory among 61 supervisors in a 2,500-person steel plant. Extraversion was slightly associated with job-related need satisfaction in the areas of autonomy and self-actualization only. A study of organizational activism (Evered, 1977) found this variable to be unrelated to extraversion. He took 96 masters of business administration graduate students and studied them for 1 academic year; he reasoned that activism within this organizational institution may be similar to activism within a work environment. Activism was behaviorally defined as spending time and energy in the organizational system beyond requirements, that is, voluntary innovative behavior. It included participation in grass roots events, counselor ratings of activism, and peer ratings of activism, all combined into one score. Activism was related only to the intuitive dimension of the Myers–Briggs Type Indicator, not to extraversion.

Turnbull (1976) found that among more than 100 male college students involved in a summer of book sales, neither Eysenck Personality Inventory extraversion scores alone nor in combination with other personality scales predicted sales success. Sales success was determined on the basis of total wholesale business and a sales index indicating amount of business per call made. In the global studies presented earlier, the sales vocations were only weakly related to extraversion. Turnbull noted a wide range of scores on the extraversion–introversion dimension among the individuals applying for the job and no personality differences between those who completed the summer of sales and those who dropped out. The author concluded that individuals of any personality type who decided to do so can become successful in sales. It was found as predicted that extraversion scores increased from the beginning of the summer to the end of the summer as a result of the summer of sales experience, an increase that was equal for more successful and less successful salesmen.

An earlier study by Cooper and Payne (1967) involving 55 female packers in a tobacco factory supported the assumption that extraverts would have more difficulty in monotonous jobs of this type than introverts. Extraversion as measured by the Eysenck Personality Inventory correlated with work variables taken over 1 full calendar year; this correlation indicated clearly that introverts were more likely to stay on the job for a longer period of time as well as receive more favorable supervisor ratings and have less absenteeism and less tardiness. Savage and Stewart (1972) also found that 100 female card punch operators in training showed negative correlations between extraversion and supervisor ratings of output per month, although there was no relationship between this personality variable and dropouts from the program.

Some effort has been devoted to determining the processes underlying such on-the-job differences. Hill (1975) attempted unsuccessfully to relate extraversion–introversion to boredom on the job. Sixty-three female press operators completed boredom ratings at the end of each of 50 consecutive working days, from "felt bored all day" to "did not feel bored at all today." The data were analyzed in such a way as to take into account the amount of variety in the workday for each subject. There was no relationship between boredom ratings and Eysenck Personality Inventory extraversion scores. The distinction between morning people and evening people has also been applied in this context. Horne and Ostberg (1977) confirmed that such types could be identified by a 19-item factor analytically derived questionnaire. In a sample of 48 adults who monitored their oral temperature every $\frac{1}{2}$ hour for 3 weeks, morning types arose almost 2 hours earlier in the morning, went to bed about $\frac{1}{2}$ hour earlier, and reached their temperature peak about 1 hour earlier during the day than evening types. This study indicates no relationship, however, of extraversion to these differences in circadian rhythms. This is in contrast to a number of studies conducted in the 1960s and early 1970s reviewed by Blake and Corcoran (1972), in which introverts' body temperature cycles and performance on laboratory tasks classified them as morning people.

Studies of mood changes are relevant. Christie and Venables (1973) asked 80 volunteers whose jobs ranged from office clerks to heads of academic departments in the public schools to complete the Mood Adjective Check List on Monday and Friday mornings and afternoons for 4 successive weeks. They combined the scales of concentration, activation, and deactivation to form an efficiency index, for which there was a significant four-way interaction effect involving day of week, time of day, extraversion, and neuroticism. Such an effect is very difficult to summarize, but the authors relate a pattern of high arousal and low euphoria experienced by neurotic introverts on Monday morning to Monday absenteeism and a pattern of high arousal and high euphoria experienced by stable extraverts on Friday afternoon to premature departures from work at that time. Bishop and Jeanrenaud (1976) related end-of-day moods to amount of change in daily activities and personality. Choosing people at random in a community, representing a number of vocations, they asked subjects to keep a diary in which entries were made each 15 minutes during both a workday and a leisure day. Mood ratings were taken from the last hour before bedtime, and again there was a four-way interaction effect. Activity variation was not related to mood on workdays but was on leisure days. The fact that activity variation was related to pleasantness of mood for stable extraverts and neurotic introverts but related to unpleasantness of mood for neurotic extraverts and stable introverts indicates how increased variation and stimulation (and its opposite, monotony) has different value for different individuals.

PLAN OF THE BOOK: A REMINDER

As stated at the outset, the content of this and the other chapters in the book is a function of the content of the published research on extraversion–introversion in the years 1972–1978. A dedicated effort has been made to include all such studies in the discussion, with the aim of informing students, researchers, and theorists in as unbiased a manner as possible of the current status and direction of research on the topic. In addition to looking at the content presented the reader should note important topics that are not discussed because there is no current relevant research. An example that applies to this chapter is the topic of achievement motivation, the relation of which to extraversion–introversion has not been addressed in recent research literature. It is hoped that this book will stimulate research on such topics as well as promote further research on issues already receiving attention.

6

PSYCHOLOGICAL DISORDERS OF EXTRAVERTS AND INTROVERTS

There are strengths and weaknesses associated with both ends of the extraversion–introversion continuum in terms of psychological and psychosocial adjustment. Nevertheless it is possible that one or the other may be either susceptible to a wider variety of psychological disorders or susceptible to more severe psychological disorders. Actually there is little evidence to support direct answers to these questions in either direction. The evidence that may be used indirectly in response to these issues consists of comparisons among groups who are currently experiencing various types of problems as to their present level of extraversion–introversion. Generally the factor-analytic studies reviewed in chapter 2 support the assumption that this personality dimension is basically unrelated to a general maladjustment dimension. But within the normal realm we have seen that social anxiety is an element of introversion and impulsiveness is an element of extraversion. This suggests that the problems encountered at either end of the continuum would be expected to be qualitatively different, though not necessarily different in severity.

GENERAL MALADJUSTMENT

Moore (1976) found no relationship of extraversion-introversion to mental health. He compared 500 flat dwellers, all female, with 188 women residing in one-family houses, under the assumption that flat dwelling is stressful. Although neuroticism scores correlated with mental health problems among the flat dwellers, extraversion did not. The mental health variables studied were scores on the Cornell Medical Index, an index of general psychiatric illness, and the number of consultations with doctors for illnesses "with an important psychiatric component." On the other hand, S. Eysenck, White, and Eysenck (1976) tested a group of normals and six groups of abnormal subjects who had been assigned to their groups on the basis of routine psychiatric diagnoses. There were 63 females and 63 males in each group labeled as criminals, schizophrenics, personality disorders, anxiety states, reactive depressives, and endogenous depressives. The extraversion scores on the Psychoticism–Extraversion–Neuroticism Scale were compared, and it was found that the normal control group had higher extraversion scores than all other groups except the criminal group, both males and females. This indicates that introversion was a factor in all but the criminal group, whereas extraversion was a factor in none.

Most likely, the relationship is more complex and may be conceptualized in several ways, all of which reach the similar conclusion that different specific disorders are related to introversion and extraversion. It may be assumed that there is a curvilinear relationship between extraversion–introversion and adjustment, such that either extreme may be related to specific disorders that are not found in the middle range of the dimension. Alternatively it may be inferred from the multidimensionality of the concept as discussed in chapter 2 that there are subcomponents of both introversion and extraversion that represent better adjustment and subcomponents of each relating to specific types of maladjustment. Where an individual's extraversion consists primarily of elevated impulsiveness rather than sociability, this probably represents a maladjusted extraversion; where one's introversion consists primarily of a lack of sociability, this is probably reflective of a maladjusted introversion. It also may be held that it is only as either introversion or extraversion is combined with elements of either neuroticism or psychoticism that specific types of maladjustment result. Heilizer (1975) suggests an additional theoretical alternative, that is, that there are two interacting bipolar dimensions involved here: introversion-extraversion and neuroticism–impulsiveness. Either pole of the latter "adjustment" dimension may be associated with extraversion or introversion; thus there are four types of maladjustment. The most common would be neurotic introversion and impulsive extraversion because of a slight positive correlation between the dimensions.

ANXIETY–RELATED DISORDERS

The terms neurotic and introverted as commonly used by the lay public overlap a great deal in meaning. Both connote shyness, social inhibition, and anxiety. Actually the individual who fits this description and who may have problems with phobias, obsessions and compulsions, guilt, and perhaps depression represents a combination of the two—neurotic introvert. And it should be recognized that there are neurotics who are not noticeably high in introversion (e.g., hysterics) as well as introverts who are quite well adjusted. Nevertheless, it is well documented that the specific disorders developed by introverts are likely to lie in this area, and both H. Eysenck (1976d) and Gray (1975) have incorporated the individual difference factor in their theories of how neurosis is learned. Eysenck's approach is also progressive in his inclusion of the concepts of incubation and preparedness in the learning process.

Other than the study by S. Eysenck, White, and Eysenck (1976) cited above, few recent studies have investigated the relationship between introversion and neurotic anxiety reactions. Negative results are reported by Farley and Mealiea (1972), who failed to find a correlation between introversion, either alone or in combination with neuroticism, and scores on a 73-item Fear Survey Schedule in a sample of 102 female college students. Hallam (1976) did find his 49 phobic patients where introverted neurotics, compared with published norms for the Eysenck scales. Hedge (1972) found that the most remarkable personality trait found in a group of adult stutterers was introversion. Scores of 106 clients of a speech and hearing center in India were significantly different from the norms for normals and the same as the introversion norms for neurotics. They were also moderately high on neuroticism. Consistently several studies (Hallam, 1976; Ingham, 1966; Levinson & Meyer, 1965; Matthews, Johnston, Shaw, & Gelder, 1974) have reported increases in extraversion scores accompanying therapeutic progress in a variety of clinical groups (mostly neurotic) and with various treatment techniques. A study in our own laboratory (Davis, 1978) found increases in sociability and in positive aspects of activation and decreases in impulsivity as a function of successful biofeedback training in a clinical population.

A topic that has ignited recent interest concerns treatment success with anxiety problems related to extraversion–introversion. With clinical phobias extraverts tend to respond better (Gelder, Marks, & Wolff, 1967; Marks, Boulougouris, & Marset, 1971) or at least faster (Hallam, 1976) to systematic desensitization, although Marks et al. (1971) found the reverse to be true for flooding techniques, and Matthews et al. (1974) found no difference. With nonclinical populations extraverts seem to be inferior, possibly because the introverts in the relatively more extraverted normal groups are more introverted than the extraverts in the relatively more introverted neurotic groups; this suggests a curvilinear relationship such that the extremes respond less readily to treatment. Extreme introvert phobics would be expected to have more persistent phobias than ambivert phobics, and extreme extraverts who are anxious would be expected to condition less readily than ambiverts. Horne (1974), using high test-anxious college students, Leboeuf (1977), using high trait-anxious students, and Stoudenmire (1972), using high trait-anxious college females, all found significant anxiety reductions following behavioral treatment for introverts only. Quereshi (1972) also found that 198 obese females who were unsuccessful in weight reduction programs were significantly more extraverted and unhappy than a group of 98 who were successful and than control subjects. The unsuccessful subjects had volunteered from across the United States and Canada for a special TOPS treatment program because they had been unsuccessful in their local TOPS weight reduction programs. In the medical realm, however, extraversion–introversion bore no relationship to behavior changes following heart attacks in a sample of nearly 500 patients.

Mallaghan and Pemberton (1977) followed patients for 1 year and found that a large percentage reduced cigarette smoking, physical activity, and weight, but the changes were unrelated to personality variables.

There is little information available from recent studies concerning the relationship of extraversion–introversion to psychosomatic disorders, but a connection may be anticipated from the anxiety-related nature of such medical problems. There is one study of dysmenorrhea (menstrual pain) that provides supportive evidence. Bloom, Shelton, and Michaels (1978) asked 200 college women to complete a Menstrual Symptom Questionnaire and thereby selected 12 sufferers who could be classified as spasmodic (pain limited to first day of menstruation), 12 congestive sufferers (more general and debilitating pain over several days prior to menstruation), and 24 nonsufferers. On a battery of personality tests including the MMPI social introversion scale, sufferers were found to evidence more neurotic traits than nonsufferers but still to be well within the normal range. In addition to being more introverted they were more anxious and depressed and had less positive social and physical self-concepts.

DEPRESSION AND SUICIDE

There is also a clear relationship between introversion and depression on the one hand and extraversion and mania on the other. In fact the clinical scale of the MMPI that relates most systematically to high scores on the extraversion dimension is the hypomania scale (Goorney, 1970; Hundleby & Connor, 1968; Lanyon, 1970), and there are relationships of introversion with depression on both the MMPI and on Cattell's Clinical Analysis Questionnaire. Krug and Laughlin (1977) administered the latter, which consists of 16 normal personality factors and 12 clinical scales, to a large group of normals, outpatients, and inpatients with various diagnoses. The seven clinical depression scales (hypochrondriasis, suicidal depression, agitated depression, anxious depression, low energy, guilt and resentment, and bored depression) clustered together to form a second-order depression factor separate from psychoticism, neuroticism, and socialization. The second-order extraversion factor derived from the normal personality factors was negatively related to this depression factor, particularly to the bored depression scale, and unrelated to the other clinical factors.

Unfortunately there are no data to indicate whether groups of manic psychotic patients score higher on the extraversion scales than do normals, but consistent group differences are being found in current studies relating depression and introversion. For example, S. Eysenck, White, and Eysenck (1976) reported both reactive depressives and endogenous depressives to be more introverted than normals. Bianchi and Fergusson (1977) indicate that depressive states have an introvertive effect on responses to self-report inventories in the same way that anxiety states elevate scores on the neuroticism scale. Serra and Pollitt (1975) examined a group of 100 depressive patients who were being treated either as outpatients or as newly admitted inpatients, divided into mild, moderate, and severe groups. The moderate and severe groups were more introverted than the mildly depressed groups and increased introversion was related to scores on the Beck Depression Inventory, particularly the cognitive component of the depressive experience. Neuroticism was similarly related to depression. A study by Paykel and Prusoff (1973) also indicates that there are meaningful differences on the extraversion–introversion dimension within a group of depressives. Using 131 recovered depressives as subjects and dividing them into the psychoanalytic personality types of obsessive, hysterical, and oral-dependent personalities on the basis of scores on the Lazare–Klerman Trait Scales, it was found that hysterical personalities were more extraverted, oral-dependent personalities were more introverted, and obsessive personalities were in between.

These findings concerning depression and introversion are corroborated by studies of suicidal behavior that show a relationship with introversion. Leonard (1977) took a group of successful suicides who were formerly psychiatric inpatients and matched them on sex and age variables with two other groups housed in the same unit. The second group was labeled serious suicidal behavior but had not committed suicide during a 3-year period following discharge from the unit. The third group was a low suicide group. High MMPI social introversion scores differentiated between female suicides and nonsuicides, and although the picture was not so clear for males, low suicide males were somewhat less socially introverted than the other groups. Recent studies have also shown suicide attempters to be introverted. A study conducted in a general hospital in Australia (Eastwood, Henderson, & Montgomery, 1972) found 92 attempters to be introverted, neurotic, and hostile in comparison to standardized norms for the general population. And Colson (1972) found graduate students who had at some time either attempted or seriously contemplated suicide to be both introverted and neurotic on the Maudsley Personality Inventory when compared with norms.

In a large-scale study Pallis and Birtchnell (1976) compared 136 attempters and 233 nonsuicidal subjects with 147° who had suicidal ideas but no attempts, all drawn from the North East Scotland Psychiatric Case Register and all of whom had completed the MMPI. Giedt and Downing's extraversion scale was one of 13 personality variables selected for study and differentiated between suicidals and nonsuicidals for the group of males and females combined. The suicidal ideation group was more introverted for females only. Following this, recognizing that suicide attempters as a group are introverted, Pallis and Jenkins (1977) attempted to relate Eysenck Personality Inventory extraversion to degree of intent to commit suicide. They administered the Beck Suicidal Intent Scale along with a dichotomous self-report of intent item to 110 attempters treated in the emergency room of a general hospital, within 48 hours following admittance. Those with more than one attempt were higher in neuroticism only. Males had higher intent scores than females. The only extraversion difference was that low-intent males scored higher on impulsiveness but not on sociability items than all other groups.

PSYCHOTIC DISORDERS

There are three studies dealing with psychotic populations that indicate that differences on the extraversion–introversion dimension within psychotic groups bear some relationship to the symptomatology and severity of the disorder. Verma and Eysenck (1973) administered various diagnostic tests to a group of 153 psychotic inpatients representing a variety of psychiatric classifications. Higher order factor analyses of intercorrelations among these scores indicated that an extraversion factor emerged along with a psychoticism factor. The indication is that relative placement on an extraversion dimension contained useful information as to the particular type of psychotic experience of individual patients. There was no clear-cut relationship between the extraversion factor and typical diagnostic classifications and no indication that individuals differing on the extraversion factor were more or less severe in their psychotic illness. Nevertheless the suggestion that differences in extraversion within psychotic populations is a major descriptive variable for those patients is informative. Eysenck suggests that a four-dimensional classification of psychoses that includes psychoticism, extraversion, neuroticism, and a lie scale would provide a better structure for classifying and categorizing psychotic experiences than does the traditional psychiatric nomenclature.

An earlier study by Armstrong, Johnson, Ries, and Holmes (1967) indicates that degree of social withdrawal (introversion) among groups of schizophrenics is related to the important process–reactive distinction among schizophrenics. Process schizophrenia comes on much more gradually, is characterized by a higher degree of social withdrawal, and is associated with a much poorer prognosis compared with reactive schizophrenia. Armstrong et al. tested 68 schizophrenic males on the Maudsley Personality Inventory extraversion scale and the Phillips Scale of Social Competence, which is a measure of the process–reactive distinction. The strong positive correlation that resulted indicates that reactive schizophrenics tend to be more extraverted than process schizophrenics. A related finding by Blackburn (1968a) was that paranoid schizophrenics, who tend to be more reactive, were more extraverted than other schizophrenics. The implication is that premorbid extraversion as well as extraversion scores during the time of psychotic episodes are positive factors in predicting an individual's ability to return to a normal life or to a person's likelihood of overcoming the schizophrenic condition. But in a study limited to chronic female residents (with an average stay of 16 years) of a closed ward, Martin and Moltmann (1977) found introversion to be associated with better treatment success. The ward was operated under a token economy system in which three levels of living arrangements on the ward were available, differing in degree of privacy and freedom, contingent on behavior. The authors reasoned that privacy and freedom were more valuable to introverted residents and thus effected greater behavior change. The impulsiveness items of the Eysenck Personality Inventory extraversion scale, not the sociability items, accounted for these differences.

There has been much speculation about the possibility that low social competence in childhood may be a predictor of schizophrenia in adulthood, that is, that deficits in social competence may be the causal link between genetic or environmental predispositions to schizophrenia and the actual development of the disorder. Rolf (1972) presents pertinent data consisting of peer sociometric ratings and teacher ratings of third and fourth graders. Overall, control subjects were judged to be the most socially competent, followed in descending order by children of neurotic depressive mothers, children currently experiencing anxiety-related problems, children of schizophrenic mothers, and children currently experiencing problems with aggression and acting out. The major point of the study is that children of high risk for schizophrenia (having schizophrenic mothers), although not currently identified as problem children, were indistinguishable particularly in the eyes of peers from the two groups of currently disturbed children. There were approximately 30 children of each sex in each group. Findings were stronger for males than for females. But what of extraversion? One cluster of items on which teachers rated the children was called positive social extraversion and would relate purely to sociability, not to impulsiveness. As we have seen for adults, the children with anxiety-related problems were significantly more introverted than all other groups, but children with aggressive problems also tended to be lower than controls on this variable. No significant differences were found for the two high-risk groups.

CRIMINAL BEHAVIOR

The relationship between extraversion and abnormality that has received the most attention revolves around the question of criminality, the psychopathic personality, and antisocial tendencies in general. Eysenck's theory suggests a connection between extraversion and antisocial behavior for one or both of two reasons: the need for stimulation and excitement and the difficulty in learning social inhibitions. There are other theoretical positions leading to similar conclusions (Lester, 1977), the most notable following the earlier work of William Sheldon on body types and temperament types. Cortes and Gatti (1972) are currently working within this framework and have devised new temperament scales. They agree with Sheldon that there are two types of extraversion, extraversion of affect (visceratonia or sociability) and extraversion of action (somatotonia or impulsiveness), both of which are contrasted with an introverted type (cerebrotonia). Only somatotonia, which is associated with the muscular, athletic body build (mesomorphy), should be related to crime and delinquency.

H. Eysenck's (1977a) book on crime and personality reviews the data supportive of his theory of criminality, whereas two literature reviews written in 1972 (Passingham, 1972; Black, 1972) present the evidence both for and against the position. Our purpose in this section is to review studies conducted on this issue since 1972. Black's (1972) review of the literature attempted to evaluate the hypothesis that criminals, psychopaths, and juvenile delinquents are high on both extraversion and neuroticism. Black reviewed 24 studies conducted as late as 1970 that used various measures of extraversion and neuroticism including Eysenck's and Cattell's. Of four studies dealing with the psychopathic personality reviewed by Black, the psychopathic group was higher in both extraversion and neuroticism in three studies with the other indicating differences on neuroticism only. However, with adult prisoners a minority of the studies were supportive of the theory, with one actually indicating that prisoners were more introverted than normals. Among juvenile delinquents one study found them to be more extraverted, three found them to be more introverted, and three found no difference between delinquent and normal groups. Black (1972) concludes that Eysenck's theory "is not adequately supported by the studies reviewed as regards criminals, although there is evidence that on the whole psychopaths may be extraverted neurotics" (p. 104). It should be noted that data involving psychopathic personalities rather than incarcerated prisoners are most relevant to the theory inasmuch as there are many additional factors that determine whether a psychopathic personality will in fact become a prisoner.

Passingham's (1972) review is slightly more recent and somewhat more comprehensive. It covers more than 60 references, some of which were published as late as 1971. His conclusions are similar. In only about one-fourth to one-third of the studies that he reviews are delinquents and adult offenders clearly more extraverted than normal controls. When higher extraversion scores are found, delinquents and criminals are higher in both extraversion and neuroticism in most cases; such scores thus support Eysenck's proposal that criminals and delinquents are neurotic extraverts. The most positive results come from studies in which personality variables taken at an early age are used to predict later delinquent behavior. Passingham states that "it must be concluded that the null hypothesis in relation to second-order factor of extraversion cannot as yet be rejected in view of the many negative findings. ... The findings in relation to neuroticism are generally more positive" (pp. 360–361).

However, Passingham goes on to suggest that the impulsivity component of the extraversion factor may differentiate criminals from normals and that it may be possible to separate subgroups of delinquents and criminals, some of which are higher on extraversion whereas others are not. The subgroup that seems to fit Eysenck's specifications might be called an aggressive psychopath group high in neuroticism and impulsiveness. Eysenck (1977a) also distinguishes between a primary psychopath, who is high only in psychoticism, and a secondary psychopath, who is high in both extraversion and neuroticism. Finally Passingham points out that the hypothesis regarding poor conditionability in criminals and delinquents has not been adequately tested. Again the suggestion is made that subgroups within the criminal population may differ in conditionability and that impulsivity rather than the larger extraversion factor may be the important variable.

Regarding the question of impulsivity and criminality, Passingham cites four studies that show differences between criminals and nonoffenders on impulsiveness but not on sociability. In fact in some instances sociability is lower in the criminal population. The type of impulsivity involved is probably best labeled liveliness. The four studies that Passingham reviews in this context are by S. Eysenck and Eysenck (1971), Field (1959), Sanocki (1967), and Schalling and Holmberg (1968). However, Hampson and Kline's (1977) comparison of 15 offenders and controls found differences in Eysenck's extraversion and in only one of the extraversion-related 16PF scales, sociability, which was higher among offenders. Nevertheless it may be that many criminal and delinquent groups score lower on the sociability items and score higher on the impulsivity items of the extraversion scales; the result is a total extraversion score that is not different from that of normals. Unfortunately the implications of these studies have not received ample attention in studies published later.

Although the findings of more recent studies concerning the relationship of extraversion and criminality is more consistent in showing higher extraversion scores in criminals than in normals, there continues to be a mixture of negative findings in the literature also. The emerging portrait of the criminal appears to be a personality high in psychoticism, neuroticism, and extraversion with extraversion perhaps being the weakest variable involved. More attention has been devoted in recent years to combinations of these variables that provide better discrimination than either variable taken separately. For example, a study by Wilson and MacLean (1974) found that 100 recidivists in London scored higher on all three variables than did a control group of 100 male adults. The criminal group was also higher on a criminal propensity scale developed by S. Eysenck and Eysenck (1971). This scale combines items from psychoticism, neuroticism, and extraversion scales but unfortunately has not been used in further published studies.

Another index of criminality called hedonism has been utilized in additional studies. A hedonism score is derived by multiplying an individual's extraversion score by neuroticism score. The implication is that individuals with a high hedonism score express their pleasure-seeking drives in an impulsive manner, whereas persons with low scores inhibit such impulsive expressions. Burgess, the author of this index, had initially completed a study (Burgess, 1972a) that was not supportive of differences between criminal and normal groups on extraversion. Utilizing a sample of 29 short-term recidivist prisoners, 49 psychopaths from the psychiatric prison, and 100 normals, Burgess found that the prisoners were higher on neuroticism but not on psychoticism or extraversion. In fact he found psychopaths to be significantly more introverted than normal controls. In another study, however,

Burgess (1972b) compared groups of 29 Canadian prisoners, 29 English prisoners, 49 English prisoners, and 62 English prisoners with appropriate control groups and found that in each case the prisoners had higher hedonism scores than the controls. This was true even though in some cases there were no differences between prisoners and controls on extraversion alone. In each case, of the subjects who scored high on both neuroticism and extraversion, a high proportion of them were prisoners. Thus even though Burgess feels that the neuroticism variable is more important than the extraversion varaible, it appears that combinations of high scores on both is highly typical of prisoner groups. S. Eysenck and Eysenck (1973) also utilized Burgess's hedonism score. In comparing 264 female prisoners with three separate control groups of adult women, the researchers found that the prisoners were higher on psychoticism, extraversion, and also neuroticism in two cases out of three and on hedonism. That is, criminals were overrepresented only in the high-extraversion, high-neuroticism quadrant of the two dimensions. The conclusion was reached that neither neuroticism without extraversion nor extraversion without neuroticism was related to criminality but that the combination of the two was. Actually psychoticism may be the most potent single variable in differentiating between normals and prisoners.

On the negative side Hughes and Johnson (1975) even failed to find differences between 20 institutionalized neurotics and 15 psychopaths drawn from a unit for the criminally insane. A chi-square analysis showed no difference in the frequency of introverts and extraverts, as determined by the Myers–Briggs Type Indicator, in the two groups. Black and Gregson (1973) found no differences among 30 recidivists, 30 first-sentence prisoners, and 30 normals in New Zealand on the extraversion dimension, though there were differences in neuroticism. Likewise Heskin, Bolton, Banister, and Smith (1977) and Heskin, Smith, Banister, and Bolton (1973) found no differences in extraversion between the normal population and 175 male long-term prisoners. Neuroticism scores were higher for the prisoners. From the preponderance of the data it does appear that taking extraversion by itself as a predictor of incarceration as a criminal is not consistently fruitful. However, it also appears that taking it in combination with neuroticism and perhaps psychoticism does predict criminal behavior.

There is another implication to be drawn from the data of Heskin et al. (1973) concerning the effect of imprisonment on personality. Dividing their long-term prisoners into groups that had been in prison 0–4 years, 4–6 years, 6–9 years, and more than 9 years, with groups matched for age, revealed that length of imprisonment was related to extraversion in that prisoners became more introverted as length of imprisonment increased (on the Eysenck Personality Inventory but not on the 16PF). Perhaps the effect of imprisonment is to encourage a degree of social withdrawal. If so, however, the change is a gradual one. Using these same groups of subjects, Bolton, Smith, Heskin, and Banister (1976) found no significant longitudinal changes upon retesting after a 19-month period. Nevertheless it is possible that criminal groups are higher in extraversion than normals prior to incarceration but that the effect of imprisonment is to reduce extraversion scores to the same level as normals. The studies of incarcerated prisoners would not show the true difference between those who have a propensity to antisocial behavior and those who do not. On the other hand, data on more than 2,000 male prisoners and controls separated into five age groups ranging from 16–59 (S. Eysenck & Eysenck, 1977a) indicate that prisoners do not follow the normal trend in the direction of introversion with age and that the only significant differences between prisoners and controls on extraversion were in the two oldest groups, above 40 years of age. In contrast prisoners of all ages were higher than controls in both neuroticism and psychoticism.

Concerning the possibility of the existence of subgroups within the criminal population who may differ in their level of extraversion, Sinclair and Chapman (1973) divided 943 male prisoners according to age (less than 30 versus 30–40) and whether they were serving their first or second sentence. Analysis of a number of variables suggested seven groups of criminals, two of whom were younger, already had a larger number of convictions and were more extraverted according to Maudsley Personality Inventory scores. They were labeled professional delinquents and aggressive delinquents. A third group was older, had few occupational or familial ties, were more introverted, and were labeled social inadequates. In terms of dimensions or factors, two were identified: (younger) working-class criminality, to which extraversion was slightly related, and (older) social inadequacy, which was related to introversion and neuroticism. S. Eysenck, Rust, and Eysenck (1977) divided prisoners into five groups on the basis of the types of crimes represented in their career history, with number of subjects per group ranging from 14 to 53: fraud, violence, property, numerous minor convictions, and nonspecialized. There were interesting differences involving psychoticism and neuroticism but only tendencies involving either sociability, impulsiveness, or extraversion as measured by the Eysenck Personality Questionnaire.

Existing evidence is consistent in indicating no extraversion differences between recidivist and nonrecidivist prisoners. This is true of earlier studies reviewed by both Black (1972) and Passingham (1972) as well as of more recent studies in New Zealand (Black & Gregson, 1973) and India (Singh, 1974). The last mentioned, for example, compared 700 nonrecidivist and 150 recidivist prisoners in jails in India, who were administered a Hindi version of the Maudsley Personality Inventory. The results indicated that there were no differences between groups on extraversion, but the recidivists had higher neuroticism scores. Even so, introversion may be related to successful rehabilitation. Sinclair, Shaw, and Troop (1974) were attempting to evaluate the effectiveness of intensive social casework in a prison setting by comparing 50 prisoners who were dealt with intensively during their final 6 months in prison with 50 who were handled in a traditional manner. Experimental subjects had a lower percentage of reconvictions at 14–26-month follow-ups. According to Eysenck Personality Inventory scores 6 months before release, successful experimental subjects were significantly more introverted than unsuccessful subjects who had been treated intensively. In contrast unsuccessful (reconvicted) control subjects were more introverted than successful ones. Thus treated introverts improved more and untreated introverts improved less than more extraverted prisoners. Correlations with other questionnaire data indicated that introverts were less likely to be involved in the prison and criminal subcultures and were less psychopathic.

ANTISOCIAL BEHAVIOR OF CHILDREN
AND YOUTH

Curiously data from delinquent youth consistently fail to show an extraversion effect, a finding agreed upon by earlier reviews and by current investigators. A book by West and Farrington (1973) makes the point well by discussing extraversion and neuroticism effects in a chapter entitled "Factors of Doubtful Importance." They present data from a longitudinal study of English youth who were given the Junior Maudsley Personality Inventory at ages 10 and 14 and the Eysenck Personality Inventory at age 16. Delinquency was defined as the number of official convictions. Only age 10 neuroticism and age 16 extraversion was related to delinquency, and it was noted that neurotic extraverts were consistently no more likely to become delinquent than other children. A study by Whitaker (1978) also failed to find differences in a group of 202 12–17-year-old delinquent boys compared with standard norms. The test used was Cattell's High School Personality Questionnaire; there were no differences on either primary scales or second-order factors of extraversion and anxiety. Similarly of the Junior Eysenck Personality Inventory scales only psychoticism was found to discriminate 200 delinquents from a like number of nondelinquent 13–16-year-old boys in Scotland (Forrest, 1977). However, further item analyses indicated that a subsample of especially problematic institutionalized delinquents scored higher on impulsiveness, autonomic anxiety, and psychoticism items and lower on sociability items than controls.

We now turn our attention to the normal population to ascertain differences between introverts and extraverts in the relative degrees of antisocial types of behaviors that would reflect differences in moral development or in the strength of conscience. The evidence supports the theory that introverts have more social inhibitions whereas extraverts are more socially impulsive. Shapland and Rushton (1975) found positive correlations between self-reported delinquent acts in a group of 54 10–12-year-old boys and two of three measures of extraversion (but not neuroticism). Allsopp and Feldman (1974) utilized a self-report measure of antisocial behavior and an objective index of school naughtiness consisting of objective records of classroom detention and other punishments inflicted by teachers for school misbehavior. It was hypothesized that scores on these measures would be positively related to both extraversion and neuroticism. In the first study approximately 50 secondary school girls in each of four grades ranging in age from 11 to 15 were used as subjects. Extraversion, neuroticism, and psychoticism were measured by the Junior Eysenck Personality Questionnaire. The 48 items of the antisocial behavior questionnaire ranged from very mild acts to serious offenses with subject responses ranging from never to three or more times. Extraversion scores were positively correlated with antisocial behavior scores only in the oldest groups and with school naughtiness scores in the youngest and the oldest groups. However, when all four groups were combined, high-extraversion subjects scored higher in both antisocial behavior and naughtiness than did low-extraversion subjects. For antisocial behavior scores there was the expected extraversion-by-neuroticism interaction effect, which is accounted for primarily by the fact that subjects who were low in both extraversion and neuroticism scored significantly lower on the self-report questionnaire. On the whole, however, the strongest effect was for psychoticism. The authors conclude that the milder types of naughtiness are more closely related to extraversion and the more serious types are more closely related to psychoticism. Neuroticism does not seem to be as strong a factor in these younger subjects as in studies of adult criminals. According to H. Eysenck, who cites a second study by Allsopp and his colleagues (H. Eysenck, 1977a, pp. 136–137), similar results have been found with boys aged 11–16. Allsopp and Feldman (1976) report data from a group of 11-16-year-old boys from whom 20 of the highest and lowest scorers on the antisocial behavior questionnaire in each of five age groups were compared on the basis of their responses to the individual items of the Junior Eysenck Personality Questionnaire. There were 15 extraversion items, both sociability and impulsiveness, that discriminated between groups, as did 11 psychoticism items. The results for neuroticism were not so clear-cut. Based on their analysis, the authors constructed a new 40-item scale for prediction of antisocial behavior tendencies. In a study of younger boys, ages 10 and 11, investigating a much more limited range of behavior problems, Saklofske (1977) found

that a group of 37 boys with a school history of discipline problems was less extraverted, surprisingly, than a similar group of
well-behaved boys. Group differences were verified by teachers'
ratings of number of classroom disturbances by the child and
of disrespectful–defiant behaviors. The misbehaved group had
higher psychoticism scores on the Junior Eysenck Personality
Questionnaire.

Among groups of college students a large group who had
been charged with cheating were found to be higher on both
extraversion and neuroticism than controls (Singh & Akhtar,
1972), and self-reported chronic shoplifters were found to be
more impulsive (MMPI hypomania scale), though not more
socially introverted, than college students who reported never
having engaged in shoplifting (Beck & McIntyre, 1977). The
hypomania scale was one of six MMPI scales that differentiated
between small groups of shoplifters and nonshoplifters of both
sexes.

A few laboratory studies of the type needed to determine
the specific psychological processes that may lie behind the
differences between introverts and extraverts and their attitudes
toward antisocial behavior have been published. In one (LaVoie,
1973), 80 14–16-year-old public high school males were tested
in a resistance-to-temptation task. Each was exposed to a free-
choice training period in which he was punished for choosing
some attractive objects and received no consequences for
choosing others. Punishment was administered by a parent and
consisted either of aversive noise, verbal instruction, both, or
neither. Following the training period, the subjects were then
left alone with the objects for a period of 30 minutes. Of six
measures of deviation or lack of resistance to temptation none
was significantly correlated with extraversion as measured by
the Eysenck Personality Inventory. There were six different
personality variables assessed, and the only one that showed
a relationship to resistance to temptation was birth order. First-
born children were less deviant or more resistant to temptation
than were later born children. The indication is that neither
punishment in general nor particular types of punishment had
differential effects on students with different personality types.
Parker (1972) was also surprised to find that more and less
extraverted third–fifth graders showed no differences in their

dislike of corporal or noncorporal punishment for misbehavior.

A complicated study by Stephenson and Barker (1972) attempted an analysis of introverts' and extraverts' complex moral decision making and of their tendencies to cheat in a laboratory situation. The conceptual basis of the study concerns the pursuit of distributive justice involving the assumption that if one perceives oneself or another to have been treated unjustly, one will condone cheating in that situation to restore equity and justice, whereas if justice has already been done, cheating to gain advantage will not be condoned. If it is true as Eysenck suggests that introverts have stronger consciences than do extraverts, it may be that introverts would be more sensitive to the distributive justice issue than extraverts and thus more attuned to the reasons behind moral or immoral actions. The subjects were 64 10-year-old British boys who had scored two standard deviations above or below the mean on the Junior Eysenck Personality Inventory. The task was a racing game preceded by an intellectual questionnaire. Subjects were told that those who scored highest on the questionnaire would have a privileged position in the racing game, that is, manning the controls, whereas subjects who performed less well on the intellectual task would be in a deprived position in the racing game, that is, picking up the cars and putting them back on the track. However, half of the assignments to the privileged and deprived groups were justified and half were unjustified. Placements that were unjustified involved the assignment of subjects to the privileged and deprived groups followed by the admission that mistakes had been made in the assignment to the privileged and deprived groups but that nevertheless the groups must remain as assigned because there was not time to correct the mistake. Thus subjects in the unjustifiably deprived groups were aware that they were there by mistake and not on the basis of their performance. The possibility of cheating was introduced following the racing game when subjects were given a very difficult quiz about racing, the criterion scores for winning certain prizes, a key to the quiz, and instructions to score their own quiz when finished. There were several significant effects involving introverts and extraverts. In the first place the interaction effect between privileged and deprived conditions and justified and unjustified conditions, that is, the distributive justice effect, was found for introverted subjects but not for extraverted subjects. Thus the normal pattern of results held only for introverts in whom a high degree of conscience is assumed. Second, extraverts showed a general tendency to cheat more than introverts, but introverts who cheated won more prizes by cheating than did extraverts. The distinction was made between calculated and spontaneous cheating. Calculated cheating was more typical of introverts who did so for a reason, that is, distributive justice, and who calculated the risks and benefits in order to maximize the latter. Extraverts, on the other hand, were typified by spontaneous cheating, which is cheating on impulse or cheating for the sake of cheating itself. The general conclusions reached by the investigators are that introverts were more susceptible to moral considerations; that is, they were more perceptive of injustice and more determined in their pursuit of distributive justice.

This study is a good example of the type of research that needs to be done in this area. Most of the research reviewed above has asked relatively simple questions with simplistic designs using large numbers of subjects to determine the differences in personality scores of different groups. The last two studies, however, have asked more specific questions in more controlled settings about the effects of specific environmental contingencies on the moral behavior of different personality groups. The person–environment interaction effect is obvious in the last study in that there is only a tendency for extraverts to cheat more in general than do introverts. And yet with regard to specific situations in which cheating is a possibility, there are differences arising that can be explained only by interaction of a personality variable along with a situational variable. Many such studies are suggested by the ideas presented in this chapter. Only when such studies are done in sufficient quantity that generalizations can be drawn will we have a more satisfactory answer to the question of extraversion–introversion and delinquent, criminal, or antisocial behavior.

AGGRESSION AND HOSTILITY

Information concerning the relationship between extraversion and aggression and hostility comes almost entirely from studies of self-report inventories, generally indicating a complex positive relationship. For example, Brand (1972) administered scales of aggressiveness, social extraversion, and behavioral extraversion (impulsivity) to 99 adult males and found them to be intercorrelated. Edmunds (1977) investigated the relationship of the Eysenck Personality Inventory scales to different types of aggression, as measured by the Buss–Durkee Hostility Inventory, among groups of college students in Scotland. The subscales included indirect aggression, irritability, verbal aggression, assault, and negativism. Correlations indicated that extraversion was related only to assault for males but to all except negativism for females. There were significant three-way interaction effects involving extraversion, neuroticism, and sex for two of the hostility scales, indirect aggression, and irritability. Extraverted neurotic females had the highest scores on these two scales, whereas introverted stable males had the lowest. Earlier studies using the Buss–Durkee inventory with U.S. college students had shown that, even though neither Maudsley Personality Inventory extraversion nor MMPI social introversion was related to a general hostility factor (Bendig, 1961), extraversion was related to overt hostility, consisting primarily of assault and verbal aggression, but not to covert hostility, including indirect aggression, irritability, and negativism (Bendig, 1962a).

Blackburn (1968a; 1972a) conducted similar studies among psychiatric groups. In his second study 165 male psychiatric offenders in a maximum security hospital were tested with the MMPI, Bendig's covert and overt hostility scales, and Fould's five hostility subscales. When factor analyzed, factors of aggression, hostility, and extraversion emerged, the latter being weakly negatively related with the other two. Neuroticism was highly related to hostility but not to aggressiveness. Blackburn (1968a) administered the MMPI and two hostility scales, one labeled general hostility and the other extrapunitiveness, to 24 paranoid and 24 nonparanoid male schizophrenic offenders. Two indices of overt aggression were utilized: extreme assault, defined as actual or attempted homicide, and persistent aggressiveness. Aside from the fact that paranoid schizophrenics were more extraverted and impulsive (MMPI repression scale), the only significant finding of interest here is that more impulsive individuals were more persistently aggressive although not more likely to be involved in extreme assault or to score higher on hostility scales.

Two studies of murderers who were not psychiatric cases, that is, they were incarcerated prisoners without psychiatric diagnoses or difficulties, have attempted to relate extraversion–introversion to Megargee's concept of overcontrolled murderers and undercontrolled murderers. Megargee's Hostility Control Scale operationalizes this distinction. Lester, Perdue, and Brookhart (1974) administered this scale, a depression scale, and the Maudsley Personality Inventory to 35 male murderers and found no relationship between extraversion and either of the hostility control scales. McGurk (1978) used the hostility control scales and the MMPI scales in an attempt to differentiate the personality types existing in a group of 40 murderers and found five types, which he felt could justifiably be reduced to two, overcontrolled and undercontrolled. The most important variable for discriminating between the two was hypomania, followed by repression. These two scales of the MMPI together constitute a good measure of impulsiveness; the extraversion and social introversion scales of the MMPI, indicating sociability, were not important discriminating variables. These studies taken together, though not actually contrasting murderers and normals, do not show a consistently strong relationship between extraversion and extreme aggression or hostility but indicate that impulsiveness rather than sociability is the important component in the relationship.

In the context of a series of studies on aggression in children and adolescents Pitkanen-Pulkinen and colleagues in Finland have come to differentiate between aggressive and controlled extraverts (Pitkanen, 1973), as well as between anxious and controlled introverts. Rather than using questionnaires to select subjects, the investigators have relied upon teacher ratings and peer ratings and then verified the accuracy of assignment to groups by behavioral measures in various experimental tasks. Their data indicate that all four groups can be reliably identified and that predictable behavioral differences occur with considerable stability and generality. Extraverts differ from introverts primarily in being more outgoing and socially dominant; introverts differ among themselves as to the signs of tension and anxiety that they display in interpersonal encounters, but neither group is aggressive; aggressive extraverts differ from controlled extraverts in that they are more disagreeable and belittling of others, less empathic and socially skilled (Pitkanen-Pulkinen & Pitkanen, 1976), and more impulsive (Pitkanen & Turunen, 1974).

LOOKING AHEAD

The principles developed in this chapter concerning introversion and the experience of anxiety and depression on the one hand and concerning extraversion and the tendency toward impulsive and antisocial behavior on the other also apply to the content of the next chapter. A more detailed summary will await the presentation of the companion material.

8

GENETIC INFLUENCE
AND EXTRAVERSION-
INTROVERSION

Chapter 2 presented one of the reasons that extraversion-introversion is considered a very important trait among those who deal with trait theories of personality. The reason presented there was that among various indices and global systems for measuring personality, extraversion-introversion consistently emerges as one of the factors that explains much of the common variance among more peripheral traits and to which most other traits in the study of personality relate in some consistent fashion. Another reason for its centrality is that this personality trait is one of the most stable over time, occupying an important role in the description of the varieties of human behavior from early childhood through adulthood. Such stability renders this dimension as more traitlike than most other personality dimensions studied. The fact that extraversion-introversion emerges as an important descriptor of people's behavior early in life and remains stable over time suggests that this personality trait may be more closely related to genetics than other personality traits, and this question continues to receive considerable attention in the research literature. An equally likely assumption

157

but one which has received much less attention is that extraversion-introversion is learned on the basis of extremely early experiences in life and remains stable beyond that point.

STABILITY OF PERSONALITY

First of all, let us examine some of the evidence for the stability of this personality trait over time. Schaie and Parham (1976) recently analyzed data from 2,500 subjects ranging in age from 21 to 84 who had completed a 75-item personality questionnaire along with numerous cognitive performance measures. All subjects were then retested 7 years later, with the original population divided into eight 7-year age intervals, so that both cross-sectional comparisons and longitudinal comparisons could be made concerning adult development. Nineteen personality factors emerged from a factor analysis of the data, including factors similar to Cattell's affectia (sociability), dominance, and group dependence, all of which are related to extraversion. The authors concluded that there is evidence for stability in these personality traits similar to the stability of intelligence across the same developmental years. Patterns of correlations, changes, and stabilities in the data led the authors to conceptualize 13 different types of traits. Sociability was categorized as an acculturated trait in which the specific pattern of early socialization might mediate the particular trait expression as an adult. The expression in the adult personality, however, remains stable.

Bronson (1966) reached similar conclusions about extraversion-introversion, that is, concerning its stability, in 5–16 year olds. The subjects were 85 children born in 1928–1929 who were rated yearly by experimenters on the basis of interviews with mother, child, other family members, and teachers. All 34 variables were described as well-defined behavioral cues. The purpose of the study was to identify what the author called central orientations, a "complex of attitudes, traits, and abilities which combine to give a characteristic flavor to all of a person's interactions" (p. 126). The investigator set two criteria for central orientations, (1) generality, which involves consistent relations with a variety of other characteristics, and (2) temporal stability. Yearly ratings were grouped into 3-year periods of early childhood, late childhood, preadolescence and adolescence. An inter-correlated cluster of reserved, somber, and shy versus expressive, gay, and socially easy, and possibly including passivity versus dominance, met the criteria. This introversion–extraversion cluster appeared at all four age levels and for both sexes, was found to be the most enduring of the variables investigated, and accounted for a large amount of variance among primary variables. The other cluster of variables that qualified as a central orientation was rebelliousness versus conformity. The article includes a good discussion of developmental aspects and sex differences in these central orientations and the implication is strong that either genetics or very early learning is operative in the formation, generality, and stability of these clusters.

The youngest subjects in Bronson's study were 5 years old. Wilson, Brown, and Matheny (1971) conducted a similar study with pairs of twins aged 3 months to 6 years. The first part of the study was aimed at identifying clusters of behavioral ratings. There were 95 identical and 73 nonidentical same-sex twin pairs who were rated quarterly or semiannually. Reliable individual differences appeared early and became increasingly important after 24 months of age. Important clusters that emerged were sociability, distress, attention span, and vocalization. By age 4 the sociability cluster, which included seeking affection, accepting people, and smiling, became even better defined and became more closely related to vocalization, a trend that continued to develop to age 6. The second part of the study was aimed at determining the evidence for the heritability of such clusters, which depends on the finding of greater similarity between identical twins on the variables studied compared with nonidentical twins. Thus the mothers were asked to report whether their twins displayed the behaviors in equal degree. In this particular study the evidence for the heritability of the clusters defined above was very weak.

These studies manifest considerable agreement that the variable of extraversion–introversion, or at least sociability, is an important and stable individual difference variable even from very young ages. Agreement is less marked when considering the reason for the existence of this situation, that is, whether it results from genetic factors or from early environmental factors. Few recent studies have highlighted or demonstrated the importance of early environmental factors on the development of extraversion–introversion, but an exception is the study of Insel (1974), who found much stronger mother–child correlations than father–child correlations among 589 members of 98 families in the London area who were tested with the psychoticism–extraversion–neuroticism scale and Junior Eysenck Personality Inventory. Results were similar for all three personality variables. For extraversion, only the mother–son and mother–daughter correlations were significant. Ages of the children ranged from 9 to 32. Whether these findings indicate a maternal genetic effect or an early environmental effect is not clear. The relationship was somewhat stronger for daughters than for sons.

One important family variable that seems to mediate socialization influences in an important way is birth order, and in general birth order has been found to be unrelated to extraversion–introversion scores. In a literature review Schooler (1972) indicates that there are no consistent differences between first borns and later borns in extraversion, neuroticism, sociability, or impulsiveness or indeed for many other important personality variables. Data provided by McCutcheon (1974) from 93 junior college students who took the 16PF and by Farley (1975) concerning females from two-sibling families agree. McCutcheon found no differences on the 16PF scales among first-, second-, and third-born children, and Farley found no differences in either extraversion or neuroticism among any of five birth-order groups. Farley used 141 college students as subjects. On the other hand, McCormick and Baer (1975) found a birth-order-by-sex-of-subject interaction effect on extraversion scores. College students coming from two-child families in which the children were fewer than 6 years apart in age were separated into groups on the basis of sex, sex of sibling, and birth order. Extraversion scores on the Eysenck Personality Inventory were higher for male first borns and female second borns compared with female first borns. The weakest interpretation of the data is that birth-order effects hold only for females, or the results may be interpreted as indicating that birth order has opposite effects on extraversion levels in boys and girls.

The finding of consistent race differences in extraversion scores might be informative in the current discussion, but such consistent differences have not emerged from recent studies. Lowe and Hildman (1972) administered the Eysenck Personality Inventory to more than 1,100 students at a predominately white university in Mississippi and to about 500 students at a totally black university in the same state. Black students scored significantly lower in extraversion, a difference that held for both females and males. Differences in neuroticism were much smaller. Levy, Murphy, and Carlson (1972) reported that black males were more extraverted on the Myers–Briggs Type Indicator than a white male standardization sample, but there were no differences between black and white females. Subjects were 758 students at a predominately black urban university. Recently, Jones (1978) conducted a more comprehensive study of white–black personality differences using 226 female and male junior college students with blacks and whites matched for socioeconomic class. A 361-item coping and defense scale consisting of both MMPI and CPI items was administered. The 179 items that discriminated best between the races were submitted to a cluster analysis; 10 clusters emerged that were significantly different for blacks and whites. Included in the 10 clusters were a social dominance and poise cluster, which was higher in blacks, and a risk-taking and adventuresomeness cluster, which was higher in whites. Both of these are related to extraversion and show different patterns of results.

GLOBAL PERSONALITY BATTERIES

The question of the importance of genetic factors in personality and in the causative picture of extraversion–introversion in particular is not a simple one to ascertain. When studies such as those reviewed in this chapter find significant differences in correlations between groups of monozygotic (identical) and dizygotic (nonidentical) twins, the results may be interpreted in different ways. On the one hand, a very loose interpretation may be drawn that the significance of these differences indicates that there is some genetic component in the data. It is well known, of course, that a statistically significant result may nevertheless account for only a small portion of the variance and may not be a psychologically significant result.

On the other hand, the degree of difference between identical and nonidentical twin groups and the resulting heritability statistic that may be computed therefrom may be taken as an estimate of the actual genetic contribution to the data in question. Thus heritability statistics ranging from .30 to .70, which is not uncommon in these studies, may be taken quite literally as percentage of variance accounted for. Some investigators do not compute a heritability statistic because of their feared tendency for lay readers to overinterpret such a percentage figure. At the very least it must be kept in mind that a heritability statistic is highly specific to the population studied and may vary markedly with the age of the subjects, the heterogeneity of the sample, and the measurement devices utilized. It is also probably better to interpret the heritability statistic as the percentage of within-family variance accounted for by genetic factors, excluding effects on the personality arising from factors outside the family.

Even in the light of these and other complexities, interpretation of the data presented in this chapter relies largely on the standpoint of the interpreter. The heritability of extraversion-introversion or of personality in general is a relative matter. If one espouses a strong environmental position, then the finding of any significant genetic component is disconfirming and worthy of note. On the other hand, if one espouses a highly constitutional orientation, the evidence for heritability in the studies presented here may not be strong enough to be satisfying. Interested readers who would like to follow these questions further are referred to a conservative review of the literature conducted by Thompson and Wilde (1973), whose stance seems to be that no firm conclusions can be drawn at this point, and to H. Eysenck's (1973a, 1973d) more optimistic discussion of the operation of genetic factors in a wide range of human characteristics.

Cattell (1973) presents the combined results of several studies investigating the heritability of the 16PF scales. Cattell estimates that surgency (enthusiasm) shows the strongest influence of all primary factors, followed closely by sociability (affectia), the second-order extraversion factor, Eysenck's extraversion scales, adventurousness, and then others not related to extraversion, in descending order of heritability. An important point is that the other 16PF components of extraversion, that is, dominance and group adherence, are much less genetically determined.

There have been several recent comprehensive studies of the scales of the California Psychological Inventory, such as that presented in a book by Loehlin and Nichols (1976). In reviewing the literature and the results of their own study, they conclude that genes and environment carry roughly equal weight in the analysis of personality variables and that the argument for the inheritance of personality traits is less strong than for measures of ability but stronger than for measures of vocational interest. Their own data were gathered from high school students, including 514 monozygotic and 336 dizygotic same-sex twin pairs. One of the methodological comments stressed in the book is that it is essential in this type of research to include large numbers, that is, hundreds of pairs of twins, in order to satisfy the statistical assumptions on which interpretations are based. This is a criterion not often met in the studies reviewed.

Unlike Loehlin and Nichols, Gottesman (1966) found some of the CPI scales to show significant genetic effects whereas others did not. Four of the seven traits of significance (dominance, sociability, social presence, and self-acceptance) have been found to load on the person-orientation or extraversion factor of that inventory, which Gottesman also found to correlate highly with the MMPI social introversion scale. Therefore in this study of 79 identical twins and 68 nonidentical twins tested while in high school there was evidence that there is a stronger genetic component for extraversion than for other personality dimensions. In another study conducted by Gottesman (1965) he found that among 34 pairs of monozygotic and dizygotic twins social introversion was the only MMPI scale that was significant for both males and females, although there was a significant genetic effect for both the depression and psychopathic deviate scales for males only. The heritability statistic for the social introversion scale in this study was an extremely high .71.

In a follow-up of these studies Dworkin, Burke, Maher, and Gottesman (1976) located 42 of the original twin pairs and tested them 12 years later with the same personality inventories. Of the 42 pairs 25 were monozygotic and 17 were dizygotic. In this small subsample of the original social introversion showed no significant effect either at the time of testing in adolescence or 12 years later. Of the CPI data only dominance maintained a significant genetic component in adulthood. Although interpretation is difficult because of the small number of twin pairs available in adulthood, the authors interpret the pattern of correlational changes to indicate that extraversion scales in general seem to be under significant genetic control in adolescence but not in adulthood and that the changes between adolescence and adulthood are not genetically controlled. A thorough discussion ensues but it is not resolved whether heritability estimates must remain the same at different ages if they truly reflect a genetic influence.

Another recent study (Horn, Plomin, & Rosenman, 1976) also used the CPI in a study of the different patterns of relationships in dizygotic and monozygotic twins, but this study was conducted in a unique fashion. First of all, the subjects were 45-55 years old and included 99 pairs of each group. The 480 items of the questionnaire were divided into those for which a genetic influence could be identified opposed to those that were environmentally controlled; 41 items fell in the former category and 74 in the latter. To be included in the genetic category the item must have shown sufficient reliability over a 3-week period of time, a sufficient difference in correlation between monozygotic and dizygotic twins, and positive correlations in both cases.

Factor analyses were performed on each set of items separately in order to specify the most powerful factors emerging from genetic items opposed to environmental items. In general, genetic items clustered together much more clearly than did environmental items and revealed a much stronger sociability component. From the loose clustering of the environmental items it may be implied that personality attributes that are primarily learned may be learned in isolation, exist in relative independence from each other, and perhaps deserve the name of habits. On the other hand, personality characteristics with a stronger genetic influence may develop together in a pattern so that the expression of each remains relatively dependent on the expression of others because of the underlying biological structure to which they relate.

Whether such speculation is valid, the findings of the study are noteworthy for the study of extraversion–introversion in that among the genetic items three of the five factors, which together accounted for 44% of the common variance, were related to this personality dimension. Factor 1 was conversational poise, particularly with strangers; factor 2 was compulsiveness, which relates to introversion; and factor 5 was social ease or dominance. On the other hand, the environmental items produced only four weak factors that might in any way be related to the dimension of extraversion–introversion. They were leadership, intellectual interest, school behavior problems, and exhibitionism; all four together accounted for only 12% of the common variance.

SPECIFIC EXTRAVERSION SCALES

The several studies just reviewed do not agree with the generalization drawn by Loehlin and Nichols (1976), who in their review of the literature were impressed to note that no specific personality variables stood out as showing more marked genetic influence than others. It is safe to say, however, that when all the difficulties and complexities of interpretation and the design of twin studies are considered, if there are any personality traits that show a strong genetic influence, the dimension of extraversion–introversion heads the list.

Considering more specific measures of extraversion–introversion, Scarr (1969) reviewed the results of numerous studies conducted between 1956 and 1969 with the conclusion that "moderate-to-high genetic contributions to social introversion–extraversion were found in all of the studies" (p. 826). In her study Scarr used as subjects 6–10-year-old twin girls, 24 identical and 28 nonidentical pairs. Mothers rated their children using Gough's Adjective Check List, and the experimenter rated children on the Fels Child Behavior Scales. Scarr computed a heritability index for each variable, derived from the differences in correlations for the identical and nonidentical groups, which is a rough estimate of the importance of genetic factors for each variable. She defined social introversion–extraversion as shy, introspective, and anxious withdrawal versus friendly, extraverted, and self-confident. The Fels friendliness and social apprehension scales showed the strongest genetic effect, followed by the Adjective Check List need-for-affiliation scale and the like-ableness variable. All of these were higher than the heritability indexes for activity, curiosity, or intelligence. One study has investigated the genetic influence on scores on the Myers–Briggs Type Indicator, and that was conducted by Vandenberg (1966). He investigated 27 nonidentical and 40 identical twins and consistent with the studies reported above found that extraversion-introversion was the only dimension with a significant genetic influence.

With regard to studies of the Eysenck scales of extraversion there are three studies using smaller samples that fail to show significant genetic influence and two comprehensive studies that yield more detailed information about genetic effects. Claridge, Canter, and Hume (1973) found surprising results in that extraversion as measured by the Eysenck Personality Inventory was not shown to have a heritable component, even though when separate tests for sociability and impulsivity were analyzed, the genetic influence was significant for each, particularly sociability. Again, however, sociability as measured by the 16PF did not show genetic influence. The study was conducted with adults in Scotland and included 44 identical and 51 nonidentical twin pairs. Young, Fenton, and Lader (1971) used Eysenck's psychoticism–extraversion–neuroticism scale as well as the Middlesex Hospital Questionnaire, which is a brief self-rating instrument for the assessment of neurotic symptoms. A very small group of 17 monozygotic and 15 dizygotic young male adults served as subjects. No genetic influence was found. Perry (1973) was interested in the genetic contribution to the consumption of alcohol, coffee, and cigarettes. Short versions of the Maudsley Personality Inventory and the Manifest Anxiety Scale were administered as part of the project; 46 monozygotic and 38 dizygotic twin pairs ranging in age from 16 to 31 completed an attitude questionnaire about alcohol, coffee, and cigarettes and rated their consumption of all three. The results indicated no genetic component in personality or attitudes and no correlation between traits, attitudes, and consumption. However, there was a significant genetic element in the consumption of the three substances, especially cigarettes. It was hoped that if such a genetic influence were found, it could be shown to be mediated by the personality varibles, but such was not the case.

Two more comprehensive studies provide analyses of the precise nature of both genetic and environmental influences that interact to mold this personality trait. In the first of these studies (Eaves, 1973) 101 pairs of monozygotic twins completed the 80-item psychoticism–extraversion–neuroticism scale. Rather than utilize scale scores, the author analyzed each of the 80 items so that a between-pairs covariance matrix reflecting genetic influences and a within-pairs covariance matrix reflecting environmental influences could be generated. Each matrix was then submitted to components analysis and the resultant structure of the two matrices compared by canonical analysis. Such an analysis of the data allows computation of a heritability statistic similar to those generated by comparison of monozygotic and dizygotic twin correlations and also allows an interpretation of the numbers of both genetic and environmental influences impinging upon each personality variable. Results of the former indicate a significant genetic component involved in all three personality variables.

The results of the environmental and genetic components analyses indicated, interestingly, that there was evidence for a unitary cluster of environmental influences operating on the development of differences in extraversion–introversion, but there were more than one, probably two, relatively independent genetic influences or structures operating on the development of the trait. Although the content of the influences cannot be specified by this type of study, it seems likely from other studies that these refer to the sociability and impulsiveness components. Said another way, for extraversion differences in this personality trait appear to be the result of the correlated, or unitary, environmental modification of more than one underlying genotypic trait.

The genetic analysis of extraversion was continued in a later study by Eaves and Eysenck (1975) in which the biometrical genetic analysis of twin data was utilized. Adult twins (837 pairs) were administered the same 80-item scale, with scales for sociability and impulsiveness scored separately. The twins were separated into five groups: identical males, identical females, nonidentical males, nonidentical females, and nonidentical mixed-sex pairs. The authors concluded that there are similar and significant genetic influences on both sociability and impulsiveness that combine to produce a situation in which the genetic component is stronger for the combined extraversion score than for either of the separate components. The estimated percentage of variance accounted for by genetic factors in the three variables ranges from 30 to 40%.

Considerable attention is devoted in the article to a discussion of the reason for the covariation or correlation or clustering together of sociability and impulsiveness into a larger extraversion dimension, and the answer seems to be more environmental than genetic. It was suggested in the earlier study that the correlation between sociability and impulsiveness might occur because of the operation of a unitary environmental influence on each, even though the genetic structure underlying the two may be independent. The most recent conclusion drawn is that the interdependence of the two dimensions is partially attributable to separate but nonindependent genetic factors, partially to a common genetic factor, and partially to a common environmental factor.

TEMPERAMENTS AND PERSONALITY TRAITS: CONCLUDING THOUGHTS

The questions raised throughout this chapter have quite often been phrased as, Are there temperaments, and if so, what are they? The word temperament has acquired the connotation as referring to those traits of personality for which there is a strong genetic component. This meaning of the term may stem largely from the early work of Sheldon concerning body types and temperament types and the correlation between the two, even though more recent research indicates that the content of Sheldon's findings was grossly overstated and this theory is not currently generating much research activity. Nevertheless the study of and the search for temperaments has continued. Some of this work was stimulated by a book by Thomas, Chess, and Birch (1968), which presented data based on a longitudinal investigation of children from birth to age 10. Several temperaments or behavioral styles were suggested including activity level, rhythmicity, approach versus withdrawal, adaptability, intensity of reaction, threshold of responsiveness, quality of mood, distractibility, attention span, and persistence, and the relationship was strong between these behavioral styles and the development of behavioral disorders.

Another recent investigative project into the temperaments is described in a book by Buss and Plomin (1975). These authors state that any trait or variable that qualifies for the term temperament must meet all of five criteria: (1) evidence for inheritance, (2) stability during development, (3) presence in adults, (4) adaptiveness, and (5) presence in animals. They assert that the four best candidates for the label are emotionality (E), activity (A), sociability (S), and impulsiveness (I). Although Buss and Plomin see Eysenck's extraversion concept as too global and factorially impure, it is obvious that sociability, impulsiveness, and perhaps activity relate to the concept. Emotionality is akin to Eysenck's neuroticism.

Taking the five criteria for temperaments in reverse order, there are obvious sociability and activity–inactivity differences in animals, although differences in impulsivity are not so obvious. Chamove, Eysenck, and Harlow (1972) factor analyzed the observed social behavior among Macaque monkeys interacting in dyads, triads, and somewhat stable groups and found the behavior to be well described by three bipolar factors: fearful behavior, hostile behavior, and affectionate behavior. If one considers the criteria of adaptiveness, sociability and unsociability, activity and inactivity, impulsivity and non-impulsivity all have their useful places in the behavior of animals and humans alike, although the introspectiveness of the human introvert as an adaptive quality may not have a parallel in the animal kingdom. Unlike a dimension such as intelligence, in which the effects of natural selection and survival value are unidirectional, all points along the extraversion–introversion dimension from one extreme to the other constitute potentially adaptive human characteristics.

Buss and Plomin's first three criteria for the definition of a temperament—presence in adults, stability during development, and evidence for inheritance—hardly deserve further comment in relation to extraversion. Differences in sociability, activity, and impulsivity have been shown clearly to be among the most important descriptors of adult personalities and to interact with other important psychological processes. Sociability in particular has been seen in the studies reviewed in this chapter to develop early stability in behavior ratings of children. Concerning genetic influence, Buss and Plomin conclude from their review of the literature that the strongest and most consistent evidence points to the heritability of sociability.

The data of this research group per se consist of the development and administration of the EASI Temperament Survey. Buss, Plomin, and Willerman (1973) used an early 20-item version of the survey with a sample of 78 monozygotic and 58 dizygotic twins ranging in age from 4 months to 16 years. Mothers completed the survey on behalf of their children. The data argued for a genetic component in all except impulsivity in girls. By 1976 Plomin had at his disposal a more elaborate EASI Temperament Survey containing 54 items and 11 separate scales. Among other changes the sociability scales included items relating both to the quantity and quality of interpersonal relationships, and the concept of impulsiveness was broadened to include sensation seeking. Parents of 60 identical and 51 nonidentical twins, ranging from 2 to 6 years old, rated their twins, themselves, and their spouses. Although the parent–child correlations were not impressive, comparisons of correlations for identical and nonidentical twins suggested a genetic component for all 11 subscales.

One of the questions with which we began this section, that is, Are there any temperaments? in akin to the broader question raised initially in chapter 1, Are there any personality traits? Although these questions demand an empirical answer in part, the evidence for the stability, consistency, and heritability of personality characteristics is such that it can neither be ignored on the one hand nor considered as factual on the other. There are three currently popular answers to the question from which one may choose, each of which represents something of a subjective value judgment but for which some evidence can be cited. One is a no-trait point of view emphasizing the situation-specific nature of behavior as controlled by the environment. The second is a trait point of view emphasizing the stable characteristics of people by which they act out their purposes on the environment and change it accordingly. The third is an interactional perspective that accepts the powerful effects of both situational forces and personality characteristics and seeks to understand how they interact to affect behavior patterns.

The question of whether there are personality characteristics that meet the criteria for consideration as temperaments is of interest but not crucial importance to interactionists. If biological predispositions, genetic or otherwise, can be shown to influence personality development, this means that the interactive process between person and environment variables may be seen operating from the moment of birth or before. It is entirely possible that ways of processing and reacting to environmental stimuli are different for different individuals from the very beginning. But it is readily apparent that these differences operate as predispositions, general tendencies, or susceptibilities that exert only a very general influence on behavior and are shaped by personal learning experiences into specific behavior patterns. Both person variables and environment variables exist only as potentialities until activated by interaction with each other.

The other question with which we began this section, If there are temperaments, what are they?, may also be broadened to include the question of personality traits in general and may be answered more specifically. The cluster of variables that together define extraversion–introversion is one of a few for which the evidence is strongest. Most characteristics that are called personality traits probably should not be so labeled in any strict sense of the word and are very unlikely to qualify as temperaments. Implications are that extraversion–introversion and related variables are likely to relate to more types of behavior for more people more of the time than most other person variables, although much is yet to be learned about the mechanics of their interaction with other important variables in determining behavior and life-styles.

BIBLIOGRAPHY

Abramson, P. R. The relationship of the frequency of masturbation to several aspects of personality and behavior. *Journal of Sex Research*, 1973, *9*, 132–142.

Allsopp, J. F., & Feldman, M. P. Extraversion, neuroticism, psychoticism, and antisocial behavior in school-girls. *Social Behavior and Personality*, 1974, *2*, 184–190.

Allsopp, J. F., & Feldman, M. P. Personality and antisocial behavior in school boys: Item analysis of questionnaire measures. *British Journal of Criminology*, 1976, *16*, 337–351.

Anthony, W. S. The development of extraversion, of ability, and of the relation between them. *British Journal of Educational Psychology*, 1973, *43*, 223–227.

Anthony, W. S. The development of extraversion and ability: An analysis of Rushton's longitudinal data. *British Journal of Educational Psychology*, 1977, *47*, 193–196.

Armstrong, H. E., Johnson, M. H., Ries, H. A., & Holmes, D. S. Extraversion-introversion and process-reactive schizophrenia. *British Journal of Social and Clinical Psychology*, 1967, *6*, 69.

Ashton, H., Millman, J. E., Telford, R., & Thompson, J. W. The effect of caffeine, nitrazepam and cigarette smoking on the contingent negative variation in man. *Electroencephalography and Clinical Neurophysiology*, 1974, *37*, 59–71.

Ashworth, C., Furman, G., Chaikin, A., & Derlega, V. Physiological responses to self-disclosure. *Journal of Humanistic Psychology*, 1976, *16*, 71–80.

Averett, M., & McManis, D. L. Relationship between extraversion and assertiveness and related personality characteristics. *Psychological Reports*, 1977, *41*, 1187–1193.

Ayers, J., Ruff, C. F., & Templer, D. I. Alcoholism, cigarette smoking, coffee drinking and extraversion. *Journal of Studies on Alcohol*, 1976, *37*, 983–985.

Baekgaard, W., & Nielson, J. Y chromosome length, extraversion–introversion and neuroticism. *British Journal of Social and Clinical Psychology*, 1975, *14*, 197–198.

Bagley, C., & Evan-Wong, L. Neuroticism and extraversion in responses to Coopersmith's Self-Esteem Inventory. *Psychological Reports*, 1975, *36*, 253–254.

Bandura, A. *Principles of behavior modification*. New York: Holt, Rinehart & Winston, 1969.

Bandura, A. *Social learning theory*. Englewood Cliffs, N.J.: Prentice-Hall, 1977.

Banks, O., & Finlayson, D. *Success and failure in the secondary school*. London: Methuen, 1973.

Barratt, E. S. Anxiety and impulsiveness. In C. D. Spielberger (Ed.), *Anxiety: Current trends in theory and research*. New York: Academic Press, 1972.

Bartol, C. R. Extraversion and neuroticism and nicotine, caffeine, and drug intake. *Psychological Reports*, 1975, *36*, 1007–1010.

Barton, K., Bartsch, T., & Cattell, R. B. Longitudinal study of achievement related to anxiety and extraversion. *Psychological Reports*, 1974, *35*, 551–556.

Barton, K., & Cattell, R. B. Marriage dimensions and personality. *Journal of Personality and Social Psychology*, 1972, *21*, 369–375.

Bascuas, J., & Eisenman, R. Study of "adventure clusters" of the Strong Vocational Interest Blank and the Personal Opinion Survey. *Perceptual and Motor Skills*, 1972, *34*, 277–278.

Bauer, S. R., & Achenbach, T. M. Self-image disparity, repression–sensitization, and extraversion–introversion: A unitary dimension? *Journal of Personality Assessment*, 1976, *40*, 46–51.

Beaubrun, M., & Knight, F. Psychiatric assessment of 30 chronic users of cannabis and 30 matched controls. *American Journal of Psychiatry*, 1973, *130*, 309–311.

Beck, E. A. & McIntyre, S. C. MMPI patterns of shoplifters within a college population. *Psychological Reports*, 1977, *41*, 1035–1040.

Becker, J. F. & Munz, D. C. Extraversion and reciprocation of interviewer disclosures. *Journal of Consulting and Clinical Psychology*, 1975, *43*, 593.

Bem, D. J., & Allen, A. On predicting some of the people some of the time: The search for cross-situational consistencies in behavior. *Psychological Review*, 1974, *81*, 506–520.

Bendig, A. W. A factor analysis of scales of emotionality and hostility. *Journal of Clinical Psychology*, 1961, *17*, 189–192.

Bendig, A. W. A factor analysis of personality scales including the Buss–Durkee Inventory. *Journal of General Psychology*, 1962, *66*, 179–183. (a)

Bendig, A. W. The Pittsburgh Scales of Social Extraversion–Introversion and Emotionality. *Journal of Psychology*, 1962, *53*, 199–209. (b)

Bendig, A. W. The relation of temperament traits of social extraversion and emotionality to vocational interests. *Journal of General Psychology*, 1963, *69*, 311–318.

Bentler, P. M., & McClain, J. A multitrait–multimethod analysis of reflection–impulsivity. *Child Development*, 1976, *47*, 218–226.

Bianchi, G. N., & Fergusson, D. M. The effect of mental state on EPI scores. *British Journal of Psychiatry*, 1977, *131*, 306–309.

Bishop, D., & Jeanrenaud, C. End-of-day moods on work and leisure days in relation to extraversion, neuroticism, and amount of change in daily activities. *Canadian Journal of Behavioral Science*, 1976, *8*, 388–400.

Black, W. A. M. Extraversion, neuroticism, and criminality. *Australian and New Zealand Journal of Criminology*, 1972, *5*, 99–106.

Black, W. A., & Gregson, R. A. Time perspective, purpose in life, extraversion and neuroticism in New Zealand prisoners. *British Journal of Social and Clinical Psychology*, 1973, *12*, 50–60.

Blackburn, R. Emotionality, extraversion and aggression in paranoid and nonparanoid schizophrenic offenders. *British Journal of Psychiatry*, 1968, *114*, 1301–1302. (a)

Blackburn, R. The scores of Eysenck's criterion groups on some MMPI scales related to emotionality and extraversion. *British Journal of Social and Clinical Psychology*, 1968, 7, 3–12. (b)

Blackburn, R. Dimensions of hostility and aggression in abnormal offenders. *Journal of Consulting and Clinical Psychology*, 1972, *38*, 20–26. (a)

Blackburn, R. Field dependence and personality structure in abnormal offenders. *British Journal of Social and Clinical Psychology*, 1972, *11*, 175–177. (b)

Blake, M. J. F., & Corcoran, D. W. J. Introversion–extraversion and circadian rhythms. *Aspects of Human Efficiency*, 1972, *5*, 261–272.

Block, J. *The challenge of response sets*. New York: Appleton–Century–Crofts, 1965.

Bloom, L. J., Shelton, J. L., & Michaels, A. C. Dysmenorrhea and personality. *Journal of Personality Assessment*, 1978, *42*, 272–276.

Blumberg, H., Cohen, S., Dronfield, E., Mordecai, E., Roberts, C., & Hanks, D. British opiate users. I. People approaching London Drug Treatment Centres. *International Journal of Addiction*, 1974, *9*, 1–23.

Blunden, D., Spring, C., & Greenberg, L. M. Validation of the Classroom Behavior Inventory. *Journal of Consulting and Clinical Psychology*, 1974, *42*, 84–88.

Boller, J. D. Differential effects of two T group styles. *Counselor Education and Supervision*, 1974, *14*, 117–123.

Bolton, N., Smith, F. V., Heskin, K. J., & Banister, P. A. Psychological correlates of long-term imprisonment. IV. A longitudinal analysis. *British Journal of Criminology*, 1976, *16*, 38–47.

Bown, O. H., & Richek, H. G. Teachers-to-be: Extraversion–introversion and self-perceptions. *Elementary School Journal*, 1969, *70*, 164–170.

Brackenridge, C. J., & Bloch, S. Smoking in medical students. *Journal of Psychosomatic Research*, 1972, *16*, 35–40.

Brand, C. R. Relations between emotional and social behavior: A questionnaire study of individual differences. *British Journal of Social and Clinical Psychology*, 1972, *11*, 10–19.

Braught, G. N., Brakarsh, D., Follingstad, D., & Berry, K. L. Deviant drug use in adolescence: A review of psychosocial correlates. *Psychological Bulletin*, 1973, *79*, 92–106.

Breen, L. J., Endler, N. S., Prociuk, T. J., & Okada, M. Person X situation interaction in personality prediction: Some specifics of the person factor. *Journal of Consulting and Clinical Psychology*, 1978, *46*, 567–568.

Bronson, W. C. Central orientations: A study of behavior organization from childhood to adolescence. *Child Development*, 1966, *37*, 125–155.

Buck, R. Nonverbal communication of affect in children. *Journal of Personality and Social Psychology*, 1975, *31*, 644–653.

Buck, R. Nonverbal communication of affect in preschool children: Relationships with personality and skin conductance. *Journal of Personality and Social Psychology*, 1977, *35*, 225–236.

Buck, R., Miller, R. E. & Caul, W. F. Sex, personality, and physiological variables in the communication of affect via facial expression. *Journal of Personality and Social Psychology*, 1974, *30*, 587–596.

Buck, R., Savin, V. J., Miller, R. E., & Caul, W. F. Communication of affect through facial expressions in humans. *Journal of Personality and Social Psychology*, 1972, *23*, 362–371.

Bull, R. H., & Strongman, K. T. Anxiety, neuroticism and extraversion. *Psychological Reports*, 1971, *29*, 1101–1102.

Burdsal, C., Greenberg, G., & Timpe, R. The relationship of marijuana usage to personality and motivational factors. *Journal of Psychology*, 1973, *85*, 45–51.

Burger, G. K., Pickett, L., & Goldman, M. Second order factors in the California Psychological Inventory. *Journal of Personality Assessment*, 1977, *41*, 58–62.

Burgess, P. K. Eysenck's theory of criminality: A new approach. *British Journal of Criminology*, 1972, *12*, 74–82. (a)

Burgess, P. K. Eysenck's theory of criminality: A test of some objections to disconfirmatory evidence. *British Journal of Social and Clinical Psychology*, 1972, *11*, 248–256. (b)

Burns, J. L. Some personality attributes of volunteers and of nonvolunteers for psychological experimentation. *Journal of Social Psychology*, 1974, *92*, 161–162.

Buss, A. The trait–situation controversy and the concept of interaction. *Personality and Social Psychology Bulletin*, 1977, *3*, 196–201.

Buss, A., & Plomin, R. A. *A temperament theory of personality development*. New York: Wiley-Interscience, 1975.

Buss, A., Plomin, R. A., & Willerman, L. The inheritance of temperaments. *Journal of Personality*, 1973, *41*, 513–524.

Byrne, D. Repression-sensitization as a dimension of personality. In B. Maher (Ed.), *Progress in experimental personality research*. New York: Academic Press, 1964, 169–220.

Cairns, E. Extraversion-introversion and conceptual tempo. *Perceptual and Motor Skills*, 1973, *37*, 470.

Campus, N. Transituational consistency as a dimension of personality. *Journal of Personality and Social Psychology*, 1974, *29*, 593–600.

Cantor, N., & Mischel, W. Traits as prototypes: Effects on recognition memory. *Journal of Personality and Social Psychology*, 1977, *35*, 38–48.

Carlson, R. Personality. *Annual Review of Psychology*, 1975, *26*, 393–414.

Carlson, R., & Levy, N. Studies of Jungian typology: I. Memory, social perception, and social action. *Journal of Personality*, 1973, *41*, 559–576.

Carlyn, M. An assessment of the Myers-Briggs Type Indicator. *Journal of Personality Assessment*, 1977, *41*, 461–473.

Carrigan, P. M. Extraversion-introversion as a dimension of personality: A reappraisal. *Psychological Bulletin*, 1960, *57*, 329–360.

Carson, R. C. *Interaction concepts of personality*. Chicago: Aldine, 1969.

Cattell, R. B. Confirmation and clarification of primary personality factors. *Psychometrika*, 1947, *12*, 197–220.

Cattell, R. B. *The scientific analysis of personality*. Chicago: Aldine, 1965.

Cattell, R. B. The 16PF and basic personality structure: A reply to Eysenck. *Journal of Behavioral Science*, 1972, *1*, 169–187.

Cattell, R. B. *Personality and mood by questionnaire*. San Francisco: Jossey-Bass, 1973.

Cattell, R. B., & Dreger, R. M. (Eds.), *Handbook of modern personality theory*. Washington: Hemisphere, 1977.

Cattell, R. B., Eber, H. W., & Tatsuoka, M. M. *Handbook for the Sixteen Personality Factor Questionnaire (16PF)*. Champaign, Ill.: Institute for Personality and Ability Testing, 1970.

Cattell, R. B., & Krug, S. Personality factor profile peculiar to the student smoker. *Journal of Counseling Psychology*, 1967, *14*, 116–121.

Cattell, R. B., & Nesselroade, J. R. Likeness and completeness theories examined by 16PF measures on stably and unstably married couples. *Journal of Personality and Social Psychology*, 1967, *7*, 351–361.

Cegalis, J. A., & Leen, D. Individual differences in responses to induced perceptual conflict. *Perceptual and Motor Skills*, 1977, *44*, 991–998.

Chamove, A. S. Eysenck, H. J., & Harlow, H. F. Personality in monkeys: Factor analyses of Rhesus social behavior. *Quarterly Journal of Experimental Psychology*, 1972, *24*, 496–504.

Cherry, N., & Kiernan, K. Personality scores and smoking behavior: A longitudinal study. *British Journal of Preventive and Social Medicine*, 1976, *30*, 123–131.

Christie, M. J., & Venables, P. H. Mood changes in reaction to age, EPI scores, time and day. *British Journal of Social and Clinical Psychology*, 1973, *12*, 61–72.

Ciotola, P. V., & Peterson, J. F. Personality characteristics of alcoholics and drug addicts in a merged treatment program. *Journal of Studies on Alcohol*, 1976, *37*, 1229–1235.

Claeson, L. E., & Malm, U. Electro-aversion therapy of chronic alcoholism. *Behaviour Research and Therapy*, 1973, *11*, 663–665.

Claridge, G., Canter, S., & Hume, W. I. *Personality differences and biological variations: A study of twins.* New York: Pergamon, 1973.

Coan, R. W. Personality variables associated with cigarette smoking. *Journal of Personality and Social Psychology*, 1973, *26*, 86–104.

Cohen, L., & Harris, R. Personal correlates of bureaucratic orientation. *British Journal of Educational Psychology*, 1972, *42*, 300–304.

Cohen, L., & Scaife, R. Self-environmental similarity and satisfaction in a college of education. *Human Relations*, 1973, *26*, 89–99.

Cohen, R. H., & Oziel, L. J. Repression–sensitization and stress effects on Maudsley Personality Inventory scores. *Psychological Reports*, 1972, *30*, 837–838.

Collins, B. E., Martin, J. C., Ashmore, R. D., & Ross, L. Some dimensions of the internal–external metaphor in theories of personality. *Journal of Personality*, 1973, *41*, 471–492.

Colson, C. E. Neuroticism, extraversion and repression–sensitization in suicidal college students. *British Journal of Social and Clinical Psychology*, 1972, *11*, 88–89.

Comrey, A. L. *Comrey Personality Scales* (Manual). San Diego: Educational and Industrial Testing Service, 1970.

Cooper, J., & Scalise, C. J. Dissonance produced by deviations from lifestyles: The interaction of Jungian typology and conformity. *Journal of Personality and Social Psychology*, 1974, *29*, 566–571.

Cooper, R., & Payne, R. Extraversion and some aspects of work behavior. *Personnel Psychology*, 1967, *20*, 45–57.

Corah, N. L. Neuroticism and extraversion in the MMPI: Empirical validation and exploration. *British Journal of Social and Clinical Psychology*, 1964, *3*, 168–174.

Cortes, J. B., & Gatti, F. M. *Delinquency and crime: A biopsychosocial approach.* New York: Academic Press, 1972.

Costa, P. T., Fozard, J. L., & McCrae, R. R. Personological interpretation of factors from the Strong Vocational Interest Blank scales. *Journal of Vocational Behavior*, 1977, *10*, 231–243.

Cunningham, M. R. Personality and the structure of the nonverbal communication of emotion. *Journal of Personality*, 1977, *45*, 564–584.

Cutter, H. S., Green, L. R., & Harford, T. C. Levels of risk taken by extraverted and introverted alcoholics as a function of drinking whiskey. *British Journal of Social and Clinical Psychology*, 1973, *12*, 83–89.

Dahlstrom, W. G., Welsh, G. S., & Dahlstrom, L. *An MMPI handbook, Vol. 1: Clinical interpretation.* Minneapolis: University of Minnesota Press, 1972.

Dana, R. H., & Cocking, R. R. Repression–sensitization and Maudsley Personality Inventory scores: Response sets and stress effects. *British Journal of Social and Clinical Psychology*, 1969, *8*, 263–269.

Davis, J. D., & Skinner, A. E. G. Reciprocity of self-disclosure in interviews: Modeling or social exchange? *Journal of Personality and Social Psychology*, 1974, *29*, 779–784.

Davis, L. *Personality change accompanying successful biofeedback training in a clinical setting*. Unpublished masters thesis, Middle Tennessee State University, 1978.

Delhees, K. H., & Cattell, R. B. *Handbook for the Clinical Analysis Questionnaire*. Champaign, Ill.: Institute for Personality and Ability Testing, 1971.

DeWinne, R., & Johnson, R. W. Extraversion–introversion: The personality characteristics of drug abusers. *Journal of Clinical Psychology*, 1976, *32*, 744–746.

DeWinne, R. F., Overton, T. D., & Schneider, L. J. Types produce types— Especially fathers. *Journal of Vocational Behavior*, 1978, *12*, 140–144.

Dorr, D., Cowen, E. L., Sandler, I., & Pratt, D. M. Dimensionality of a test battery for nonprofessional mental health workers. *Journal of Consulting and Clinical Psychology*, 1973, *41*, 181–185.

Doyle, J. A. Field-independent introverts, extraverts, and psychological health. *Perceptual and Motor Skills*, 1976, *42*, 196. (a)

Doyle, J. A. Self-actualization, neuroticism, and extraversion revisited. *Psychological Reports*, 1976, *39*, 1081–1082. (b)

Drake, L. E. A social I–E scale for the MMPI. *Journal of Applied Psychology*, 1946, *30*, 51–54.

Dworkin, R. H., Burke, B. W., Maher, B. A., & Gottesman, I. I. A longitudinal study of the genetics of personality. *Journal of Personality and Social Psychology*, 1976, *34*, 510–518.

Dworkin, R. H., & Kihlstrom, J. F. An S–R inventory of dominance for research on the nature of person–situation interactions. *Journal of Personality*, 1978, *46*, 43–56.

Eastwood, M. R., Henderson, A. S., & Montgomery, I. M. Personality and para-suicide: Methodological problems. *Medical Journal of Australia*, 1972, *1*, 170–175.

Eaves, L. J. The structure of genotypic and environmental covariations for personality measurements: An analysis of the PEN. *British Journal of Social and Clinical Psychology*, 1973, *12*, 275–282.

Eaves, L. J., & Eysenck, H. J. Genetics and the development of social attitudes. *Nature*, 1974, *249*, 288–289.

Eaves, L. J., & Eysenck, H. J. The nature of extraversion: A genetical analysis. *Journal of Personality and Social Psychology*, 1975, *32*, 102–112.

Edmunds, G. Extraversion, neuroticism, and different aspects of self-reported aggression. *Journal of Personality Assessment*, 1977, *41*, 66–70.

Edwards, G., Chandler, C., & Hensman, C. Drinking in a London suburb:

I. Correlates of normal drinking. *Journal of Studies on Alcohol,* 1972, *33*(Suppl. No. 6), 69-93.

Edwards, G., Chandler, C., Hensman, C., & Peto, J. Drinking in a London suburb: II. Correlates of trouble with drinking among men. *Journal of Studies on Alcohol,* 1972, *33*(Suppl. No. 6), 94-119.

Edwards, G., Hensman, C., & Peto, J. Drinking in a London suburb: III. Comparisons of drinking troubles among men and women. *Journal of Studies on Alcohol,* 1972, *33*(Suppl. No. 6), 120-128.

Eisinger, A. J., Huntsman, R. G., Lord, J., Merry, J., Polani, P., Tanner, J. M., Whitehouse, R. H., & Griffiths, P. D. Female homosexuality. *Nature,* 1972, *238,* 106.

Eliot, J., & Hardy, R. C. Internality and extraversion-introversion. *Perceptual and Motor Skills,* 1977, *45,* 430.

Elliott, C. D. Personality factors and scholastic attainment. *British Journal of Educational Psychology,* 1972, *42,* 23-32.

Endler, N. S., Hunt, J. McV., & Rosenstein, A. J. An S-R Inventory of Anxiousness. *Psychological Monographs,* 1962, *76*(17, Whole No. 536), 1-33.

Endler, N. S., & Magnusson, D. (Eds.). *Interactional psychology and personality.* Washington, D.C.: Hemisphere, 1976.

Entwistle, N. J. Personality and academic attainment. *British Journal of Educational Psychology,* 1972, *42,* 137-151.

Epstein, S. The self-concept revisited, or a theory of a theory. *American Psychologist,* 1973, *28,* 404-416.

Euse, F. J., & Haney, J. N. Clarity, controllability, and emotional intensity of image: Correlations with introversion, neuroticism, and subjective anxiety. *Perceptual and Motor Skills,* 1975, *40,* 443-447.

Evered, R. D. Organizational activism and its relation to "reality" and mental imagery. *Human Relations,* 1977, *30,* 311-334.

Exner, J. E., Jr., Wylie, J., Leura, A., & Parrill, T. Some psychological characteristics of prostitutes. *Journal of Personality Assessment,* 1977, *41,* 474-485.

Eysenck, H. J. Types of personality: A factorial study of seven hundred neurotics. *Journal of Mental Science,* 1944, *90,* 851-861.

Eysenck, H. J. *The structure of human personality.* London: Methuen, 1953.

Eysenck, H. J. *Manual of the Maudsley Personality Inventory.* London: University of London Press, 1959.

Eysenck, H. J. *Smoking, health, and personality.* New York: Basic, 1965.

Eysenck, H. J. Personality and attitudes to sex: A factorial study. *Personality,* 1970, *1,* 335-376.

Eysenck, H. J. Hysterical personality and sexual adjustment, attitudes and behaviour. *Journal of Sex Research,* 1971, *7,* 274-281. (a)

Eysenck, H. J. Masculinity-femininity, personality and sexual attitudes. *Journal of Sex Research,* 1971, *7,* 83-88. (b)

Eysenck, H. J. Personality and sexual adjustment. *British Journal of Psychiatry,* 1971, *118,* 593-608. (c)

Eysenck, H. J. Personality and sexual behaviour. *Journal of Psychosomatic Research*, 1972, *16*, 141–152. (a)

Eysenck, H. J. Primaries or second-order factors: A critical consideration of Cattell's 16PF battery. *British Journal of Social and Clinical Psychology*, 1972, *11*, 265–269. (b)

Eysenck, H. J. *Psychology is about people*. London: Allen Lane, 1972/1978. (c)

Eysenck, H. J. Genetic factors in personality development. In A. R. Kaplan (Ed.), *Human behaviour genetics*. Springfield, Ill.: Thomas, 1973, 198–229. (a)

Eysenck, H. J. Personality and attitudes to sex in criminals. *Journal of Sex Research*, 1973, *9*, 295–306. (b)

Eysenck, H. J. Personality and the maintenance of the smoking habit. In W. L. Dunn (Ed.), *Smoking behavior: Motives and incentives*. Washington, D.C.: Winston, 1973, 113–146. (c)

Eysenck, H. J. *The inequality of man*. London: Temple Smith, 1973. (d)

Eysenck, H. J. Personality, premarital sexual permissiveness and assortative mating. *Journal of Sex Research*, 1974, *10*, 47–51.

Eysenck, H. J. Personality and participation in group sex: An empirical study. *Revista Latinoamericana de psicologia*, 1976, (a)

Eysenck, H. J. *Sex and personality*. Austin: University of Texas Press, 1976. (b)

Eysenck, H. J. The biology of morality. In T. Likona (Ed.), *Moral development and behavior*. New York: Holt, Rinehart & Winston, 1976, 108–123. (c)

Eysenck, H. J. The learning theory model of neurosis: A new approach. *Behaviour Research and Therapy*, 1976, *14*, 251–267. (d)

Eysenck, H. J. (Ed.). *The measurement of personality*. Baltimore: University Park Press, 1976. (e)

Eysenck, H. J. *Crime and personality*. London: Palladin, 1964/1970; Routledge and Kegan Paul, 1977. (a)

Eysenck, H. J. Personality and factor analysis: A reply to Guilford. *Psychological Bulletin*, 1977, *84*, 405–411. (b)

Eysenck, H. J., & Eysenck, S. B. *Manual: Eysenck Personality Inventory*. San Diego: Educational and Industrial Testing Service, 1968.

Eysenck, H. J., & Eysenck, S. B. *Personality structure and measurement*. London: Routledge and Kegan Paul, 1969.

Eysenck, H. J., & Eysenck, S. B. *Manual of the EPQ (Eysenck Personality Questionnaire)*. San Diego: Educational and Industrial Testing Service, 1976. (a)

Eysenck, H. J., & Eysenck, S. B. *Psychoticism as a personality dimension*. London: Hodder & Stroughton, 1976. (b)

Eysenck, M. W. Extraversion, verbal learning, and memory. *Psychological Bulletin*, 1976, *83*, 75–90.

Eysenck, M. W. *Human memory: Theory, research, and individual differences*. New York: Pergamon, 1977.

Eysenck, S. B. *The Junior Eysenck Personality Inventory*. London: University of London Press, 1965.

Eysenck, S. B., & Eysenck, H. J. On the dual nature of extraversion. *British Journal of Social and Clinical Psychology*, 1963, *2*, 46–55.

Eysenck, S. B., & Eysenck, H. J. Scores on three personality variables as a function of age, sex, and social class. *British Journal of Social and Clinical Psychology*, 1969, *8*, 69–76.

Eysenck, S. B., & Eysenck, H. J. Crime and personality: Item analysis of questionnaire responses. *British Journal of Criminology*, 1971, *11*, 44–62.

Eysenck, S. B., & Eysenck, H. J. The questionnaire measurement of psychoticism. *Psychological Medicine*, 1972, *2*, 50–55.

Eysenck, S. B., & Eysenck, H. J. The personality of female prisoners. *British Journal of Psychiatry*, 1973, *123*, 693–698.

Eysenck, S. B., & Eysenck, H. J. Personality and recidivism in borstal boys. *British Journal of Criminology*, 1974, *14*, 385–387.

Eysenck, S. B., & Eysenck, H. J. Personality differences between prisoners and controls. *Psychological Reports*, 1977, *40*, 1023–1028. (a)

Eysenck, S. B., & Eysenck, H. J. The place of impulsiveness in a dimensional system of personality description. *British Journal of Social and Clinical Pyschology*, 1977, *16*, 57–68. (b)

Eysenck, S. B., Eysenck, H. J., & Shaw, L. The modification of personality and lie scale scores by special "honesty" instructions. *British Journal of Social and Clinical Psychology*, 1974, *13*, 41–50.

Eysenck, S. B., Rust, J., & Eysenck, H. J. Personality and the classification of adult offenders. *British Journal of Criminology*, 1977, *17*, 169–179.

Eysenck, S. B., White, O., & Eysenck, H. J. Personality and mental illness. *Psychological Reports*, 1976, *39*, 1011–1022.

Farley, F. H. Birth order and a two-dimensional assessment of personality. *Journal of Personality Assessment*, 1975, *39*, 151–153.

Farley, F. H. The stimulation-seeking motive and extraversion in adolescents and adults. *Adolescence*, 1977, *12*, 65–71.

Farley, F. H., & Davis, S. A. Arousal, personality, and assortative mating in marriage. *Journal of Sex and Marital Therapy*, 1977, *3*, 122–127.

Farley, F. H., & Goh, D. S. PENmanship: Faking the P-E-N. *British Journal of Social and Clinical Psychology*, 1976, *15*, 139–148.

Farley, F. H., Goh, D. S., Sewell, T., Davis, S. A., & Dyer, M. American and British data on a three-dimensional assessment of personality in college students. *Journal of Personality Assessment*, 1977, *41*, 160–163.

Farley, F. H., & Mealiea, W. L. Personality and fears. *Journal of Personality Assessment*, 1972, *36*, 451–453.

Farley, F. H., & Soper, R. E. Global self-rating validation of the measurement of extraversion and neuroticism. *Educational and Psychological Measurement*, 1976, *36*, 487–490.

Feinberg, L. Faculty-student interaction: How students differ. *Journal of College Student Personnel*, 1972, *13*, 24–27.

Fenigstein, A., Scheier, M., & Buss, A. Public and private self-consciousness:

Assessment and theory. *Journal of Consulting and Clinical Psychology,* 1975, *43,* 522-527.

Field, J. G. *The personality of criminals.* Paper presented at the Annual Conference of the British Psychological Society, 1959.

Fine, B. J. Field-dependent introvert and neuroticism: Eysenck and Witkin united. *Psychological Reports,* 1972, *31,* 939-956.

Fine, B. J., & Danforth, A. V. Field-dependence, extraversion and perception of the vertical: Empirical and theoretical perspectives of the Rod and Frame Test. *Perceptual and Motor Skills,* 1975, *40,* 683-693.

Fine, B. J., & Kobrick, J. L. Note on the relationship between introversion-extraversion, field-dependence–independence and accuracy of visual target detection. *Perceptual and Motor Skills,* 1976, *42,* 763-766.

Forrest, R. Personality and delinquency: A multivariate examination of Eysenck's theory with Scottish delinquent and nondelinquent boys. *Social Behavior and Personality,* 1977, *5,* 157-167.

Foulds, M. L., & Hannigan, P. S. A Gestalt marathon workshop: Effects on extraversion and neuroticism. *Journal of College Student Personnel,* 1976, *17,* 50-54.

Fouts, G. T. The effects of being imitated and awareness on the behavior of introverted and extraverted youth. *Child Development,* 1975, *46,* 296-300.

Fouts, G. T., & Click, M. *The effects of live and TV models on imitation in introverted and extraverted children.* Paper presented at the meeting of the Society for Research in Child Development, Philadelphia, March 1973.

Fowles, D. C., Roberts, R., & Nagel, K. E. The influence of introversion-extraversion on the skin conductance response to stress and stimulus intensity. *Journal of Research in Personality,* 1977, *11,* 129-146.

Francis, R. D., & Diespecker, D. D. Extraversion and volunteering for sensory isolation. *Perceptual and Motor Skills,* 1973, *36,* 244-246.

Frigon, J. Extraversion, neuroticism and strength of the nervous system. *British Journal of Psychology,* 1976, *67,* 467-474.

Fuher, M. J., Baer, P. E., & Cowan, C. O. Orienting responses and personality variables as predictors of differential conditioning of electrodermal responses and awareness of stimulus relations. *Journal of Personality and Social Psychology,* 1973, *27,* 287-296.

Geen, R. G. *Personality: The skein of behavior.* St. Louis: Mosby, 1976.

Gelder, M. G., Marks, I. M., & Wolff, H. Desensitization and psychotherapy in the treatment of phobic states: A controlled inquiry. *British Journal of Psychiatry,* 1967, *113,* 53-73.

Gellens, H. K., Gottheil, E., & Alterman, A. I. Drinking outcome of specific alcoholic subgroups. *Journal of Studies on Alcohol,* 1976, *37,* 986-989.

Genthner, R. W., & Moughan, J. Introverts' and extraverts' response to nonverbal attending behavior. *Journal of Counseling Psychology,* 1977, *24,* 144-146.

Ghuman, P. A. S. An exploratory study of Witkin's dimension in relation to social class, personality factors and Piagetian tests. *Social Behavior and Personality*, 1977, *5*, 87–91.

Gibson, H. B. The two faces of extraversion: A study attempting validation. *British Journal of Social and Clinical Psychology*, 1974, *13*, 91–92.

Gibson, H. B., & Corcoran, M. E. Personality and differential susceptibility to hypnosis: Futher replication and sex differences. *British Journal of Psychology*, 1975, *66*, 513–520.

Gibson, H. B., Corcoran, M. E., & Curran, J. D. Hypnotic susceptibility and personality: The consequences of diazepam and the sex of the subjects. *British Journal of Psychology*, 1977, *68*, 51–59.

Gibson, H. B., & Curran, J. D. Hypnotic susceptibility and personality: A replication study. *British Journal of Psychology*, 1974, *65*, 283–291.

Giedt, F. H., & Downing, L. An extraversion scale for the MMPI. *Journal of Clinical Psychology*, 1961, *17*, 156–159.

Gilliland, J. C. *Social anxiety factors: Relation to neuroticism, extraversion, and self-disclosure.* Unpublished masters thesis, Middle Tennessee State University, 1977.

Goh, D. S., & Moore, C. Personality and academic achievement in three educational levels. *Psychological Reports*, 1978, *43*, 71–79.

Goodyear, R. K., & Frank, A. C. Introversion–extraversion: Some comparisons of the SVIB and OPI scales. *Measurement and Evaluation in Guidance*, 1977, *9*, 206–211.

Goorney, A. B. MPI and MMPI scores, correlations and analysis for a military aircrew population. *British Journal of Social and Clinical Psychology*, 1970, *9*, 164–170.

Gorsuch, R. L., & Butler, M. C. Initial drug abuse: A review of predisposing social psychological factors. *Psychological Bulletin*, 1976, *83*, 120–137.

Gossop, M. R. A comparative study of oral and intravenous drug-dependent patients on three dimensions of personality. *The International Journal of the Addictions*, 1978, *13*, 135–142.

Gossop, M. R., & Kristjansson, I. Crime and personality: A comparison of convicted and non-convicted drug-dependent males. *British Journal of Criminology*, 1977, *17*, 264–273.

Gottesman, I. I. Personality and natural selection. In S. G. Vandenberg (Ed.), *Methods and goals in human behaviour genetics.* New York: Academic Press, 1965, 63–80.

Gottesman, I. I. Genetic variance in adaptive personality traits. *Journal of Child Psychology and Psychiatry*, 1966, *7*, 199–208.

Gotz, K. O., & Gotz, K. Introversion–extraversion and neuroticism in gifted and ungifted art students. *Perceptual and Motor Skills*, 1973, *36*, 675–678.

Gough, H. G. *Manual for the California Psychological Inventory.* Palo Alto, Calif.: Consulting Psychologists Press, 1975.

Graham, J. R., & Schroeder, H. E. Abbreviated Mf and Si scales of the MMPI. *Journal of Personality Assessment*, 1972, *36*, 436–439.

Graham, J. R., Schroeder, H. E., & Lilly, R. S. Factor analysis of items on the Social Introversion and Masculinity–Femininity scales of the MMPI. *Journal of Clinical Psychology*, 1971, *27*, 367–370.

Gray, J. A. The psychophysiological nature of introversion–extraversion: A modification of Eysenck's theory. In V. D. Nebylistsyn & J. A. Gray (Eds.), *Biological bases of individual behavior*. New York: Academic Press, 1972, 182–205.

Gray, J. A. *Elements of a two-process theory of learning*. London: Academic Press, 1975.

Griffiths, A. K., & Crocker, R. K. Achievement in individualized and conventional chemistry courses and its interactions with selected academic and personality variables. *Alberta Journal of Educational Research*, 1976, *22*, 97–105.

Grotevant, H. D., Scarr, S., & Weinberg, R. A. Patterns of interest similarity in adoptive and biological families. *Journal of Personality and Social Psychology*, 1977, *35*, 667–676.

Guilford, J. P. Factors and factors of personality. *Psychological Bulletin*, 1975, *82*, 802–814.

Guilford, J. P. Will the real factor of extraversion–introversion please stand up? A reply to Eysenck. *Psychological Bulletin*, 1977, *84*, 412–416.

Gupta, B. S. Adaptation of a Hindi version of the Junior Eysenck Personality Inventory. *British Journal of Social and Clinical Psychology*, 1971, *10*, 189–190.

Gupta, B. S. Extraversion and reinforcement in verbal operant conditioning. *British Journal of Psychology*, 1976, *67*, 47–52.

Gupta, B. S., & Nagpal, M. Impulsivity/sociability and reinforcement in verbal operant conditioning. *British Journal of Psychology*, 1978, *69*, 203–206.

Hallam, R. S. The Eysenck personality scales: Stability and change after therapy. *Behaviour Research and Therapy*, 1976, *14*, 369–372.

Hampson, S. E., & Kline, P. Personality dimensions differentiating certain groups of abnormal offenders from non-offenders. *British Journal of Criminology*, 1977, *17*, 310–331.

Handel, A. Personality factors among adolescent boys. *Psychological Reports*, 1976, *39*, 435–445.

Harkins, S., Becker, L. A., & Stonner, D. Extraversion–introversion and the effects of favorability and set size on impression formation. *Bulletin of the Psychonomic Society*, 1975, *5*, 300–302.

Hedge, M. N. Stuttering, neuroticism and extraversion. *Behaviour Research and Therapy*, 1972, *10*, 395–397.

Heilizer, F. The law of initial values (LIV) and personality. *Journal of General Psychology*, 1975, *92*, 273–290.

Hekmat, H., Khajavi, F., & Mehryar, A. Psychoticism, neuroticism, and extraversion: The personality determinants of empathy. *Journal of Clinical Psychology*, 1974, *30*, 559–561.

Hendrick, C., & Brown, S. R. Introversion, extraversion, and interpersonal attraction. *Journal of Personality and Social Psychology*, 1971, *20*, 31–36.

Heskin, K. J., Bolton, N., Banister, P. A., & Smith, F. V. Prisoners' personality: A factor analytically derived structure. *British Journal of Social and Clinical Psychology*, 1977, *16*, 203–206.

Heskin, K. J., Smith, F. V., Banister, P. A., & Bolton, N. Psychological correlates of long-term imprisonment, II: Personality variables. *British Journal of Criminology*, 1973, *13*, 323–330.

Hill, A. B. Work variety and individual differences in occupational boredom. *Journal of Applied Psychology*, 1975, *60*, 128–131.

Hinton, J. W., & Craske, B. Differential effects of test stress on the heart rates of extraverts and introverts. *Biological Psychology*, 1977, *5*, 23–28.

Hogan, H. W. Construct validity of self-estimated IQ scores. *Journal of Social Psychology*, 1976, *100*, 321–322.

Holland, J. L. *Making vocational choices: A theory of careers*. Englewood Cliffs, N.J.: Prentice–Hall, 1973.

Holland, T. R. Multivariate analysis of personality correlates of alcohol and drug abuse in a prison population. *Journal of Abnormal Psychology*, 1977, *86*, 644–650.

Honess, T., & Kline, P. Extraversion, neuroticism and academic attainment in Uganda. *British Journal of Educational Psychology*, 1974, *44*, 74–75.

Horn, J. Plomin, R. A., & Rosenman, R. Heritability of personality traits in adult male twins. *Behavior Genetics*, 1976, *6*, 17–30.

Horn, J. M., Turner, R. G., & Davis, L. S. Personality differences between both intended and actual social sciences and engineering majors. *British Journal of Educational Psychology*, 1975, *45*, 293–298.

Horne, A. M. Effect of personality type in reducing specific anxiety with behavioral and psychodynamic therapy. *Journal of Counseling Psychology*, 1974, *21*, 340–341.

Horne, J. A., & Ostberg, O. Individual differences in human circadian rhythms. *Biological Psychology*, 1977, *5*, 179–190.

Horrocks, J. E., & Jackson, D. *Self and role: A theory of self-process and role behavior*. Boston: Houghton Mifflin, 1972.

Howarth, E. An hierarchical oblique factor analysis of Eysenck's rating study of 700 neurotics. *Social Behavior and Personality*, 1973, *1*, 81–87.

Howarth, E. A psychometric investigation of Eysenck's personality inventory. *Journal of Personality Assessment*, 1976, *40*, 173–185. (a)

Howarth, E. Were Cattell's "personality sphere" factors correctly identified in the first instance? *British Journal of Psychology*, 1976, *67*, 213–230. (b)

Howarth, E., & Browne, J. A. An item-factor-analysis of the 16PF. *Personality*, 1971, *2*, 117–139.

Howarth, E., & Browne, J. A. An item-factor-analysis of the Eysenck Personality Inventory. *British Journal of Social and Clinical Psychology*, 1972, *11*, 162–174.

Huba, G. J., Segal, B., & Singer, J. L. Organization of needs in male and female drug and alcohol users. *Journal of Consulting and Clinical Psychology*, 1977, *45*, 34–44.

Hughes, R. C., & Johnson, R. W. Introversion–extraversion and psychiatric diagnosis: A test of Eysenck's hypothesis. *Journal of Clinical Psychology*, 1975, *31*, 426–427.

Hundleby, J. D., & Connor, W. H. Interrelationships between personality inventories: The 16PF, the MMPI and the MPI. *Journal of Consulting and Clinical Psychology*, 1968, *32*, 152–157.

Ingham, J. C. Change in MPI scores in neurotic patients: A three year follow-up. *British Journal of Psychiatry*, 1966, *112*, 931–939.

Insel, P. M. Maternal effects in personality. *Behavior Genetics*, 1974, *4*, 133–143.

Irfani, S. Eysenck's Extraversion, Neuroticism, and Psychoticism Inventory in Turkey. *Psychological Reports*, 1977, *41*, 1231–1234.

Iwawaki, S., Eysenck, S. B., & Eysenck, H. J. Differences in personality between Japanese and English. *Journal of Social Psychology*, 1977, *102*, 27–33.

Jaccard, J. J. Predicting social behavior from personality traits. *Journal of Research in Personality*, 1974, *7*, 358–367.

Jamison, K. A note on the relationship between extraversion and aesthetic preferences. *Journal of General Psychology*, 1972, *87*, 301–302.

Jensen, A. R. Personality and scholastic achievement in three ethnic groups. *British Journal of Educational Psychology*, 1973, *43*, 115–125.

Johansson, C. B. Strong Vocational Interest Blank introversion–extraversion and occupational membership. *Journal of Counseling Psychology*, 1970, *17*, 451–455.

Johnson, J. H., & Overall, J. E. Factor analysis of the Psychological Screening Inventory. *Journal of Consulting and Clinical Psychology*, 1973, *41*, 57–60.

Johnson, R. W., Flammer, D. P., & Nelson, J. G. Multiple correlations between personality factors and SVIB Occupational scales. *Journal of Counseling Psychology*, 1975, *22*, 217–222.

Johnson, R. W., Nelson, J. G., Nolting, E., Roth, J. D., & Taylor, R. G. Stability of canonical relationships between the Strong Vocational Interest Blank and the Minnesota Counseling Inventory. *Journal of Counseling Psychology*, 1975, *22*, 247–251.

Jones, E. E. Black–white personality differences: Another look. *Journal of Personality Assessment*, 1978, *42*, 244–252.

Joubert, C. E. Multidimensionality of locus of control and the Eysenck Personality Inventory. *Psychological Reports*, 1978, *43*, 338.

Jung, C. G. *Psychological types*. London: Routledge & Kegan Paul, 1923; Princeton, N.J.: Princeton University Press, 1971.

Kaldegg, A. Aspects of personal relationships in heroin dependent young men: An experimental study. *British Journal of Addiction*, 1975, *70*, 277–286.

Kanekar, S., & Mukerjee, S. Intelligence, extraversion, and neuroticism in relation to season of birth. *Journal of Social Psychology*, 1972, *86*, 309–310.

Kanthamani, B. K., & Rao, K. R. Personality characteristics of ESP subjects: III. Extraversion and ESP. *Journal of Parapsychology*, 1972, *36*, 198–212.

Kassebaum, G. G., Couch, A. S., & Slater, P. E. The factorial dimensions of the MMPI. *Journal of Consulting Psychology*, 1959, *23*, 226-236.

Kay, E. J., Lyons, A., Newman, W., Mankin, D., & Loeb, R. C. A longitudinal study of the personality correlates of marijuana use. *Journal of Consulting and Clinical Psychology*, 1978, *46*, 470–477.

Kelly, G. A. *The psychology of personal constructs*. New York: Norton, 1955.

Kendon, A., & Cook, M. The consistency of gaze patterns in social interaction. *British Journal of Psychology*, 1969, *60*, 481–494.

Khavari, K. A., Mabry, E., & Humes, M. Personality correlates of hallucinogen use. *Journal of Abnormal Psychology*, 1977, *86*, 172-178.

Kirton, M. J., & Mulligan, G. Correlates of managers' attitudes toward change. *Journal of Applied Psychology*, 1973, *58*, 101-107.

Kline, P. The use of the Cattell 16PF test and Eysenck's EPI with a literate population in Ghana. *British Journal of Social and Clinical Psychology*, 1967, *6*, 97-107.

Knapp, R. Relationship of a measure of self-actualization to neuroticism and extraversion. *Journal of Consulting Psychology*, 1965, *29*, 168–172.

Knudson, R. M., & Golding, S. L. Comparative validity of traditional versus S-R format inventories of interpersonal behavior. *Journal of Research in Personality*, 1974, *8*, 111-127.

Kokosh, J. Psychology of scientist: XXXIV. MMPI characteristics of physical and social science students: Replication and reanalysis. *Psychological Reports*, 1976, *39*, 1067-1071.

Krasner, L., & Ullmann, L. P. *Behavior influence and personality: The social matrix of human action*. New York: Holt, Rinehart & Winston, 1973.

Krebs, D. & Adinolfi, A. A. Physical attractiveness, social relations, and personality style. *Journal of Personality and Social Psychology*, 1975, *31*, 245-253.

Krug, S. E., & Laughlin, J. E. Second-order factors among normal and pathological primary personality traits. *Journal of Consulting and Clinical Psychology*, 1977, *45*, 575-582.

Kurtines, W. M., Ball, L. R., & Wood, G. H. Personality characteristics of long-term recovered alcoholics: A comparative analysis. *Journal of Consulting and Clinical Psychology*, 1978, *46*, 971-977.

Lanyon, R. I. Development and validation of a Psychological Screening Inventory. *Journal of Consulting and Clinical Psychology Monograph*, 1970, *35*(1, Pt. 2).

Lanyon, R. I. *Psychological Screening Inventory: Manual*. Goshen, N.Y.: Research Psychologists Press, 1973.

Lanyon, R. I. Factor structure of Psychological Screening Inventory scales. *Psychological Reports*, 1978, *42*, 383-386.

Lanyon, R. I., Johnson, J. H., & Overall, J. E. Factor structure of the Psychological Screening Inventory items in a normal population. *Journal of Consulting and Clinical Psychology*, 1974, *42*, 219–223.

LaVoie, J. C. Individual differences in resistance-to-temptation behavior in adolescents: An Eysenck analysis. *Journal of Clinical Psychology*, 1973, *29*, 20–22.

Lawlis, G. F. & Rubin, S. E. 16PF study of personality patterns in alcoholics. *Journal of Studies on Alcohol*, 1971, *32*, 318–327.

Lazarus, A. A. Has behavior therapy outlived its usefulness? *American Psychologist*, 1977, *32*, 550–554.

Leboeuf, A. The effects of EMG feedback training on state anxiety in introverts and extraverts. *Journal of Clinical Psychology*, 1977, *33*, 251–253.

Leith, G. O. M. The relationships between intelligence, personality, and creativity under two conditions of stress. *British Journal of Educational Psychology*, 1972, *42*, 240–247.

Leith, G. O. M. The effects of extroversion and methods of programmed instruction on achievement. *Educational Research*, 1973, *15*, 150–153.

Leonard, C. V. The MMPI as a suicide predictor. *Journal of Consulting and Clinical Psychology*, 1977, *45*, 367–377.

Lester, D. *A physiological basis for personality traits*. Springfield, Ill.: Thomas, 1974.

Lester, D. Extraversion in police officers. *Psychological Reports*, 1976, *39*, 578. (a)

Lester, D. Preferences among Sheldon's temperaments. *Psychological Reports*, 1976, *38*, 722. (b)

Lester, D. The relationship between some dimensions of personality. *Psychology*, 1976, *13*, 58–60. (c)

Lester, D. Three psychological descriptions of delinquents: A synthesis. *Corrective and Social Psychiatry & Journal of Behavior Technology, Methods and Therapy*, 1977, 23, 33–35.

Lester, D., McLaughlin, S., & Nosal, G. Graphological signs for extraversion. *Perceptual and Motor Skills*, 1977, *44*, 137–138.

Lester, D., Perdue, W. C., & Brookhart, D. Murder and the control of aggression. *Psychological Reports*, 1974, *34*, 706.

Levinson, F., & Meyer, V. Personality changes in relation to psychiatric status following orbital cortex undercutting. *British Journal of Psychiatry*, 1965, *111*, 207–218.

Levy, N. Murphy, C., Jr., & Carlson, R. Personality types among Negro college students. *Educational and Psychological Measurement*, 1972, *32*, 641–653.

Lippa, R. Expressive control and the leakage of dispositional introversion-extraversion during role-played teaching. *Journal of Personality*, 1976, *44*, 541–559.

Lippa, R. Expressive control, expressive consistency, and the correspondence between expressive behavior and personality. *Journal of Personality*, 1978, *46*, 438–461.

Loehlin, J. C., & Nichols, R. C. *Heredity, environment, and personality.* Austin: University of Texas Press, 1976.

Long, G. T., Calhoun, L. G., & Selby, J. W. Personality characteristics related to cross-situational consistency of interpersonal distance. *Journal of Personality Assessment,* 1977, *41,* 274-278.

Loo, R. Field dependence and the Eysenck Personality Inventory. *Perceptual and Motor Skills,* 1976, *43,* 614.

Loo, R., & Townsend, P. J. Components underlying the relation between field dependence and extraversion. *Perceptual and Motor Skills,* 1977, *45,* 528-530.

Lorefice, L., Steer, R. A., Fine, E. W., & Schut, J. Personality traits and moods of alcoholics and heroin addicts. *Journal of Studies on Alcohol,* 1976, *37,* 687-689.

Lorr, M., & Youniss, R. P. An inventory of interpersonal style. *Journal of Personality Assessment,* 1973, *37,* 165-173.

Lowe, J. D., & Hildman, L. K. EPI scores as a function of race. *British Journal of Social and Clinical Psychology,* 1972, *11,* 191-192.

Lynn, R. *Personality and national character.* Oxford: Pergamon Press, 1971.

Lynn, R. National differences in anxiety and the consumption of caffeine. *British Journal of Social and Clinical Psychology,* 1973, *12,* 92-93.

Lynn, R., & Hampson, S. L. National differences in extraversion and neuroticism. *British Journal of Social and Clinical Psychology,* 1975, *14,* 223-240.

Lynn, R., & Hampson, S. L. Fluctuations in national levels of neuroticism and extraversion. *British Journal of Social and Clinical Psychology,* 1977, *16,* 131-138.

Lynn, R., & Hayes, B. Some international comparisons of tobacco consumption and personality. *Journal of Social Psychology,* 1969, *79,* 13-17.

McClain, E. W. Personality differences between intrinsically religious and nonreligious students: A factor analytic study. *Journal of Personality Assessment,* 1978, *42,* 159-166.

McCormick, K., & Baer, D. J. Birth order, sex of subject and sex of sibling as factors in extraversion and neuroticism in two-child families. *Psychological Reports,* 1975, *37,* 259-261.

McCutcheon, L. E. Birth order and selected student characteristics. *Catalog of Selected Documents in Psychology,* 1974, *4,* 44-45.

McGurk, B. J. Personality types among "normal" homicides. *British Journal of Criminology,* 1978, *18,* 146-161.

McLaughlin, R. J., & Harrison, N. W. Extraversion, neuroticism and the volunteer subject. *Psychological Reports,* 1973, *32,* 1131-1134.

MacRae, K. D., & Power, R. P. An analysis of items of the Eysenck Personality Inventory. *British Journal of Psychology,* 1975, *66,* 501-511.

McWithey, K. O. *Differential relationship of locus of control to components of extraversion: Sociability and impulsivity.* Unpublished masters thesis, Middle Tennessee State University, 1978.

Magnusson, D., & Endler, N. S. (Eds.). *Personality at the crossroads: Current issues in interactional psychology.* Hillsdale, N.J.: Erlbaum, 1977.

Mahoney, M. J. *Cognition and behavior modification.* Cambridge, Mass.: Ballinger, 1974.

Mallaghan, M., & Pemberton, J. Some behavioural changes in 493 patients after an acute myocardial infarction. *British Journal of Preventive and Social Medicine,* 1977, *31,* 86–90.

Mann, W. R., & Rizzo, J. L. Composition of the Achiever Personality Scale of the OAIS. *Psychological Reports,* 1972, *31,* 218.

Marin, G. Social–psychological correlates of drug use among Colombian university students. *International Journal of Addiction,* 1976, *11,* 199–207.

Marks, I. M., Boulougouris, J., & Marset, P. Flooding versus desensitization in the treatment of phobic patients: A crossover study. *British Journal of Psychiatry,* 1971, *119,* 353–375.

Marsteller, R. A., & Slocum, J. W. Prediction of psychological need satisfaction. *Training and Development Journal,* 1972, *26,* 50–59.

Martin, R. B., & Moltmann, M. L. Extraversion and neuroticism in chronic residents of a state hospital. *Journal of Behavior Therapy and Experimental Psychiatry,* 1977, *8,* 11–14.

Matthews, A. M., Johnston, D. W., Shaw, P. M., & Gelder, M. G. Process variables and the prediction of outcome in behaviour therapy. *British Journal of Psychology,* 1974, *125,* 256–264.

Mayo, P. R., & Bell, J. M. A note on the taxonomy of Witkin's field-independence measures. *British Journal of Psychology,* 1972, *63,* 255–256.

Megargee, E. I. *The California Psychological Inventory handbook.* San Francisco: Jossey-Bass 1972.

Mehryar, A. H. Some data on the Persian translation of the EPI. *British Journal of Social and Clinical Psychology,* 1970, *9,* 257–263.

Mehryar, A. H., Hekmat, H., & Khajavi, F. Some personality correlates of self-rated academic success. *Perceptual and Motor Skills,* 1975, *40,* 1007–1010.

Mehryar, A. H., Khajavi, F., & Hekmat, H. Comparison of Eysenck's PEN and Lanyon's Psychological Screening Inventory in a group of American students. *Journal of Consulting and Clinical Psychology,* 1975, *43,* 9–12.

Mehryar, A. H., Khajavi, F., Razavieh, A., & Hosseini, A. Some personality correlates of intelligence and educational attainment in Iran. *British Journal of Educational Psychology,* 1973, *43,* 8–16.

Mendhiratta, S. S., Wig, N. N., & Verma, S. K. Some psychological correlates of long-term heavy cannabis users. *British Journal of Psychiatry,* 1978, *132,* 482–486.

Messer, S. B. Reflection–impulsivity: A review. *Psychological Bulletin,* 1976, *83,* 1026–1052.

Michaelsson, G. Short-term effects of behaviour therapy and hospital treatment of chronic alcoholics. *Behaviour Research and Therapy*, 1976, *14*, 69–72.

Miller, G. A., Galanter, E., & Pribram, K. H. *Plans and the structure of behavior*. New York: Holt, Rinehart & Winston, 1960.

Miller, I. W. & Magaro, P. A. Toward a multivariate theory of personality styles: Measurement and reliability. *Journal of Clinical Psychology*, 1977, *33*, 460–466.

Mirante, T. J., & Rychman, D. B. Classroom Behavior Inventory: Factor verification. *Journal of Research in Personality*, 1974, *8*, 291–293.

Mischel, W. *Personality and assessment*. New York: Wiley, 1968.

Mischel, W. Toward a cognitive social learning reconceptualization of personality. *Psychological Review*, 1973, *80*, 252–283.

Mischel, W. The interaction of person and situation. In D. Magnusson & N. S. Endler (Eds.), *Personality at the crossroads: Current issues in international psychology*. Hillsdale, N.J.: Erlbaum, 1977.

Mobbs, N. A. Eye-contact in relation to social introversion/extraversion. *British Journal of Social and Clinical Psychology*, 1968, *7*, 305–306.

Moore, N. C. The personality and mental health of flat dwellers. *British Journal of Psychiatry*, 1976, *128*, 259–261.

Myers, I. B. *The Myers–Briggs Type Indicator: Manual*. Princeton, N.J.: Educational Testing Service, 1962.

Nauss, A. The ministerial personality: Myth or reality? *Journal of Religion and Health*, 1973, *12*, 77–96.

Nerviano, V. J. The second stratum factor structure of the 16PF for alcoholic males. *Journal of Clinical Psychology*, 1974, *30*, 83–85.

Nerviano, V. J., & Gross, W. F. A multivariate delineation of two alcoholic profile types on the 16PF. *Journal of Clinical Psychology*, 1973, *29*, 371–374.

Nerviano, V. J., & Weitzel, W. D. The 16PF and CPI: A comparison. *Journal of Clinical Psychology*, 1977, *33*, 400–406.

Nias, D. K. B. Attitudes to the Common Market: A case study in conservatism. In G. D. Wilson (Ed.), *The psychology of conservatism*. London: Academic Press, 1973, 239–255. (a)

Nias, D. K. B. Measurement and structure of children's attitudes. In G. D. Wilson (Ed.), *The psychology of conservatism*. London: Academic Press, 1973, 93–113. (b)

Nideffer, R. M. Test of Attentional and Interpersonal Style. *Journal of Personality and Social Psychology*, 1976, *34*, 394–404.

Norman, R. M. G., & Watson, L. D. Extraversion and reactions to cognitive inconsistency. *Journal of Research in Personality*, 1976, *10*, 446–456.

Orford, J. A. A study of the personalities of excessive drinkers and their wives, using the approaches of Leary and Eysenck. *Journal of Consulting and Clinical Psychology*, 1976, *44*, 534–545.

Organ, D. W. Extraversion, locus of control, and individual differences in conditionability in organizations. *Journal of Applied Psychology*, 1975, *60*, 401–404.

Orpen, C. The cross-cultural validity of the Eysenck Personality Inventory:

A test in Afrikaans-speaking South Africa. *British Journal of Social and Clinical Psychology*, 1972, *11*, 244–247.

Orpen, C. Personality and academic attainment: A cross-cultural study. *British Journal of Educational Psychology*, 1976, *46*, 220–222.

Overall, J. E., & Patrick, J. H. Unitary alcoholism factor and its personality correlates. *Journal of Abnormal Psychology*, 1972, *79*, 303–309.

Overton, W. F., & Reese, H. W. Models of development: Methodological implications. In J. R. Nesselroade & H. W. Reese (Eds.), *Lifespan developmental psychology: Methodological issues*. New York: Academic Press, 1973.

Pallis, D. J., & Birtchnell, J. Personality and suicidal history in psychiatric patients. *Journal of Clinical Psychology*, 1976, *32*, 246–253.

Pallis, D. J., & Jenkins, J. S. Extraversion, neuroticism, and intent in attempted suicides. *Psychological Reports*, 1977, *41*, 19–22.

Palmiere, L. Intro-extra-version as an organizing principle in fantasy production. *Journal of Analytical Psychology*, 1972, *17*, 116–131.

Paramesh, C. R. Dimensions of personality and achievement in scholastic subjects. *Indian Journal of Psychology*, 1976, *51*, 302–306.

Parker, J. L. Introversion/extraversion and children's aversion to social isolation and corporal punishment: A note on a failure to replicate Eysenck. *Australian Journal of Psychology*, 1972, *24*, 141–143.

Passingham, R. E. Crime and personality: A review of Eysenck's theory. In V. D. Nebylitsyn & J. Gray (Eds.), *Biological bases of behavior*. New York: Academic Press, 1972, 342–351.

Patterson, M. L., & Strauss, M. E. An examination of the discriminant validity of the Social Avoidance and Distress Scale. *Journal of Consulting and Clinical Psychology*, 1972, *39*, 169.

Paykel, E. S., & Prusoff, B. A. Relationships between personality dimensions: Neuroticism and extraversion against obsessive, hysterical and oral personality. *British Journal of Social and Clinical Psychology*, 1973, *12*, 309–318.

Pearson, P. R., & Sheffield, B. F. Is personality related to social attitudes? An attempt at replication. *Social Behavior and Personality*, 1976, *4*, 109–111.

Penk, W. E., & Robinowitz, R. Personality differences of volunteer and nonvolunteer heroin and nonheroin drug users. *Journal of Abnormal Psychology*, 1976, *85*, 91–100.

Perry, A. Heredity, personality traits, product attitude and product comsumption: An exploratory study. *Journal of Marketing Research*, 1973, *10*, 376–379.

Peterson, D. R. Scope and generality of verbally defined personality factors. *Psychological Review*, 1965, 72, 48–59.

Phares, E. J., & Lamiell, J. T. Personality. *Annual Review of Psychology*, 1977, *28*, 113–140.

Pilkonis, P. A. Shyness, public and private, and its relationship to other measures of social behavior. *Journal of Personality*, 1977, *45*, 585–595. (a)

Pilkonis, P. A. The behavioral consequences of shyness. *Journal of Personality*, 1977, *45*, 596-611. (b)

Pillai, P. G. A study of factors related to the disparity between occupational aspirations and value choices of high school students. *Indian Journal of Social Work*, 1975, *36*, 61-73.

Pitkanen, L. An aggression machine. I: The intensity of aggressive defence aroused by aggressive offence; II: Interindividual differences in the aggressive defence responses aroused by varying stimulus conditions; III: The stability of aggressive and nonaggressive patterns of behaviour. *Scandinavian Journal of Psychology*, 1973, *14*, 56-77.

Pitkanen, L., & Turunen, A. Psychomotor reactions of aggressive and nonaggressive extrovert children. *Scandinavian Journal of Psychology*, 1974, *15*, 314-319.

Pitkanen-Pulkinen, L., & Pitkanen, M. Social skills of aggressive and nonaggressive adolescents. *Scandinavian Journal of Psychology*, 1976, *17*, 10-14.

Platt, J. J., Pomeranz, D., & Eisenman, R. Validation of the Eysenck Personality Inventory by the MMPI and internal-external control scale. *Journal of Clinical Psychology*, 1971, *27*, 104-105.

Plomin, R. A. A twin and family study of personality in young children. *Journal of Psychology*, 1976, *94*, 233-235. (a)

Plomin, R. A. Extraversion: Sociability and impulsivity? *Journal of Personality Assessment*, 1976, *40*, 24-30. (b)

Power, C. N. Effects of student characteristics and level of teacher-student interaction on achievement and attitudes. *Contemporary Educational Psychology*, 1977, *2*, 265-274.

Power, R. P., & MacRae, K. D. Characteristics of items in the Eysenck Personality Inventory which affect responses when students simulate. *British Journal of Psychology*, 1977, *68*, 491-498.

Power, R. P., MacRae, K. D., & Muntz, H. J. Separation of normals, neurotics and simulating malingerers on the MPI by means of discriminant function analysis. *British Journal of Social and Clinical Psychology*, 1974, *13*, 65-72.

Power, R. P., Muntz, H. J., & MacRae, K. D. Man or machine as diagnostic tool: A comparison between clinical psychologists and discriminant function analysis. *British Journal of Social and Clinical Psychology*, 1975, *14*, 413-422.

Quereshi, M. Y. Some psychological factors that distinguish between the remediably and irremediably obese. *Journal of Clinical Psychology*, 1972, *28*, 17-22.

Quereshi, M. Y., & Soat, D. M. Perception of self and significant others by alcoholics and nonalcoholics. *Journal of Clinical Psychology*, 1976, *32*, 189-194.

Rae, G. Extraversion, neuroticism, and cigarette smoking. *British Journal of Social and Clinical Psychology*, 1975, *14*, 429-430.

Rae, G., & McCall, J. Some international comparisons of cancer mortality rates and personality: A brief note. *Journal of Psychology*, 1973, *85*, 87-88.

Ramsay, R. W. Personality and speech. *Journal of Personality and Social Psychology*, 1966, *4*, 116–118.

Randall, J. L. Card-guessing experiments with schoolboys. *Journal of the Society for Psychical Research*, 1974, *47*, 421–432.

Revelle, W., Amaral, P., & Turiff, S. Introversion–extraversion, time stress, and caffeine: Effect on verbal performance. *Science*, 1976, *192*, 149–150.

Roberts, C. A., & Johansson, C. B. The inheritance of cognitive interest styles among twins. *Journal of Vocational Behavior*, 1974, *4*, 237–243.

Robertson, I. T. Relationships between learning strategy, attention deployment and personality. *British Journal of Educational Psychology*, 1978, *48*, 86–91.

Rolf, J. E. The social and academic competence of children vulnerable to schizophrenia and other behavior pathologies. *Journal of Abnormal Psychology*, 1972, *80*, 225–243.

Romine, P. G., & Crowell, O. Construct validity: Person-orientation and value-orientation scales of the California Psychological Inventory. *Psychological Reports*, 1978, *42*, 317–318.

Rosenbluh, E. S., Owens, G. B., & Pohler, M. J. Art preferences and personality. *British Journal of Psychology*, 1972, *63*, 441–443.

Rosenthal, D. A., & Lines, R. Handwriting as a correlate of extraversion. *Journal of Personality Assessment*, 1978, *42*, 45–48.

Rotter, J. B., Chance, J. E., & Phares, E. J. *Applications of a social learning theory of personality*. New York: Holt, Rinehart & Winston, 1972.

Rowell, J. A., & Renner, V. J. Personality, mode of assessment and student achievement. *British Journal of Educational Psychology*, 1975, *45*, 232–238.

Rustin, R. M., Kittel, F., Dramaix, M., Kornitzer, M., & DeBacker, G. Smoking habits and psycho–socio–biological factors. *Journal of Psychosomatic Research*, 1978, *22*, 89–99.

Rutter, D. R., Morley, I. E., & Graham, J. C. Visual interaction in a group of introverts and extraverts. *European Journal of Social Psychology*, 1972, *2*, 371–384.

Saklofske, D. H. Personality and behavior problems of school boys. *Psychological Reports*, 1977, *41*, 445–446.

Sanocki, W. The use of Eysenck's inventory for testing of young prisoners. *Przeglad Penitenyermy (Warszawa)*, 1967, *7*, 53–68.

Savage, R. D., & Stewart, R. R. Personality and the success of card-punch operators in training. *British Journal of Psychology*, 1972, *63*, 445–450.

Scarr, S. Social introversion–extraversion as a heritable response. *Child Development*, 1969, *40*, 823–832.

Schaefer, E. S. Development of hierarchical, configural models for parent behavior and child behavior. In S. P. Hill (Ed.), *Minnesota symposium on child psychology* (Vol. 5). Minneapolis: University of Minnesota Press, 1971.

Schaie, K. W., & Parham, I. A. Stability of adult personality traits: Fact or fable? *Journal of Personality and Social Psychology*, 1976, *34*, 146–158.

Schalling, D. The trait–situation interaction and the physiological correlates of behavior. In D. Magnusson & N. S. Endler (Eds.), *Personality at the crossroads*. Hillsdale, N.J.: Erlbaum, 1977, 129–141.

Schalling, D., & Holmberg, M. *Extraversion in criminals*. Unpublished manuscript, 1968.

Schleuter, S. L. An investigation of the interrelation of personality traits, musical aptitude, and musical achievement. In E. Gordon (Ed.), *Experimental Research in the Psychology of Music*, 1972, *8*, 90–102.

Schoolar, J. C. White, E. H., & Cohen, C. P. Drug abusers and their clinic-patient counterparts: A comparison of personality dimensions. *Journal of Consulting and Clinical Psychology*, 1972, *39*, 9–14.

Schooler, C. Birth order effects: Not here, not now! *Psychological Bulletin*, 1972, *78*, 161–175.

Schwartz, S. Multimethod analysis of three measures of six common personality traits. *Journal of Personality Assessment*, 1973, *37*, 559–567.

Schwartz, S., & Burdsal, C. A factor-analytic examination of the relationship of personality variables to hypnotizability. *Journal of Clinical Psychology*, 1977, *33*, 356–360.

Sechrest, L. Personality. *Annual Review of Psychology*, 1976, *27*, 1–27.

Seddon, G. M. The effects of chronological age on the relationship of intelligence and academic achievement with extraversion and neuroticism. *British Journal of Psychology*, 1975, *66*, 493–500.

Seddon, G. M. The effects of chronological age on the relationship of academic achievement with extraversion and neuroticism: A follow-up study. *British Journal of Educational Psychology*, 1977, *47*, 187–192.

Serra, A. V., & Pollitt, J. The relationship between personality and the symptoms of depressive illness. *British Journal of Psychiatry*, 1975, *127*, 211–218.

Shadbolt, D. R. Interactive relationships between measured personality and teaching strategy variables. *British Journal of Educational Psychology*, 1978, *48*, 227–231.

Shanthamani, V. S., & Hafeez, A. Some personality variables among engineering students and employed engineers. *Indian Journal of Social Work*, 1973, *33*, 323–330.

Shapiro, K. J. & Alexander, I. E. Extraversion-introversion, affiliation, and anxiety. *Journal of Personality*, 1969, *37*, 387–406.

Shapiro, K. J., & Alexander, I. E. *The experience of introversion: An integration of phenomenological, empirical, and Jungian approaches*. Durham, N.C.: Duke University Press, 1975.

Shapland, J., & Rushton, J. P. Crime and personality: Further evidence. *Bulletin of the British Psychological Society*, 1975, *28*, 66–67.

Shaw, D. M., MacSweeney, D. A., Johnson, A. L., & Merry, J. Personality characteristics of alcoholic and depressed patients. *British Journal of Psychiatry*, 1975, *126*, 56–59.

Sheppard, C., Ricca, E., Fracchia, J., & Merlis, S. Personality characteristics of urban and suburban heroin abusers: More data and another reply to Sutker and Allain (1973). *Psychological Reports*, 1973, *33*, 999–1008.

Shriberg, L. D. Intercorrelations among repression-sensitization, extraversion, neuroticism, social desirability, and locus of control. *Psychological Reports*, 1972, *31*, 925–926.

Sieveking, N. A. A child-adult research form of the Pittsburgh Scales of Social Extraversion–Introversion and Emotionality. *Journal of Psychology*, 1973, *83*, 49–56.

Simmons, D. D. Personal values and Eysenck's two basic personality factors. *Psychological Reports*, 1976, *38*, 912–914.

Sinclair, I. A., & Chapman, B. A typological and dimensional study of a sample of prisoners. *British Journal of Criminology*, 1973, *13*, 341–353.

Sinclair, I. A., Shaw, M. J., & Troop, J. The relationship between introversion and response to casework in a prison setting. *British Journal of Social and Clinical Psychology*, 1974, *13*, 51–60.

Singh, U. P. Another study of Hindi version of the Maudsley Personality Inventory (MPI). *Indian Psychological Review*, 1966, *3*, 57–58.

Singh, U. P. Personality profiles of recidivists and nonrecidivists. *Indian Journal of Social Work*, 1974, *35*, 227–232.

Singh, U. P., & Akhtar, S. N. Personality variables and cheating in examinations. *Indian Journal of Social Work*, 1972, *32*, 423–428.

Skinner, N. F. Personality characteristics of heavy smokers and abstainers as a function of perceived predispositions toward marijuana use. *Social Behavior and Personality*, 1974, *2*, 157–160.

Smith, G. M. Personality correlates of cigarette smoking in students of college age. *Annals of the New York Academy of Sciences*, 1967, *142*, 308–321.

Smith, G. M. Relations between personality and smoking behavior in preadult subjects. *Journal of Consulting and Clinical Psychology*, 1969, *33*, 710–715.

Smith, J. C. Personality correlates of continuation and outcome in meditation and erect sitting control treatments. *Journal of Consulting and Clinical Psychology*, 1978, *46*, 272–279.

Smithers, A. G. & Lobley, D. M. Dogmatism, social attitudes and personality. *British Journal of Social and Clinical Psychology*, 1978, *17*, 135–142.

Snyder, M., & Monson, T. C. Persons, situations, and the control of social behavior. *Journal of Personality and Social Psychology*, 1975, *32*, 637–644.

Staats, A. W. *Social behaviorism*. Homewood, Ill.: Dorsey, 1975.

Stagner, R. Traits are relevant: Theoretical analysis and empirical evidence. In N. S. Endler & D. Magnusson (Eds.), *Interactional psychology and personality*. Washington, D.C.: Hemisphere, 1976, 109–124.

Stagner, R. On the reality and relevance of traits. *Journal of General Psychology*, 1977, *96*, 185-207.

Stedman, J. M., & Adams, R. L. Achievement as a function of language competence, behavior adjustment, and sex in young, disadvantaged Mexican-American children. *Journal of Educational Psychology*, 1972, *63*, 411-417.

Steele, R. S., & Kelly, T. J. Eysenck Personality Questionnaire and Jungian Myers–Briggs Type Indicator correlation of extraversion–introversion. *Journal of Consulting and Clinical Psychology*, 1976, *44*, 690-691.

Steer, A. B. Sex differences, extraversion and neuroticism in relation to speech rate during the expression of emotion. *Language and Speech*, 1974, *17*, 80-86.

Stephenson, G. M., & Barker, J. Personality and the pursuit of distributive justice: An experimental study of children's moral behaviour. *British Journal of Social and Clinical Psychology*, 1972, *11*, 207-219.

Stoudenmire, J. Effects of muscle relaxation training on state and trait anxiety in introverts and extraverts. *Journal of Personality and Social Psychology*, 1972, *24*, 273-275.

Strassberg, D., & Kangas, J. MMPI correlates of self-disclosure. *Journal of Clinical Psychology*, 1977, *33*, 739-740.

Stricker, L. J., & Ross, J. An assessment of some structural properties of the Jungian personality typology. *Journal of Abnormal and Social Psychology*, 1964, *68*, 62-71.

Stroup, A. L., & Manderscheid, R. W. CPI and 16PF second-order factor congruence. *Journal of Clinical Psychology*, 1977, *33*, 1023-1026.

Sutker, P. B., & Allain, A. B. Incarcerated and street heroin addicts: A personality comparison. *Psychological Reports*, 1973, *32*, 243-246.

Thayer, R. W. The interrelation of personality traits, musical achievement, and different measures of musical aptitude. In E. Gordon (Ed.), *Experimental Research in the Psychology of Music*, 1972, *8*, 103-118.

Thomas, A., Chess, S., & Birch, H. *Temperament and behavior disorders in children.* New York: New York University Press, 1968.

Thompson, W. R., & Wilde, G. J. S. Behavior genetics. In B. B. Wolman (Ed.), *Handbook of general psychology.* Englewood Cliffs, N.J.: Prentice-Hall, 1973, 206-229.

Tolor, A. Effects of procedural variations in measuring interpersonal distance by means of representational space. *Psychological Reports*, 1975, *36*, 475-491. (a)

Tolor, A. Introversion–extraversion and topological representations of self and others. *Journal of Clinical Psychology*, 1975, *31*, 662-663. (b)

Trown, E. A., & Leith, G. O. Decision rules for teaching strategies in primary schools: Personality–treatment interactions. *British Journal of Educational Psychology*, 1975, *45*, 130-140.

Turnbull, A. A. Selling and the salesman: Prediction of success and personality change. *Psychological Reports*, 1976, *38*, 1175-1180.

Turner, R. G. Consistency, self-consciousness, and the predictive validity of typical and maximal personality measures. *Journal of Research in Personality*, 1978, *12*, 117-132.

Vagg, P. R., & Hammond, S. B. The number and kind of invariant personality (Q) factors: A partial replication of Eysenck and Eysenck. *British Journal of Social and Clinical Psychology*, 1976, *15*, 121–129.

Vandenberg, S. G. Contributions of twin research to psychology. *Psychological Bulletin*, 1966, *66*, 327–352.

Vandenberg, S. G. Assortative mating, or who marries whom? *Behavior Genetics*, 1972, *2*, 127–157.

Vandenberg, S. G., & Price, R. A. Replication of the factor structure of the Comrey Personality Scales. *Psychological Reports*, 1978, *42*, 343–352.

Verma, R. M., & Eysenck, H. J. Severity and type of psychotic illness as a function of personality. *British Journal of Psychiatry*, 1973, *122*, 573–585.

Vestewig, R. E. Extraversion and risk preference in portfolio theory. *Journal of Psychology*, 1977, *97*, 237–245.

Vestewig, R. E., & Moss, M. K. The relationship of extraversion and neuroticism to two measures of assertive behavior. *Journal of Psychology*, 1976, *93*, 141–146.

Vine, I. Stereotypes in the judgment of personality from handwriting. *British Journal of Social and Clinical Psychology*, 1974, *13*, 61–64.

Vingoe, F. J., & Antonoff, S. R. Personality characteristics of good judges of others. *Journal of Counseling Psychology*, 1968, *15*, 91–93.

Wakefield, J. A., Bradley, P. E., Doughtie, E. B., & Kraft, I. A. Influence of overlapping and nonoverlapping items on the theoretical interrelationships of MMPI scales. *Journal of Consulting and Clinical Psychology*, 1975, *43*, 851–857.

Wakefield, J. A., Sasek, J., Brubaker, M. L., & Friedman, A. F. Validity study of the Eysenck Personality Questionnaire. *Psychological Reports*, 1976, *39*, 115–120.

Wakefield, J. A., Yom, B. L., Bradley, P. E., Doughtie, E. B., Cox, J. A., & Kraft, I. A. Eysenck's personality dimensions: Model for the MMPI. *British Journal of Social and Clinical Psychology*, 1974, *13*, 413–420.

Wallach, M. A., & Thomas, H. L. Graphic constriction and expansiveness as a function of induced social isolation and social interaction: Experimental manipulations and personality effects. *Journal of Personality*, 1963, *31*, 491–509.

Walsh, W. B. *Theories of person-environment interaction: Implications for the college student.* Iowa City, Iowa: American College Testing Program, 1973.

Ward, G. R., Cunningham, C. H., & Wakefield, J. A. Relationships between Holland's VPI and Cattell's 16PF. *Journal of Vocational Behavior*, 1976, *8*, 307–312.

Watkins, D. Sex differences among correlates of extraversion and neuroticism. *Psychological Reports*, 1976, *38*, 695–698.

Watson, D. & Friend, R. Measurement of social-evaluative anxiety. *Journal of Consulting and Clinical Psychology*, 1969, *33*, 448–457.

Wells, B. W. P., & Stacey, B. G. A further comparison of cannabis (marijuana) users and non-users. *British Journal of Addiction*, 1976, *71*, 161–165. (a)

Wells, B. W. P., & Stacey, B. G. Social and psychological features of young drug misusers. *British Journal of Addiction*, 1976, *71*, 243–251. (b)

Welsh, G. S. Factor dimensions A and R. In G. S. Welsh & W. G. Dahlstrom (Eds.), *Basic readings on the MMPI in psychology and medicine*. Minneapolis: University of Minnesota Press, 1956.

West, D. J., & Farrington, D. P. *Who becomes delinquent?* London: Heinemann, 1973.

Wheeless, L. R. Attitude and credibility in the prediction of attitude change: A regression approach. *Speech Monographs*, 1974, *41*, 277–281.

Whitaker, E. M. The personality structure of boys in a regional assessment centre. *British Journal of Educational Psychology*, 1978, *48*, 92–97.

Wigglesworth, M. J. & Smith, B. D. Habituation and dishabituation of the electrodermal orienting reflex in relation to extraversion and neuroticism. *Journal of Research in Personality*, 1976, *10*, 437–445.

Wilde, G. J. S. Trait description and measurement by personality questionnaires. In R. B. Cattell & R. M. Dreger (Eds.), *Handbook of modern personality theory*. Washington, D.C.: Hemisphere, 1977, 69–103.

Willerman, L., Turner, R. G., & Peterson, M. A comparison of the predictive validity of typical and maximal personality measures. *Journal of Research in Personality*, 1976, *10*, 482–492.

Williams, M., Berg–Cross, G., & Berg–Cross, L. Handwriting characteristics and their relationship to Eysenck's extraversion–introversion and Kagan's impulsivity–reflectivity dimensions. *Journal of Personality Assessment*, 1977, *41*, 291–298.

Williams, P., Francis, A., & Durham, R. Personality and meditation. *Perceptual and Motor Skills*, 1976, *43*, 787–792.

Wilson, G. D. Introversion/extraversion. In T. Blass (Ed.), *Personality variables in social behavior*. New York: Halsted, 1977.

Wilson, G. D., & Brazendale, A. H. Social attitude correlates of Eysenck's personality dimensions. *Social Behavior and Personality*, 1973, *1*, 115–118.

Wilson, G. D., & MacLean, A. Personality, attitudes and humor preferences of prisoners and controls. *Psychological Reports*, 1974, *34*, 847–854.

Wilson, R., Brown, A., & Matheny, A. Emergence and persistence of behavioral differences in twins. *Child Development*, 1971, *42*, 1381–1398.

Wilson, S., & Kennard, D. The extraverting effect of treatment in a therapeutic community for drug abusers. *British Journal of Psychiatry*, 1978, *132*, 296–299.

Wishnie, H. *The impulsive personality: Understanding people with destructive character disorders*. New York: Plenum Press, 1977.

Witkin, H., & Goodenough, D. Field dependence and interpersonal behavior. *Psychological Bulletin,* 1977, *84,* 661–689.

Young, J. P. R., Fenton, G. W., & Lader, M. H. The inheritance of neurotic traits: A twin study of the Middlesex Hospital Questionnaire. *British Journal of Psychiatry,* 1971, *119,* 393–398.

Zeichner, A., Pihl, R. O., & Wright, J. C. A comparison between volunteer drug-abusers and non-drug-abusers on measures of social skills. *Journal of Clinical Psychology,* 1977, *33,* 585–590.

Zelhart, P. Types of alcoholics and their relationship to traffic violations. *Journal of Studies on Alcohol,* 1972, *33,* 811–813.

Ziller, R. C. *The social self.* New York: Pergamon, 1973.

Zuckerman, M., Bone, R. N., Neary, R., Mangelsdorff, D., & Brustman, B. What is the sensation-seeker? Personality trait and experience correlates of the Sensation-Seeking Scales. *Journal of Consulting and Clinical Psychology,* 1972, *39,* 308–321.

Zuckerman, M., Sola, S., Masterson, J., & Angelone, J. V. MMPI patterns in drug abusers before and after treatment in therapeutic communities. *Journal of Consulting and Clinical Psychology,* 1975, *43,* 286–296.

AUTHOR INDEX

Abramson, P. R., 55, 173
Achenbach, T. M., 79, 81, 174
Adams, R. L., 94, 198
Adinolfi, A. A., 54, 188
Akhtar, S. N., 130, 197
Alexander, I. E., 6, 37, 45, 196
Allain, A. B. 148, 198
Allen, A., 17, 174
Allsopp, J. F., 128, 129, 173
Alterman, A. I., 145, 183
Amaral, P., 141, 195
Angelone, J. V., 149, 150, 201
Anthony, W. S., 92, 94, 173
Antonoff, S. R., 50, 199
Armstrong, H. E., 120, 173
Ashmore, R. D., 69, 71, 178
Ashton, H., 138, 173
Ashworth, C., 57, 174
Averett, M., 73, 174
Ayers, J., 143, 174

Baekgaard, W., 174
Baer, D. J., 160, 190

Baer, P. E., 183
Bagley, C., 82, 174
Ball, L. R., 143, 188
Bandura, A., 9, 174
Banister, P. A., 125, 126, 176, 186
Banks, O., 96, 174
Barker, J., 131, 198
Barratt, E. S., 27, 174
Bartol, C. R., 141, 174
Barton, K., 52, 95, 174
Bartsch, T., 95, 174
Bascuas, J., 107, 174
Bauer, S. R., 79, 81, 174
Beaubrun, M., 151, 174
Beck, E. A., 130, 174
Becker, J. F., 57, 174
Becker, L. A., 50, 185
Bell, J. M., 76, 191
Bem, D. J., 17, 174
Bendig, A. W., 37, 103, 133, 175
Bentler, P. M., 27, 175
Berg-Cross, G., 62, 200
Berg-Cross, L., 62, 200

Berry, K. L., 142, 147, 176
Bianchi, G. N., 118, 175
Birch, H., 168, 198
Birtchnell, J., 119, 193
Bishop, D., 111, 175
Black, W. A., 122, 125, 127, 175
Blackburn, R., 34, 76, 120, 133, 175
Blake, M. J. F., 110, 175
Bloch, S., 141, 176
Block, J., 33, 175
Bloom, L. J., 117, 175
Blumberg, H., 147, 175
Blunden, D., 38, 175
Boller, J. D., 46, 175
Bolton, N., 125, 126, 176, 186
Bone, R. N., 74, 201
Boulougouris, J., 116, 191
Bown, O. H., 81, 176
Brackenridge, C. J., 141, 176
Bradley, P. E., 34, 199
Brakarsh, D., 142, 147, 176
Brand, C. R., 133, 176
Braught, G. N., 142, 147, 176
Brazendale, A. H., 85, 200
Breen, L. J., 83, 176
Bronson, W. C., 158, 176
Brookhart, D., 134, 189
Brown, A., 159, 200
Brown, S. R., 51, 64, 185
Browne, J. A., 26, 29, 186
Brubaker, M. L., 37, 199
Brustman, B., 74, 201
Buck, R., 59, 60, 176
Bull, R. H., 83, 176
Burdsal, C., 62, 63, 151, 176, 196
Burger, G. K., 31, 176
Burgess, P. K., 124, 125, 176
Burke, B. W., 163, 179
Burns, J. L., 61, 176
Buss, A., 14, 84, 169, 170, 176, 177, 182
Butler, M. C., 147, 184
Byrne, D., 78, 177

Cairns, E., 27, 177
Calhoun, L. G., 17, 190

Campus, N., 17, 177
Canter, S., 166, 178
Cantor, N., 16, 177
Carlson, R., 8, 37, 58, 107, 161, 177, 189
Carlyn, M., 37, 177
Carrigan, P. M., 23, 177
Carson, R. C., 9, 11, 177
Cattell, R. B., 15, 28–30, 52, 95, 139, 162, 174, 177, 179
Caul, W. F., 59, 176
Cegalis, J. A., 76, 177
Chaikin, A., 57, 174
Chamove, A. S., 169, 177
Chance, J. E., 9, 195
Chandler, C., 142, 179, 180
Chapman, B., 126, 197
Cherry, N., 139, 177
Chess, S., 168, 198
Christie, M. J., 110, 178
Ciotola, P. V., 147, 178
Claeson, L. E., 145, 178
Claridge, G., 166, 178
Click, M., 47, 183
Coan, R. W., 139, 178
Cocking, R. R., 73, 78, 179
Cohen, C. P., 150, 196
Cohen, L., 44, 45, 86, 87, 178
Cohen, R. H., 78, 178
Cohen, S., 147, 175
Collins, B. E., 69, 71, 178
Colson, C. E., 78, 119, 178
Comrey, A. L., 32, 178
Connor, W. H., 29, 34, 117, 187
Cook, M., 56, 188
Cooper, J., 48, 178
Cooper, R., 110, 178
Corah, N. L., 34, 178
Corcoran, D. W. J., 110, 175
Corcoran, M. E., 63, 184
Cortes, J. B., 122, 178
Costa, P. T., 102, 178
Couch, A. S., 34, 188
Cowan, C. O., 183
Cowen, E. L., 107, 179
Cox, J. A., 34, 199
Craske, B., 50, 186
Crocker, R. K., 98, 185

Crowell, O., 32, 195
Cunningham, C. H., 103, 199
Cunningham, M. R., 58, 178
Curran, J. D., 63, 184
Cutter, H. S., 145, 178

Dahlstrom, L., 33, 178
Dahlstrom, W. G., 33, 178
Dana, R. H., 73, 78, 179
Danforth, A. V., 183
Davis, J. D., 57, 179
Davis, L., 116, 179
Davis, L. S., 105, 186
Davis, S. A., 52, 182
DeBacker, G., 139, 195
Delhees, K. H., 30, 179
Derlega, V., 57, 174
DeWinne, R., 104, 147, 179
Diespecker, D. D., 61, 183
Dorr, D., 107, 179
Doughtie, E. B., 34, 199
Downing, L., 33, 184
Doyle, J. A., 77, 85, 179
Drake, L. E., 33, 179
Dramaix, M., 139, 195
Dreger, R. M., 177
Dronfield, E., 147, 175
Durham, R., 46, 200
Dworkin, R. H., 19, 163, 179
Dyer, M., 182

Eastwood, M. R., 119, 179
Eaves, L. J., 85, 167, 179
Eber, H. W., 29, 177
Edmunds, G., 133, 179
Edwards, G., 142, 179, 190
Eisenman, R., 68, 107, 174, 194
Eisinger, A. J., 55, 180
Eliot, J., 70, 180
Elliott, C. D., 95, 180
Endler, N. S., 10, 19, 83, 176, 180,
    191
Entwistle, N. J., 92, 101, 180
Epstein, S., 9, 180
Euse, F. J., 107, 180
Evan-Wong, L., 82, 174

Evered, R. D., 109, 180
Exner, J. E., Jr., 108, 180
Eysenck, H. J., 6-8, 24-29, 52, 54,
    55, 71, 81, 85, 99, 114, 115,
    118-127, 129, 138, 152, 162,
    167, 169, 177, 179-182, 187,
    199
Eysenck, M. W., 99, 181
Eysenck, S. B., 6, 24, 25, 27-29,
    71, 114, 115, 118, 123-127,
    152, 181, 182, 187

Farley, F. H., 52, 74, 115, 160, 182
Farrington, D. P., 128, 200
Feinberg, L., 44, 182
Feldman, M. P., 128, 129, 173
Fenigstein, A., 84, 182
Fenton, G. W., 166, 201
Fergusson, D. M., 118, 175
Field, J. G., 123, 183
Fine, B. J., 76, 183
Fine, E. W., 147, 190
Finlayson, D., 96, 174
Flammer, D. P., 31, 102, 187
Follingstad, D., 142, 147, 176
Forrest, R., 128, 183
Foulds, M. L., 183
Fouts, G. T., 47, 64, 183
Fowles, D. C., 7, 183
Fozard, J. L., 102, 178
Fracchia, J., 148, 197
Francis, A., 46, 200
Francis, R. D., 61, 183
Frank, A. C., 103, 105, 184
Friedman, A. F., 37, 199
Friend, R., 83, 84, 199
Frigon, J., 183
Fuher, M. J., 183
Furman, G., 57, 174

Galanter, E., 13, 192
Gatti, F. M., 122, 178
Geen, R. G., 72, 78, 183
Gelder, M. G., 116, 183, 191
Gellens, H. K., 145, 183
Genthner, R. W., 45, 183

Ghuman, P. A. S., 76, 183
Gibson, H. B., 25, 63, 184
Giedt, F. H., 33, 184
Gilliland, J. C., 57, 83, 184
Goh, D. S., 97, 182, 184
Golding, S. L., 20, 188
Goldman, M., 31, 176
Goodenough, D., 75, 201
Goodyear, R. K., 103, 105, 184
Goorney, A. B., 34, 117, 184
Gorsuch, R. L., 147, 184
Gossop, M. R., 148, 184
Gottesman, I. I., 163, 179, 184
Gottheil, E., 145, 183
Gotz, K., 106, 184
Gotz, K. O., 106, 184
Gough, H. G., 31, 184
Graham, J. C., 56, 195
Graham, J. R., 33, 34, 184, 185
Gray, J. A., 7, 115, 185
Green, L. R., 145, 178
Greenberg, G., 151, 176
Greenberg, L. M., 38, 175
Gregson, R. A., 125, 127, 175
Griffiths, A. K., 98, 185
Griffiths, P. D., 55, 180
Gross, W. F., 145, 192
Grotevant, H. D., 104, 185
Guilford, J. P., 30, 185
Gupta, B. S., 25, 48, 185

Hafeez, A., 105, 196
Hallam, R. S., 115, 116, 185
Hammond, S. B., 27, 199
Hampson, S., 123, 152, 185, 190
Handel, A., 25, 185
Haney, J. N., 107, 180
Hanks, D., 147, 175
Hannigan, P. S., 183
Hardy, R. C., 70, 180
Harford, T. C., 145, 178
Harkins, S., 50, 185
Harlow, H. F., 169, 177
Harris, R., 86, 87, 178
Harrison, N. W., 61, 190
Hayes, B., 152, 190

Hedge, M. N., 115, 185
Heilizer, F., 115, 185
Hekmat, H., 36, 74, 98, 185, 191
Henderson, A. S., 119, 179
Hendrick, C., 51, 64, 185
Hensman, C., 142, 179, 180
Heskin, K. J., 125, 126, 176, 186
Hildman, L. K., 161, 190
Hill, A. B., 110, 186
Hinton, J. W., 50, 186
Hogan, H. W., 99, 186
Holland, J. L., 103, 186
Holland, T. R., 146, 186
Holmberg, M., 123, 196
Holmes, D. S., 120, 173
Honess, T., 97, 186
Horn, J., 164, 186
Horn, J. M., 105, 186
Horne, A. M., 116, 186
Horne, J. A., 110, 186
Horrocks, J. E., 9, 186
Hosseini, A., 98, 191
Howarth, E., 26, 29, 186
Huba, G. J., 144, 186
Hughes, R. C., 125, 187
Hume, W. I., 166, 178
Humes, M., 150, 188
Hundleby, J. D., 29, 34, 117, 187
Hunt, J. McV., 19, 180
Huntsman, R. G., 55, 180

Ingham, J. C., 116, 187
Insel, P. M., 160, 187
Irfani, S., 25, 187
Iwawaki, S., 152, 187

Jaccard, J. J., 20, 187
Jackson, D., 9, 186
Jamison, K., 107, 187
Jeanrenaud, C., 111, 175
Jenkins, J. S., 119, 193
Jensen, A. R., 95, 187
Johansson, C. B., 35, 102, 104,
    187, 195
Johnson, A. L., 144, 196
Johnson, J. H., 36, 187, 188

Johnson, M. H., 120, 173
Johnson, R. W., 31, 35, 102, 103, 125, 147, 179, 187
Johnston, D. W., 116, 191
Jones, E. E., 161, 187
Joubert, C. E., 68, 187
Jung, C. G., 6, 37, 187

Kaldegg, A., 147, 187
Kanekar, S., 105, 187
Kangas, J., 57, 198
Kanthamani, B. K., 63, 188
Kassebaum, G. G., 34, 188
Kay, E. J., 150, 188
Kelly, G. A., 9, 188
Kelly, T. J., 37, 198
Kendon, A., 56, 188
Kennard, D., 149, 200
Khajavi, F., 36, 74, 98, 185, 191
Khavari, K. A., 150, 188
Kiernan, K., 139, 177
Kihlstrom, J. F., 19, 179
Kirton, M. J., 108, 188
Kittel, F., 139, 195
Kline, P., 25, 97, 123, 185, 186, 188
Knapp, R., 85, 188
Knight, F., 151, 174
Knudson, R. M., 20, 188
Kobrick, J. L., 183
Kokosh, J. 105, 188
Kornitzer, M., 139, 195
Kraft, I. A., 34, 199
Krasner, L., 9, 188
Krebs, D., 54, 188
Kristjansson, I., 148, 184
Krug, S., 30, 117, 139, 177, 188
Kurtines, W. M., 143, 188

Lader, M. H., 166, 201
Lamiell, J. T., 8, 193
Lanyon, R. I., 35, 36, 117, 188
Laughlin, J. E., 30, 117, 188
LaVoie, J. C., 130, 189
Lawlis, G. F., 144, 189

Lazarus, A. A., 9, 189
Leboeuf, A., 116, 189
Leen, D., 76, 177
Leith, G. O., 99, 106, 189, 198
Leonard, C. V., 118, 189
Lester, D., 62, 73, 76, 78, 82, 107, 122, 134, 189
Leura, A., 108, 180
Levinson, F., 116, 189
Levy, N., 37, 58, 107, 161, 177, 189
Lilly, R. S., 33, 185
Lines, R., 62, 195
Lippa, R., 53, 189
Lobley, D. M., 87, 197
Loeb, R. C., 150, 188
Loehlin, J. C., 163, 165, 190
Long, G. T., 17, 190
Loo, R., 76, 190
Lord, J., 55, 180
Lorefice, L., 147, 190
Lorr, M., 12, 38, 190
Lowe, J. D., 161, 190
Lynn, R., 152, 190
Lyons, A., 150, 188

Mabry, E., 150, 188
McCall, J., 152, 194
McClain, E. W., 87, 190
McClain, J., 27, 175
McCormick, K., 160, 190
McCrae, R. R., 102, 178
McCutcheon, L. E., 160, 190
McGurk, B. J., 134, 190
McIntyre, S. C., 130, 174
McLaughlin, R. J., 61, 190
McLaughlin, S., 62, 189
MacLean, A., 124, 200
McManis, D. L., 73, 174
MacRae, K. D., 190, 194
MacSweeney, D. A., 144, 196
McWithey, K. O., 71, 190
Magaro, P. A., 79, 192
Magnusson, D., 10, 180, 191
Maher, B. A., 163, 179
Mahoney, M. J., 9, 191

Mallaghan, M., 117, 191
Malm, U., 145, 178
Manderscheid, R. W., 32, 198
Mangelsdorff, D., 74, 201
Mankin, D., 150, 188
Mann, W. R., 98, 191
Marin, G., 151, 191
Marks, I. M., 116, 183, 191
Marset, P., 116, 191
Marsteller, R. A., 109, 191
Martin, J. C., 69, 71, 178
Martin, R. B., 120, 191
Masterson, J., 149, 150, 201
Matheny, A., 159, 200
Matthews, A. M., 116, 191
Mayo, P. R., 76, 191
Mealiea, W. L., 115, 182
Megargee, E. I., 31, 191
Mehryar, A. H., 25, 36, 74, 98,
    185, 191
Mendhiratta, S. S., 151, 191
Merlis, S., 148, 197
Merry, J., 55, 144, 180, 196
Messer, S. B., 27, 191
Meyer, V., 116, 189
Michaels, A. C., 117, 175
Michaelsson, G., 145, 192
Miller, G. A., 13, 192
Miller, I. W., 79, 192
Miller, R. E., 59, 176
Millman, J. E., 138, 173
Mirante, T. J., 38, 192
Mischel, W., 9, 10, 15, 16, 177, 192
Mobbs, N. A., 56, 192
Moltmann, M. L., 120, 191
Monson, T. C., 47, 197
Montgomery, I. M., 119, 179
Moore, C., 97, 184
Moore, N. C., 114, 192
Mordecai, E., 147, 175
Morley, I. E., 56, 195
Moss, M. K., 73, 199
Moughan, J., 45, 183
Mukerjee, S., 105, 187
Mulligan, G., 108, 188
Muntz, H. J., 194
Munz, D. C., 57, 174

Murphy, C., Jr., 161, 189
Myers, I. B., 36, 192

Nagel, K. E., 7, 183
Nagpal, M., 48, 185
Nauss, A., 107, 192
Neary, R., 74, 201
Nelson, J. G., 31, 35, 102, 103,
    187
Nerviano, V. J., 29, 32, 144, 145,
    192
Nesselroade, J. R., 52, 177
Newman, W., 150, 188
Nias, D. K. B., 86, 192
Nichols, R. C., 163, 165, 190
Nideffer, R. M., 16, 38, 192
Nielson, J., 174
Nolting, E., 35, 103, 187
Norman, R. M. G., 49, 192
Nosal, G., 62, 189

Okada, M., 83, 176
Orford, J. A., 144, 192
Organ, D. W., 99, 192
Orpen, C., 25, 97, 192, 193
Ostberg, O., 110, 186
Overall, J. E., 36, 143, 187, 188,
    193
Overton, T. D., 104, 179
Overton, W. F., 14, 193
Owens, G. B., 107, 195
Oziel, L. J., 78, 178

Pallis, D. J., 119, 193
Palmiere, L., 107, 193
Paramesh, C. R., 98, 193
Parham, I. A., 158, 196
Parker, J. L., 130, 193
Parrill, T., 108, 180
Passingham, R. E., 122, 123, 127,
    193
Patrick, J. H., 143, 193
Patterson, M. L., 83, 193
Paykel, E. S., 118, 193

Payne, R., 110, 178
Pearson, P. R., 86, 193
Pemberton, J., 117, 191
Penk, W. E., 148, 150, 193
Perdue, W. C., 134, 189
Perry, A., 166, 193
Peterson, D. R., 23, 193
Peterson, J. F., 147, 178
Peterson, M. A., 19, 200
Peto, J., 142, 180
Phares, E. J., 8, 9, 193, 195
Pickett, L., 31, 176
Pihl, R. O., 148, 201
Pilkonis, P. A., 58, 84, 193, 194
Pillai, P. G., 105, 194
Pitkanen, L., 134, 135, 194
Pitkanen, M., 135, 194
Pitkanen-Pulkinen, L., 135, 194
Platt, J. J., 68, 194
Plomin, R. A., 28, 164, 169, 170,
      177, 186, 194
Pohler, M. J., 107, 195
Polani, P., 55, 180
Pollitt, J., 118, 196
Pomeranz, D., 68, 194
Power, C. N., 101, 194
Power, R. P., 190, 194
Pratt, D. M., 107, 179
Pribram, K. H., 13, 192
Price, R. A., 32, 74, 199
Prociuk, T. J., 83, 176
Prusoff, B. A., 118, 193

Quereshi, M. Y., 116, 143, 194

Rae, G., 139, 152, 194
Ramsay, R. W., 56, 195
Randall, J. L., 63, 195
Rao, K. R., 63, 188
Razavieh, A., 98, 191
Reese, H. W., 14, 193
Renner, V. J., 100, 195
Revelle, W., 141, 195
Ricca, E., 148, 197
Richek, H. G., 81, 176

Ries, H. A., 120, 173
Rizzo, J. L., 98, 191
Roberts, C., 147, 175
Roberts, C. A., 104, 195
Roberts, R., 7, 183
Robertson, I. T., 101, 195
Robinowitz, R., 148, 150, 193
Rolf, J. E., 121, 195
Romine, P. G., 32, 195
Rosenbluh, E. S., 107, 195
Rosenman, R., 164, 186
Rosenstein, A. J., 19, 180
Rosenthal, D. A., 62, 195
Ross, J., 37, 198
Ross, L., 69, 71, 178
Roth, J. D., 35, 103, 187
Rotter, J. B., 9, 195
Rowell, J. A., 100, 195
Rubin, S. E., 144, 189
Ruff, C. F., 143, 174
Rushton, J. P., 128, 196
Rust, J., 127, 182
Rustin, R. M., 139, 195
Rutter, D. R., 56, 195
Rychman, D. B., 38, 192

Saklofske, D. H., 129, 195
Sandler, I., 107, 179
Sanocki, W., 123, 195
Sasek, J., 37, 199
Savage, R. D., 110, 195
Savin, V. J., 59, 176
Scaife, R., 44, 45, 178
Scalise, C. J., 48, 178
Scarr, S., 104, 165, 185, 195
Schaefer, E. S., 38, 195
Schaie, K. W., 158, 196
Schalling, D., 27, 123, 196
Scheier, M., 84, 182
Schleuter, S. L., 106, 196
Schneider, L. J., 104, 179
Schoolar, J. C., 150, 196
Schooler, C., 160, 196
Schroeder, H. E., 33, 34, 184, 185
Schut, J., 147, 190
Schwartz, S., 62, 63, 68, 196

Sechrest, L., 8, 196
Seddon, G. M., 96, 97, 196
Segal, B., 144, 186
Selby, J. W., 17, 190
Serra, A. V., 118, 196
Sewell, T., 182
Shadbolt, D. R., 100, 196
Shanthamani, V. S., 105, 196
Shapiro, K. J., 6, 37, 45, 196
Shapland, J., 128, 196
Shaw, D. M., 144, 196
Shaw, L., 182
Shaw, M. J., 127, 197
Shaw, P. M., 116, 191
Sheffield, B. F., 86, 193
Shelton, J. L., 117, 175
Sheppard, C., 148, 197
Shriberg, L. D., 68, 78, 197
Sieveking, N. A., 38, 197
Simmons, D. D., 88, 197
Sinclair, I. A., 126, 127, 197
Singer, J. L., 144, 186
Singh, U. P., 25, 127, 130, 197
Skinner, A. E. G., 57, 179
Skinner, N. F., 151, 197
Slater, P. E., 34, 188
Slocum, J. W., 109, 191
Smith, B. D., 7, 200
Smith, F. V., 125, 126, 176, 186
Smith, G. M., 139, 197
Smith, J. C., 46, 197
Smithers, A. G., 87, 197
Snyder, M., 47, 197
Soat, D. M., 143, 194
Sola, S., 149, 150, 201
Soper, R. E., 182
Spring, C., 38, 175
Staats, A. W., 9, 197
Stacey, B. G., 151, 200
Stagner, R., 16, 197, 198
Stedman, J. M., 94, 198
Steele, R. S., 37, 198
Steer, A. B., 59, 198
Steer, R. A., 147, 190
Stephenson, G. M., 131, 198
Stewart, R. R., 110, 195
Stonner, D., 50, 185

Stoudenmire, J., 116, 198
Strassberg, D., 57, 198
Strauss, M. E., 83, 193
Stricker, L. J., 37, 198
Strongman, K. T., 83, 176
Stroup, A. L., 32, 198
Sutker, P. B., 148, 198

Tanner, J. M., 55, 180
Tatsuoka, M. M., 29, 177
Taylor, R. G., 35, 103, 187
Telford, R., 138, 173
Templer, D. I., 143, 174
Thayer, R. W., 106, 198
Thomas, A., 168, 198
Thomas, H. L., 199
Thompson, J. W., 138, 173
Thompson, W. R., 162, 198
Timpe, R., 151, 176
Tolor, A., 57, 81, 198
Townsend, P. J., 76, 190
Troop, J., 127, 197
Trown, E. A., 99, 198
Turiff, S., 141, 195
Turnbull, A. A., 109, 198
Turner, R. G., 18, 19, 105, 186,
    198, 200
Turunen, A., 135, 194

Ullmann, L. P., 9, 188

Vagg, P. R., 27, 199
Vandenberg, S. G., 32, 52, 74, 166,
    199
Venables, P. H., 110, 178
Verma, R. M., 119, 199
Verma, S. K., 151, 191
Vestewig, R. E., 73, 74, 199
Vine, I., 62, 199
Vingoe, F. J., 50, 199

Wakefield, J. A., 34, 37, 103, 199
Wallach, M. A., 199

Walsh, W. B., 10, 199
Ward, G. R., 103, 199
Watkins, D., 44, 199
Watson, D., 83, 84, 199
Watson, L. D., 49, 192
Weinberg, R. A., 104, 185
Weitzel, W. D., 32, 192
Wells, B. W. P., 151, 200
Welsh, G. S., 33, 178, 200
West, D. J., 128, 200
Wheeless, L. R., 60, 200
Whitaker, E. M., 128, 200
White, E. H., 150, 196
White, O., 114, 115, 118, 182
Whitehouse, R. H., 55, 180
Wig, N. N., 151, 191
Wigglesworth, M. J., 7, 200
Wilde, G. J. S., 23, 162, 198,
    200
Willerman, L., 19, 170, 177, 200
Williams, M., 62, 200

Williams, P., 46, 200
Wilson, G. D., 85, 124, 200
Wilson, R., 159, 200
Wilson, S., 149, 200
Wishnie, H., 150, 200
Witkin, H., 75, 201
Wolff, H., 116, 183
Wood, G. H., 143, 188
Wright, J. C., 148, 201
Wylie, J., 108, 180

Yom, B. L., 34, 199
Young, J. P. R., 166, 201
Youniss, R. P., 12, 38, 190

Zeichner, A., 148, 201
Zelhart, P., 144, 201
Ziller, R. C., 9, 201
Zuckerman, M., 74, 149, 150, 201

SUBJECT INDEX

Academic performance, 92–101
  age differences, 92–94, 101
  older students, 96–99
  teaching methods, 98–101
  younger children, 94–96
Addiction (*See* Alcohol; Caffeine;
  Heroin; LSD; Marijuana;
  Tobacco)
Adjustment–maladjustment and
  extraversion–introversion,
  113–115, 152–155
Affect Expression Rating Scale,
  60
Affection, 11–12, 54, 73–74, 144
Affiliation, 43–45, 54, 87, 89
Aggression, 121, 123, 126–127,
  132–135, 153
  (*See also* Hostility)
Alcohol, 142–147, 152–153, 155,
  166
Anxiety:
  and academic performance, 95
  and drug use, 145, 148, 149,
    151, 166

Anxiety (*Cont.*):
  and extraversion–introversion,
    80–85
  and field dependence, 77
  and interpersonal behavior, 45,
    55, 57, 59, 62–63, 134
  and juvenile delinquency, 128
  as personality factor, 24, 27, 29,
    32, 33
  and repression–sensitization, 77–
    78
  therapeutic reduction of, 46–47,
    116, 149
  (*See also* Anxiety-related dis-
    orders; Neuroticism; Social
    anxiety; Stress)
Anxiety-related disorders, 114–117,
  121, 145, 154–155
  (*See also* Neurotics)
Assertiveness, 60–61, 73, 148
  (*See also* Dominance)
Attitude change, 48–49, 60–61
Attraction, 50–53
Authoritarianism, 85–86

Birth order, 160

Caffeine, 138, 141-142, 152, 166
California Psychological Inventory, 31-32, 36, 40, 50-51, 61, 78, 83, 87, 102, 143, 150-151, 161, 163-165
Classroom Behavior Inventory, 38, 94-95
Clinical Analysis Questionnaire (see 16 Personality Factor Questionnaire)
Cognition-learning interaction (see Interactionism)
Cognitive dissonance, 48-50
Cognitive processes:
 extraversion-introversion and, 38-40, 87-88, 99-101
 (See also Interactionism)
Communication (see Emotional expression; Nonverbal communication; Self-disclosure)
Comrey Personality Scales, 32-33, 40, 74
Conformity, 47-50
Conscience development, 121-122, 128-132
Conservatism, 85-87
Creativity, 106-107
Criminals, 114, 121-127, 133-134, 146-150, 152-154
 (See also Delinquents; Psychopaths)
Cross-cultural comparisons, 25, 151-152

Delinquents, 121-123, 128-130, 132, 153
 (See also Criminals; Psychopaths)
Depression, 30, 34-35, 80, 114, 117-118, 134, 135, 143, 149, 154
 (See also Suicide)
Dogmatism, 80, 85-88

Dominance:
 as component of extraversion, 29, 31-32, 39-41, 74, 87, 102, 134, 158
 and drug use, 144, 150, 151
 genetic influence on, 158, 159, 162-165
 innovative assessment of, 18-20, 38-40
 and interpersonal behavior, 11-12, 53, 153-154, 158-159
 and sensation seeking, 74
 (See also Assertiveness)
Drug use (see Alcohol; Caffeine; Heroin; LSD; Marijuana; Tobacco)

Emotional expression, 39, 57-60, 89
 (See also Affect Expression Rating Scale; Nonverbal communication)
Empathy, 32-33, 74, 135
Extrasensory perception, 63
Extraversion-introversion:
 components of, 25-34, 38-41, 88-89, 114, 122, 153-154, 167-168
 definition of, 5-8, 28, 36-37, 41, 88-89
Eysenck Personality Inventory, 25, 26, 32, 39, 40, 44, 47, 49, 50, 53, 55, 56, 61, 62, 68-71, 73-77, 80, 82-85, 87, 98, 100, 101, 105, 109, 110, 119, 121, 126-128, 130, 133, 139, 142-144, 147, 150, 160, 161, 166
 junior version, 63, 86, 95, 96, 128, 131, 160
Eysenck Personality Questionnaire, 25, 28, 32, 37, 40, 45, 62, 71, 97, 127, 148
 junior version, 129-130
Eysenckian theory, 6-8, 121-122, 137-138

Field dependence, 75-77, 79-80

Guilford-Zimmerman Temperament Survey, 30-32, 37-38, 40, 78

Handwriting, 61-62
Heritability, 159, 161-171
Heroin, 146-150
High School Personality Questionnaire (see 16 Personality Factor Questionnaire)
Hostility, 73, 132-134
(See also Aggression)
Hypnotic susceptibility, 62-63

Impulsivity:
    and antisocial behavior, 27, 123-124, 127-130, 133-135, 154
    and birth order, 160
    as component of extraversion, 25-28, 31, 34, 36, 38-40, 70-74, 76, 78, 88-89, 114
    components of, 27-28, 71-72, 76
    and drug use, 142-143, 145-151
    and emotional expression, 60
    genetic influence on, 166-170
    and locus of control, 71-72
    and maladjustment, 34, 113-116, 119-121
    as personality factor, 24, 27, 31, 33, 87, 169
    and repression-sensitization, 78-79
    and sensation seeking, 74
    sociability and, 25-28, 30-31, 34, 38, 39
    and vocational preference, 105
Interactionism:
    cognitive processes and, 9-13, 15-17, 38-39
    defining characteristics of, 8-9, 13-15

Interactionism (Cont.):
    extraversion-introversion and, 15-22, 40-41, 63-64
    humanistic theory and, 9-10
    interpersonal processes and, 9, 11-13, 38-39, 63-64
    Neo-Freudian theory and, 9-13
    personality assessment and, 17-20, 38-40
    personality traits and, 15-20, 170-171
    social-learning theory and, 9-11, 13
Internal-external control of reinforcement (see Locus of control)
Interpersonal style inventories, 11-12, 16, 38-40, 144, 150
Introspectiveness, 31, 40, 41, 78, 88-89, 107, 147, 154, 169

Jungian theory, 6

Locus of control, 67-72, 80
LSD, 147, 150

Marijuana, 144, 150-151
Maudsley Personality Inventory, 25, 28, 29, 34, 36-40, 46, 51, 68, 77, 78, 103, 105, 106, 119, 120, 126, 127, 133, 134, 139, 146, 166
    junior version, 27, 86, 128
Minnesota Multiphasic Personality Inventory, 33-36, 68, 77, 117, 119, 130, 133, 134, 143, 146-149, 161, 163
    extraversion scale, 33, 34, 40, 79, 119, 134
    hypomania scale, 33-36, 40, 57, 74, 105, 117, 130, 134, 143, 147-150
    psychopathic deviate scale, 35, 143, 147, 149, 150, 163

Minnesota Multiphasic Personality
Inventory (*Cont.*):
repression scale, 33, 34, 40, 79,
133, 134
social introversion scale, 33–40,
44–45, 57, 74, 76, 78, 80,
105, 108, 117, 118, 130,
133, 134, 143, 148–150,
163
Myers–Briggs Type Indicator, 36–37,
40, 45, 48, 70, 76, 78, 81,
107, 109, 125, 147, 161, 166

Narcotics (*see* Heroin)
Neo-Freudian theory (*see* Interactionism)
Neuroticism:
and academic performance, 96,
98–101
and antisocial behavior, 122–
130, 133
cross-cultural comparisons, 151–
152
and drug use, 139–145, 147,
148, 151
and field dependence, 77
genetic and familial influence
on, 160, 166, 167, 169
and interpersonal behavior, 46,
47, 52, 55, 57, 58, 61–63,
74
and locus of control, 68, 71–72
and maladjustment, 114–120,
154
as personality factor, 24–27, 29,
30, 32–37, 39, 66, 68, 81
and repression–sensitization, 78
and social anxiety, 82–84
and social attitudes, 86, 88
and vocational behavior, 105,
106, 108, 111
(*See also* Anxiety)
Neurotics, 34, 115–116, 125
(*See also* Anxiety-related disorders)
Nonverbal communication, 56–60

Observational learning, 47–48, 64
Occupational Introversion-
Extraversion Scale (*see*
Strong Vocational Interest
Blank)
Operant conditioning, 48

Person–environment interaction,
8–9, 19–20, 45, 49, 63–64,
132, 138
(*See also* Interactionism)
Person perception, 50–54, 56
Personal Orientation Inventory, 77,
85
Personality, definition of, 1–5
Pittsburgh social extraversion scale,
37–38, 40, 83
Psychological Screening Inventory,
35–36, 40, 98–99
Psychopaths, 34, 121–125, 127,
154
Psychosomatic disorders, 117
Psychoticism:
and academic performance, 98,
101
and antisocial behavior, 123–
130, 144, 148, 151, 154
cross-cultural comparisons, 152
genetic and familial influences
on, 160, 166, 167
and interpersonal behavior, 52,
55, 74
as personality factor, 24–25, 34–
36, 120
Psychoticism–Extraversion-
Neuroticism Scale, 25, 36,
46, 98, 114, 152, 160, 166,
167

Racial differences, 160–161
Reflection–impulsivity, 27
Religious orientation, 85–87
Repression–sensitization, 77–82, 89
Risk taking, 74–75, 145–146, 161
(*See also* Impulsivity)

Schizophrenics, 114, 120, 121, 133
Self-actualization (see Personal Orientation Inventory)
Self-consciousness, 84–85
  (See also Introspectiveness)
Self-disclosure, 56–57
Self-esteem, 59, 70, 79–82
Self-monitoring, 47, 58, 84
Sensation seeking, 52, 74–76, 79–80, 147, 150, 170
Sexual behavior, 54–56, 86, 108
Shyness, 60, 84–85, 115
  (See also Social anxiety)
16 Personality Factor Questionnaire, 28–30, 32, 40, 46, 52–53, 61, 68–69, 74, 77, 87, 92, 94, 98, 102, 103, 122–124, 126, 144–145, 147, 149, 151, 160, 162–163, 166
  children's version, 30, 76
  clinical version, 30, 62–63, 117–118
  early school version, 30
  high school version, 30, 63, 95–96, 106, 128
Sociability:
  and adjustment, 34, 46, 114, 116, 119–121, 153, 154
  and antisocial behavior, 123–124, 127–129, 134, 143, 149, 151
  and birth order, 160
  as component of extraversion, 25–26, 31–34, 39–40, 68–69, 73, 88–89, 167–168
  and field dependence, 76
  genetic influence, 158–159, 162–164, 166–170
  and interpersonal behavior, 50–51, 53, 54, 60–63
  and locus of control, 68–69, 71, 72
  as personality factor, 26–32, 38, 54, 158–159
  and repression–sensitization, 78
  and sensation seeking, 74
  and social anxiety, 83–84

Sociability (Cont.):
  and vocational behavior, 102, 107
Social anxiety, 50, 80–85, 113, 148
  (See also Anxiety)
Social attitudes, 85–88
  (See also Authoritarianism; Conservatism; Dogmatism)
Social competence, 120, 121
Social desirability, 58, 68–69
Social introversion (see Minnesota Multiphasic Personality Inventory)
Social-learning theory, 9–11, 13, 47–48
Stress, 45–46, 61, 77, 106, 114, 141–142
Strong Vocational Interest Blank, occupational introversion-extraversion scale, 35, 54, 102–103, 107
Stuttering, 115–116
Suicide, 118–119, 152, 154

Temperaments, 73, 82, 122, 146, 168–171
Test of Attentional and Interpersonal Style (see Interpersonal style inventories)
Therapy, 46–47, 116–117, 120–121, 127, 145, 149, 155
Tobacco, 137–142, 151, 152, 166
Trait-state interaction (see Interactionism)

Vocational performance, 108–111
Vocational preference, 102–108
  artist, 106–107
  college major, 103–105
  inventories of, 102–104, 106–108
  minister, 107
Volunteering for experiments, 61